In the
SHADOW
of His
WINGS

In the
SHADOW
of His
WINGS

CHRISTIAN ART
PUBLISHERS

Originally published in Afrikaans by Christelike Uitgewersmaatskappy
under the title *In die skadu van Sy vleuels*

© 2003

English edition © 2003
Christian Art Publishers
PO Box 1599, Vereeniging, 1930, RSA

First edition 2003
Second edition 2010

Translated by Louise Emerton
Cover designed by Christian Art Publishers

Images used under license from Shutterstock.com

Scripture taken from the *Holy Bible*, New International Version® NIV®.
Copyright © 1973, 1978, 1984 by International Bible Society.
Used by permission of Zondervan Publishing House. All rights reserved.

Scripture taken from *The Message*. Copyright © by Eugene H. Peterson,
1993, 1994, 1995. Used by permission of NavPress Publishing Group.

Set in 11 on 13 pt Leawood Bk BT by Christian Art Publishers

Printed in China

ISBN 978-1-86920-121-0

10 11 12 13 14 15 16 17 18 19 – 10 9 8 7 6 5 4 3 2 1

Because you are my help, I sing in the shadow of your wings. My soul clings to you; your right hand upholds me.

~ Psalm 63:7-8 ~

January

In the shadow of His wings

Today's woman can testify with the psalmist that God is her help and she can sing in the shadow of His wings.

In our hectic daily programs, crammed with stress and anxiety, we desperately need the shadow of God's wings.

We need to personally experience God's peace and presence every day.

And yet, we often get the feeling that God is far away.

Brother Lawrence writes in his book *The Practice of the Presence of God*: "I cannot imagine how religious persons can live satisfied without the practice of the presence of God."

This month we are going to learn how to seek God's presence so that we can live in the shadow of His wings all day long.

Jesus is the key to God's presence in the lives of His children: 2 Corinthians 4:14 says, *"We know that the one who raised the Lord Jesus from the dead will also raise us with Jesus and will bring us with you in his presence."*

It is my prayer that, after completing this month's daily readings, you will experience God's presence in a completely new way in your life.

Joy in the presence of God

Read Acts 2:15-28

You have made known to me the paths of life; you will fill me with joy in your presence (Acts 2:28).

Children of God know that there is no other place where they experience so much joy as in the presence of God. Rowland Croucher writes that his father's epitaph comes from Psalm 16:11: *"In Thy presence is fullness of joy."* His father knew the art of living in the presence of God. This epitaph proves that for him, death was not the end, but rather the beginning – the beginning of a joyous life with God, testifies Croucher.

We don't need to wait until we are dead to experience the joy of God's presence. You can experience it right here and now when you glorify and worship Him during your quiet time. You can hear God speaking to you in person, every time you open His Word. You can obey His commandments and live for His kingdom. You can look forward to the glory that the future holds for the children of God.

To live in the presence of God is both a choice and a responsibility. If you want to experience the joy of God's presence in your life, you will have to make a positive decision. You will have to be willing to sacrifice other things that you enjoy to have more time to spend in His presence. Are you willing to try?

Heavenly Father, thank You so much for the bubbling joy that my prayer time with You injects into my life. Help me, once again, to make a positive decision to spend more time with You. Amen.

Be silent before God

Read Habakkuk 2:18-3:2

But the LORD is in his holy temple; let all the earth be silent before him (Hab. 2:20).

The prophet Habakkuk calls on the whole earth to be silent in the presence of the Lord and to worship Him. *Quiet time*, we call the time that we reserve for God – when we read from His Word, listen to His voice and talk to Him in person. Every Christian woman needs quiet time in her day. A time when we can be refreshed, when our strength can be renewed, when we can be comforted in times of sorrow, when we can get courage to face the problems that confront us daily.

Your quiet time is the time to feel God's arms around you, and to delight in His presence. If you are not spending enough time with God before starting your busy day, do something about it *now*. Find a special time when you can focus on God, when you can sit in the shadow of His wings and listen to His voice. It is essential that you *find* time for this. God wants to equip you for the demanding day that awaits you.

God is there for all who seek Him. He is near to those who call on Him, writes the psalmist (Ps. 145:18). All you have to do is find time for Him and be silent before Him. There, in the shadow of His healing wings, He will provide you with everything you need.

Heavenly Father, thank You for the wonder of communicating with You. Thank You for drawing near when I call on You. I praise You for my quiet time in which I can be silent before You, while You equip me for the day ahead. Amen.

Thirst for God's presence

Read Psalm 42

As the deer pants for streams of water, so my soul pants for you, O God. My soul thirsts for God, for the living God. When can I go and meet with God? (Ps. 42:1-2).

In Psalm 42, the poet declares his yearning for God. As the deer in the desert pants for water, so his soul pants for God's presence in his life. At the beginning of the psalm, he is not aware of this presence, but at the end of the psalm he comes to the conclusion that those who put their hope in God will yet praise Him because He is our Savior and our God.

Henri Nouwen maintains that, at the beginning of our spiritual life, it is often difficult to experience God's presence, because there are so many things that we worry about. However, when we purposefully thirst for God, God will allow us to find Him and to become aware of His Spirit in our lives.

"If, however, we are faithful to our disciplines, a new hunger will make itself known. This new hunger is the first sign of God's presence. When we remain attentive to this divine presence, we will be led always deeper into the kingdom. There, to our joyful surprise, we will discover that all things are being made new," writes Nouwen.[1]

"If you seek him, he will be found by you … ," David promises his son Solomon (1 Chron. 28:9). If you purposefully seek God's presence, God will answer you.

Heavenly Father, my heart thirsts for Your presence. I pray that I will find You, so that I may experience Your lasting presence in my life. Amen.

Focus on God

O God, you are my God, earnestly I seek you; my soul thirsts for you, my body longs for you, in a dry and weary land where there is no water (Ps. 63:1).

To become truly silent before God, you first need to calm down and forget about all the things that keep you busy every day. You need to tune in to God and focus on Him alone. *"Be still, and know that I am God; I will be exalted among the nations, I will be exalted in the earth,"* God says in Psalm 46:10.

There, in your room, close to God, it is possible to forget about yourself and all your problems. "The real fact of being in the presence of God is that you either forget yourself altogether or see yourself as a small, dirty object. It is better to forget about yourself altogether," writes C. S. Lewis, tongue in cheek.[2]

If you long for God's presence, and if you draw near to Him in your quiet time, you cannot but realize His grandeur, power and majesty anew. When you communicate with Him, you will be able to forget about all the demands awaiting you, about the flurry of the day ahead, about the anxieties that threaten to overwhelm you.

There in the shadow of the wings of the God you seek, close to the God whom you seek and for whom you thirst, you can spend your time focusing on Him and His love for you, and be at peace with yourself.

Lord, how great and wonderful You are! I want to forget about all things – including myself – and focus on You alone. Please give me Your peace in my life. Amen.

Worshiping God!

Read Revelation 22:6-12

But he said to me, "Do not do it! I am a fellow-servant with you and with your brothers the prophets and of all who keep the words of this book. Worship God!" (Rev. 22:9).

As John is about to prostrate himself in worship before the angel who showed him the Revelation of things to come, the angel stops him. He reminds him that only God should be worshiped, that only He is worthy of our devotion and worship. Your quiet time is the right time to worship God. Do you know the secret of how God should be worshiped? Ask the Holy Spirit to give you the right words with which to worship God.

To worship is to realize that you are in the presence of the holy God. Worship entails a heart of reverence and deference towards Him and words that express your love for Him.

To worship is to kneel in awe before the majesty of God, to glorify God with your entire being.

It remains a miracle that such a great God offers His love to the sinful child of man and that He allows us to address Him as our Father. When we worship Him, we may rest assured in the knowledge that this omnipotent God commits Himself to caring for us as a worldly father would care for his children. Never forget to glorify and worship Him for this!

Holy Spirit, I pray that You help me to worship God in such a way that I will be deeply aware of His love for me, so that I will never lose my sense of wonder about it. Please give me the right words to worship Him. Amen.

Being still in the morning

> *Read Psalm 5*

In the morning, O LORD, you hear my voice; in the morning I lay my requests before you and wait in expectation (Ps. 5:3).

Are you willing to find time in your busy daily schedule to be totally still and listen to God's voice? We all need a time to rest from the day's activities, a time when we can be quiet in God's presence and place ourselves in His shadow, so that we can gain strength for the day ahead. Most people find it best to have their quiet time in the morning. *"Awake, my soul! Awake, harp and lyre! I will awaken the dawn,"* says the psalmist (Ps. 57:8).

And yet, many Christians still have difficulties with their quiet time – not only because they cannot find sufficient time for it, but because it makes them uncomfortable. Being still is a discipline that has disappeared from the lives of many believers, and yet, we cannot truly live without it.

"I want to be still Lord, and wait on You," writes Jörg Zink. "I want to be still so that, amongst the many voices I can recognize Your voice. I want to be still and stand in awe because You can spare a word for me."[3]

Maybe it's time to learn how to be truly still in the presence of God. Give it a try, and your quiet time will develop a new dimension!

Heavenly Father, I am one of those people who has difficulty being still, because there are so many thoughts milling around in my mind when I should be busy with You. I pray that You will enable me to become so quiet that I will recognize Your voice and clearly hear Your message to me. Amen.

Being still in the evening

> *Read Psalm 92*

It is good to praise the LORD and make music to your name, O Most High, to proclaim your love in the morning and your faithfulness at night (Ps. 92:1-2).

It is not enough to communicate with God only in the morning. At night, before going to bed, you also need to study His Word and to talk to Him. Discuss the activities of your day with Him and thank Him for what He has done for you during the course of the day. You need to fit this into your busy daily schedule, but don't postpone your quiet time until you are so sleepy that you fall asleep on your knees from sheer exhaustion.

The custom of praying at night originates from the Old Testament. The Levites were to stand every morning to thank and praise the Lord and *"they were to do the same in the evening,"* reports 1 Chronicles 23:30.

The world really doesn't need more busy people, maybe not even more intelligent people. The world needs people who know what they need, claims Don Postema: "Silence, if their words are to mean anything; reflection, if their actions are to have any significance; contemplation, if they are to see the world as it really is; prayer, if they are going to be conscious of God, if they are to 'know God and enjoy God forever.'"[4]

Do you now realize how much you need your quiet time at night?

Heavenly Father, thank You for pointing out my need to find time for You in the evening. I really want to get to know You better. Thank You for being there to carry me day after day and to provide for all my needs. Amen.

Finding time to pray

Read Mark 1:32-39

Very early in the morning, while it was still dark, Jesus got up, left the house and went off to a solitary place, where he prayed (Mark 1:35).

When Jesus walked the earth, He was very busy. People were constantly coming to Him with the sick and the disabled. With all the people who wanted help and who came to listen to Him, He could hardly find time to be alone to talk to His Father. But Jesus was not deterred by His busy schedule. He *found* the time to be quiet – even though it meant that He had to get up very early, *"while it was still dark,"* says Mark.

Sometimes you do not have the time and sometimes you do not feel like praying – because you are so busy.

When a friend of Martin Luther asked his advice on how to pray, Luther replied in his characteristic humorous fashion: I will tell you to the best of my ability what I do and may the Lord help you to do it better than me! On days when I don't feel like praying because of all the things that clutter my thoughts, I simply go to my room and read the Ten Commandments, something that Jesus said and a psalm.

When you need advice about prayer, pick up your Bible and use the words of Scripture for your prayer. Learn your favorite Bible verse off by heart, then you will be able to communicate with God, using the words from His Word, regardless of the place.

Lord, help me to find the time to pray, even when I do not feel like it. Please teach me to use the words from Your Word to communicate with You. Amen.

Praying is a good habit

Read James 4:1-4

You do not have, because you do not ask God. When you ask, you do not receive, because you ask with wrong motives (James 4:2-3).

Martin Luther was of the opinion that it is a good thing to pray first thing in the morning and last thing at night, so that prayer becomes a fixed routine in your life. When we become accustomed to doing something, it eventually becomes part of our routine and we don't have to think about whether we have the time for it or not. None of us would, for example, get up or go to bed without brushing our teeth and combing our hair – the force of habit is too strong for that.

If you acquire the good habit of having a quiet time twice a day every day, you will find that God, in turn, will give you those things for which you ask, provided they correspond with His will for your life. Perhaps you do not have, because you do not ask God often enough (see James 4: 2).

Try to make praying a habit. If you don't, there is a danger that something else could become more important to you than your time with God. If your day is going to be extra busy, rather go to bed an hour earlier, so that you can get up earlier for your appointment with God. Guard against neglecting your prayer time because of a busy schedule. Rather pray for a little while longer when a full program awaits you!

Lord, thank You that, in spite of my busy schedule, I can acquire the good habit of making time for You every day. Thank You for being ever ready to listen to my requests. Amen.

Pray continually

Read 1 Thessalonians 5:16-24

Pray continually (1 Thess. 5:17).

Prayer should be a way of life for God's children, something you cannot imagine living without. God is always ready to help and support His children. When I get up off my knees, I experience something very unusual: What James writes is true – the prayer of a righteous man is powerful and effective! (see James 5:16). Not only because God hears our prayers, but because we physically experience His strength and support in our lives when we pray.

Through prayer, God's children become strong and refreshed. Moreover, when you pray, God makes His wonder-working power available to you, so that you realize anew each day that you can do all things through Him who strengthens you (see Phil. 4:13).

This is why it is a such a good thing to learn to pray continually. Every day, during your quiet time, you can be equipped with strength, so that you can face the problems and challenges of the day with God's strength, guidance and wisdom. But you can also pray on your way to work, in the shower, or while cleaning the house.

God can be reached every moment of every day. Talk to Him continually, worship Him, praise Him, thank Him and feel free to ask Him for those things that you really want.

Lord, I praise You for always being available to me, every moment of the day or night – and, making Your wonder-working power available to me when I pray. Thank You that I can pray continually, secure in the knowledge that You always listen. Amen.

Listen to the voice of God

Read 1 Kings 19:9-12

*After the earthquake came a fire, but the LORD was not in the fire.
And after the fire came a gentle whisper* (1 Kings 19:12).

When Elijah fled from Jezebel, God talked to him in a gentle whisper. Elijah had to listen carefully in order to hear God's voice. But when he was aware of the voice of God, he talked freely with Him. Sometimes the voice of God is only a whisper in your life, requiring you to listen carefully.

Praying includes listening to the voice of God. It is amazing to experience God's presence, to *know* that He loves you, just the way you are, sins and all; to know that nothing on earth can ever separate you from His love; to know that when you talk to Him, He is near, eager to listen to you and to surround you with His love.

Saint Theresa of Avila writes that most of the problems we have in our prayer life are because of one fatal blunder: we pray as though God were absent. God's message is easily missed if you do not take time to listen to Him. When you pray, listen attentively to God, *know* that God is there and that He is listening to you, that He wants to tell you in person: Be still and know that I am the Lord. Keep watch and pray, persevere in faith. I am with you, as I promised.

Father, thank You for being near me, even though, at times, I cannot hear Your voice all that clearly. Please make me sensitive to those times when You want to talk to me in person, so that I will clearly know what it is that You want to tell me. Amen.

Procrastination is the thief of time

Be self-controlled and alert. Your enemy the devil, prowls around like a roaring lion looking for someone to devour. Resist him, standing firm in the faith (1 Pet. 5:8-9).

There is one thing you must know: The devil is going to do his level best to sabotage your prayer time, because there is nothing that he fears more than a praying Christian.

Luther warns those who pray against the danger of continually postponing our prayer time because there are other urgent matters that need attention. Be careful of the thought, "I will pray in an hour's time or so, I just need to do this or that first," Luther writes. In this way we postpone out prayer time. Eventually, it will no longer be a matter of course for us, and we might even lose the habit of praying regularly.

Heed this warning today – if you want to pray and there are numerous things distracting you, things that seem to be more important than your daily prayer time, do not become lazy or careless in your prayers. This is the one thing that you cannot lay at the door of the devil who wants to take away your desire to pray! He does not know the meaning of the word defeat. Therefore, be alert, stand firm in your faith and resist him. Prevent him at all costs from succeeding in persuading you to shorten or postpone you prayer time.

Heavenly Father, You know that I often fall in battle against the devil. Please help me to be self-controlled and alert, never allowing him to sabotage my prayer time. Amen.

What God wants

He knelt down and prayed, "Father, if you are willing, take this cup from me; yet not my will, but yours be done" (Luke 22:41-42).

Jesus knew the secret of successful prayer: making God's will our priority. In Gethsemane when He prayed fervently for God to take the cup of bitterness from Him, He closes His prayer with the words, *"Yet not my will, but yours be done"* (Luke 22:42). "I've learned that prayer is not a magic wand to wave about so I can get what I want. It's opening my heart to Him in surrender, so He can get what He wants," writes Brenda Waggoner.[5]

Do your prayers still consist of a long list, filled with requests, which you recite to God? Then you can *learn* to pray in accordance with God's will. Make a list of the things that you are grateful for, as well as things you want to ask of God. Then, first allow God the opportunity to tell you what He wants to do for you and give to you – allow Him to remind you of all the things you should be grateful for. It is not wrong to reveal your heart's desire to God, as long as your prayers do not only consist of requests.

God created you especially to have a relationship with Him and to communicate with Him. Your relationship with God will demand time, attention and patience. Remember this next time you kneel down to pray.

Heavenly Father, please forgive me for bombarding You with selfish requests to the extent that I forget the main objective of prayer – to seek Your glory and Your will. Please teach me to pray in accordance with Your will. Amen.

In the presence of God

> *Read Psalm 145:14-21*

The LORD is near to all who call to him, to all who call on him in truth. He fulfils the desires of those who fear him (Ps. 145:18-19).

When you kneel in prayer, God is with you – the Bible is very clear about this. He is near to all who call on Him in truth, writes the psalmist. Therefore, when you pray, you find yourself in the presence of God.

Lewis Smedes wrote a phenomenal book called *Everything Is Alright, Even Though Everything Is Wrong*. In order to put everything right in your wrong world, it is necessary for you to linger in the presence of God. He writes, "If you experience God's presence, then you will know that everything is alright in your life, at that moment, as well as in every moment that follows. Deep inside you, you will know that God is holding you, and you will know that everything is alright, even though everything seems wrong."[6]

When you pray, you have the assurance that the God who has created the world and who preserves it every day, is holding you. That He knows all there is to know about you and still loves you, that He only wants the best for you. So you can rest assured that when you kneel down in prayer, you are in the presence of God, and that everything is right with you, regardless of all the problems that cause you so much heartache.

Heavenly Father, thank You so much for being there when I pray, that You are near me when I call upon You and that You answer all my prayers. I praise You for the assurance that everything will be alright with me if I live close to You. Amen.

How great is God!

Read Job 36:22-29

God is exalted in his power. Who has prescribed his ways for him? How great is God – beyond our understanding! (Job 36:22-23, 26).

Before you busy yourself with God, it is good to know that He knows you completely (see Ps. 139), but that you will never get to know Him in full. "We are surrounded by God," Anthony de Mello writes, "but we do not notice Him, because we think that we know Him."

Some people judge God by man-made criteria. They even expect Him to account for His deeds. Even worse, sometimes we are so presumptuous as to think that God is not treating us fairly – as Job did. God is omnipotent – His power is infinite. He cannot be fathomed by the human mind. All that you need to know is that God is so great that He is beyond your understanding and that you may never question His deeds.

God is totally righteous, even though it may not seem like that to you right now – He does not make any mistakes, because He is God. If He sometimes answers your prayers in a way that is different from what you wanted, rest assured that He is omnipotent and always knows best.

Although God is beyond your understanding, you can get to know Him better by studying His Word and studying His deeds. Do this during your quiet time.

Father, Your power is great – and I know full well that no one can prescribe Your ways, nor can anyone comprehend You. Teach me to get to know You better and better and to abide by Your will for my life. Amen.

God created us for Himself

Read Acts 17:24-28

God did this so that men would seek him, and perhaps reach out for him and find him, though he is not far from each one of us. For in him we live and move and have our being (Acts 17:27-28).

When Paul wanted to explain to the people of Athens who God is, he used an altar to an unknown God to drive the message home: This God whom he worships, created men to seek Him. He is near to us, for in Him we live and move and have our being.

"Being in the dazzling presence of God is a wondrous experience; realizing God's majestic, just and compassionate action in the world and in our lives urges us to let all thanks break loose! We come so often to God as beggars. We ask and beg: give me; bless me; help me; guide me; grant me. And that's one necessary level of our existence. But in thanksgiving and adoration we come to God not to ask, but to give! We come not whimpering but shouting praise, not in guilt but in gratitude. We feel not distant from God, but close to God. We are like a traveler who is home again at last, the prodigal at a banquet. Those moments may be seldom, but when they happen, we know that we were created for God," writes Don Postema.[7]

God has created you to seek Him and, for this reason, you will never be truly happy until you have found Him. If you do not know Him yet, do not wait any longer to invite Him into your life.

Heavenly Father, thank You for creating me to seek You. I praise You because I can believe in You and because I can live and exist in You every day. Amen.

With God in the sanctuary

Read Psalm 63

I have seen you in the sanctuary and beheld your power and your glory (Ps. 63:2).

For the Israelites, the temple was the one place where they experienced God's presence. Today we know that we are the temples of God, that He dwells in us. Therefore, we do not have to spend hours in a church building in order to be near to God. We don't all have the time to spend hours with God every day. But if you are going to be extra busy on a particular day, you can ask God to be with you every minute of your busy day.

In his book, *The Practice of the Presence of God*, Brother Lawrence writes: "The time of business does not, with me, differ from the time of prayer; and in the noise and clutter of my kitchen, while several persons are at the same time calling for different things, I possess God in as great a tranquility as if I were upon my knees at the Blessed Sacrament."[8] And Brother Lawrence really practiced what he preached. His fellow-priests testified how they were able to physically observe God's presence in him – even when he was at his busiest.

You too can make time for God in your busy daily schedule by thinking of Him while doing your work, so that you will not only experience His presence in your life, but that it will also become evident to others in the new tranquility that will be part of your life.

Lord, thank You that I can experience Your presence in my life, even when I am very busy. Help me to find extra time on my busiest days to be still in Your presence. Amen.

Think about God

Read Psalm 63

On my bed, I remember you; I think of you through the watches of the night. Because you are my help, I sing in the shadow of your wings (Ps. 63:6-7).

Many Christians are wary of the word meditation, because it is so characteristic of Eastern religions. And yet, meditation is a practice that is propagated in the Bible. David often confesses that he thinks about God, that he reflects on Him when he is alone. Eastern meditation – which requires that you totally empty your thoughts – and Christian meditation – which requires that you reflect upon God – are indeed poles apart.

Maybe it's time to drop your prejudices about meditation and to *find* the time to reflect upon God, to teach yourself to meditate, and to fill your thoughts with God. If you think about God often, your quiet time will be filled with God. It will no longer only be a time for telling God what you want from Him.

For your next quiet time, reflect upon each of God's characteristics. Think about His greatness and kindness, His majesty and omnipotence, and reflect upon the miracle of His creation. At the end of your quiet time, you too can pray: *"May the words of my mouth and the meditation of my heart be pleasing in your sight, O Lord, my Rock and my Redeemer"* (Ps. 19:14).

Father, how wonderful it is to be able to fill my thoughts with Your attributes and to admire the beauty of Your creation. I praise You for Your strength and love, for Your power and majesty and for Your creation! Amen.

Quietly trusting

Read Isaiah 30:15-18

"In repentance and rest is your salvation, in quietness and trust is your strength" (Isa. 30:15).

The prophet, Isaiah, promises God's people that they will be saved if they repent and come to rest. He also assures them that the Lord longs to be gracious to them, that He rises to show them compassion, and adds that all who wait for Him are blessed (v. 18). Unfortunately, the people do not pay attention to God's promises. They prefer to remain disobedient.

Most women rush about from early morning till late at night in an effort to do all the things expected of them; to fit the demands of their homes, children, husband and career into the hours available. Many a day we feel as though things are getting out of hand – as though we have no strength left for the challenges facing us.

There is a wonderful tranquility captured in today's text: *"In quietness and trust is your strength."* Your quiet time ought to be an oasis of stillness in your busy day. A place where you can draw on the grace of God and renew your strength for the day ahead. Learn to trust in God anew every day, to become quiet in His presence. He is worthy of your trust. He fulfills each of His many promises, and is true to His word. He has never disappointed anyone who trusted in Him. He will never forsake you either.

Lord, how good it is to know that my strength lies in quietness with You and trust in You. Thank You for my daily quiet time with You when You fill me with Your strength. Amen.

God will be with you

Read Exodus 33:12-17

Then Moses said to him, "If your Presence does not go with us, do not send us up from here. What else will distinguish me and Your people from all the other people on the face of the earth?" (Exod. 33:15-16).

When the Israelites tried the Lord's patience, He told Moses that He would not go with them (see Exod. 33:3), because He might destroy them on the way. But Moses absolutely refused to go one step on their journey through the desert without the assurance of God's presence. He explained that what distinguishes God's people from all the other people on earth, is His presence.

In the end, God agreed to go with them. On the journey through the desert, the people were reminded every day of God's presence – through a pillar of fire at night and a pillar of cloud during the day. In this way, God revealed Himself to them in a visible manner, so that they could face the dangerous journey with confidence every day. Over and over again they saw that God's presence guaranteed their safety.

"Do not be afraid, for I am with you," God promises (Isa. 43:5). This promise still holds true for you today. If you belong to God, you can be assured of His continued presence in your life.

Heavenly Father, thank You so much for the assurance that You are with me every day; that I do not have to undertake my life's journey without You. I pray that You will make me aware of Your guidance and Your presence every day. Amen.

God provides for His children

Read Nehemiah 9:16-23

For forty years you sustained them in the desert; they lacked nothing, their clothes did not wear out nor did their feet become swollen. You gave them kingdoms and nations (Neh. 9:21-22).

During the journey through the desert, which lasted forty years, the Israelites witnessed things that were nearly unbelievable: God provided for all their needs in the desert. Every day they had enough food and water. Their clothes did not wear out and they won the wars against the hostile nations they encountered. God provided for them every day and protected them from danger.

Apart from the women and children, approximately 600,000 men set out on the journey through the desert with Moses. The journey itself was a miracle – normally, nobody can survive for more than a few days in the desert, but God's people journeyed for forty years through the desert. And in these forty years, He not only saw to it that they had sufficient food and water, but also that their clothes didn't wear out.

God also protected them against disease. *"I will not bring on you any of the diseases I brought on the Egyptians, for I am the* LORD, *who heals you,"* He promised them (Exod. 15:26).

If you belong to God, you can still count on God's care and protection today. He wants to be a Father to you and provide for all your needs.

Heavenly Father, I praise You for Your presence and protection in my own life every day. Thank You for providing so abundantly in all my needs and for protecting me from danger. Amen.

God becomes more and you become less

Read Galatians 2:15-21

I have been crucified with Christ and I no longer live, but Christ lives in me (Gal. 2:20).

When sinners repent, a revolutionary change takes place in their lives. We no longer try to earn our salvation through good deeds. We already partake of eternal life because we believe in Jesus. We already share in the benefits of Jesus' death. Not only do we become new people, but through the Holy Spirit, Christ takes over the core of our personality. Now it is no longer we who live, but Christ who lives in us.

I once saw a sketch that neatly illustrates this. In it was a see-saw with a Christian at the one end and Jesus at the other. When Jesus is up, the Christian is down but when the Christian is up, He is down. Take a good look at the position that Jesus takes in your life. What do you do when you have to make an important decision? Do you first find out what the Lord's will for you is, or do you do what you think is best for you?

God's way requires that you must lose to be able to win. You must become less so that He can become more. And the true winners are those people who are prepared to deny themselves, to take up their crosses and follow Him.

Heavenly Father, I confess that so often I still occupy the most important position in my own life. Make me willing to put You first in everything, so that I will no longer live but that You will live in me. Amen.

January 23

God walks the road ahead of you

Read Deuteronomy 31:6-8

The LORD himself goes before you and will be with you; he will never leave you nor forsake you. Do not be afraid; do not be discouraged (Deut. 31:8).

When Joshua succeeded Moses as leader of the Israelites, Moses assured him of God's presence. Joshua need not worry or be afraid, because God would lead him and never fail him.

In January we are still at the beginning of the road into the new year. None of us knows exactly what this year has in store for us. However, we know that if we walk with the Lord every day, nothing can really go wrong in our lives. God wants to promise you today that He will be with you, that He will go before you on the road through the new year; that He will lead you and show you how to live every day.

For this reason, you can leave your fears and anxieties in His hands and trust Him. He promises to help you in danger and in temptation. This does not mean that you can be slack or that no crises will cross your path. You are still engaged in a battle with the devil. But you can be assured that through it all you will be more than a conqueror through the power of God.

Heavenly Father, I praise You for Your promise that You will go before me on the road through the new year. Thank You that I need not fear anything, but that I can cast all my troubles on You because I know that You will sustain me. Amen.

The God of all comfort

Read 2 Corinthians 1:3-11

Praise be to the God and Father of our Lord Jesus Christ, the Father of compassion and the God of all comfort, who comforts us in all our troubles (2 Cor. 1:3).

Paul shared the secret of how Christians can continue to praise the Lord under difficult circumstances with the congregation in Corinth. The fact that we belong to God does not safeguard us against heartache and suffering. *"For just as the sufferings of Christ flow over into our lives, so also through Christ our comfort overflows"* (v. 5). However, we have the assurance that God is with us when things are difficult and we know that He will comfort us.

Because God helps us, He equips us, through our suffering, to help others who are facing a crisis. *"We can comfort those in any trouble with the comfort we ourselves have received from God. For just as the sufferings of Christ flow over into our lives, so also through Christ our comfort overflows,"* writes Paul in verses 4 and 5.

When your load is heavy, try to follow Paul's example and praise God when you face problems, because they engender in you greater sympathy for the problems of others. Crises teach you to assist others with similar problems with greater success. Besides, you have the assurance that God is with you and that He will take you by the hand and give you the strength to persevere.

Lord, I find it very difficult to thank You for my problems. Please help me to utilize negative experiences in a positive way by helping others who find themselves in difficult circumstances. Amen.

Learn to experience God

Read John 12:20-26

Now there were some Greeks among those who went up to worship at the Feast. They came to Philip with a request. "Sir," they said, "we would like to see Jesus" (John 12:20-21).

When Jesus walked this earth, it was possible for people such as the Greeks (mentioned in this verse) to meet Him, to see Him and to touch Him. Today it is somewhat more difficult to experience God's presence physically. You can experience God physically during your quiet time when you reflect on His love and grace in the warmth of the sun of righteousness with healing in its wings (see Mal. 4:2).

We do not only experience the presence of God while studying His Word or while praying. We can also see Him in nature when we look at a sunset or a delicate spider's web. The things that God has created prove to us how magnificent He is. When I walk along the beach and see the sun disappear in a blaze of gold and amber behind the horizon, when the moon rises and casts a silver shadow over the sea, when it rains while the sun shines, when I pick the first daffodil of spring, or when I find a delicately shaded feather of a pheasant, I know for sure that God lives. All these marvels make me intensely aware of God's presence in my life.

Experience God in the miracles surrounding you, experience His presence in nature, and glorify Him for it.

Lord, how wondrously You have created the world! Thank You that I may become intensely aware of Your presence when reading Your Word, when talking to You and when observing the wonders of nature. Amen.

God's love

Read Hosea 11:4-9

How can I give you up, Ephraim? How can I hand you over, Israel? My heart is changed within me; all my compassion is aroused (Hosea 11:8).

Sometimes disappointment and pain can cause us to doubt God's presence. These things may even cause us to doubt God's love for us. If there is one thing you need never doubt, it is God's love for you. Just as God could not give up His disobedient people, He cannot give you up either, because all His compassion is aroused for you.

One of the members of our congregation lost her fiancé in a car accident. There was a time when she could not pray at all, she told us. However, she knew for certain that, regardless of the pain that God had allowed in her life, He still loved her. She just kept on repeating, "I know that You love me, I want to love You too, Lord."

God's love for you generates mutual love. We love because God first loved us, writes John (see 1 John 4:19). And God proved that fervent love by sacrificing His Son to be crucified, so that you need never be without Him ever again.

Know that God loves you, even if you are not experiencing His love right now. When the going gets tough, hold on to His love. God Himself promises that nothing in all creation will ever be able to separate us from His love (see Rom. 8:39).

Heavenly Father, thank You that I can love You because You first loved me and sent Your Son to die for me. I glorify You for the promise that nothing in all creation will ever be able to separate me from Your love. Amen.

The extent of God's love

Read Ephesians 3:14-21

I pray that you may have power, together with all the saints, to grasp how wide and long and high and deep is the love of Christ, and to know this love that surpasses knowledge (Eph. 3:17-19).

God's love for you knows no bounds, it is unconditional and does not depend on anything you have done. His love is wider, longer, higher and deeper than human love and surpasses human understanding. It is an all-encompassing and immeasurable love.

Amy Carmichael wrote a very special song about this love:

Lord Beloved, I would ponder
breadth and depth and length and height
of Thy love's eternal wonder
all embracing, infinite.

What was that to Thee: The measure
of Thy love was Calvary.
Stooping low, love found a treasure
in the least of things that be.

O, the passion of Thy loving,
O, the flame of Thy desire!
Melt my heart with Thy great living
Set me all aglow, afire.[9]

Lord, I praise You for Your all-embracing love for me – help me to reflect upon it often, to define it for myself, so that I may become intensely aware of Your presence in my life. Amen.

God is all around you

Read Isaiah 52:7-12

But you will not leave in haste or go in flight; for the Lord will go before you, the God of Israel will be your rearguard (Isa. 52:12).

The prophet Isaiah brings to God's people the wonderful tidings that their God is King; that He reigns and that He will bring about their deliverance. They do not have to leave in haste, because the Lord promises them that He Himself will go before them and that He will be their rearguard. He surrounds His people with His love. And within this circle of love, they are completely safe and secure – they will no longer live in exile.

The psalmist also writes about God's encompassing love. *"You hem me in – behind and before; you have laid your hand upon me. Such knowledge is too wonderful for me, too lofty for me to attain"* (Ps. 139:5-6).

If you belong to God, you may claim this promise. Not only is God with you, He surrounds you with His love day after day. He will go before you and He will be your rearguard. Because He loves you in this way, you need not fear anything. Your God is King, He knows your situation. You are safe in the circle of His love and you can rest assured that God will take care of you every day. Therefore, from now on, you can live like a child of God.

Heavenly Father, I worship You as the King of my life, the God who surrounds me with Your infinite love day after day, who undertakes to help me, as You have always helped Your people. Teach me to live like Your child every day. Amen.

Glory be to God!

Read Jude 24 and 25

To the only God our Savior be glory, majesty, power and authority, through Jesus Christ our Lord, before all ages, now, and for evermore! (Jude 25).

Jude concludes his short letter with moving praise. He glorifies the *"only God and our Savior through Jesus Christ."* To this God be the glory and the majesty, the power and the authority, for evermore. The psalmist, too, realizes the importance of praise in the life of a believer. *"I will extol the LORD at all times; his praise will always be on my lips"* (Ps. 34:1).

When you linger in the shadow of God's wings, you can learn from your Bible how to praise and glorify God. Find a core passage where God is being praised and glorified, and read it out loud like a prayer. Always remember: The most important thing to focus on during your quiet time, is the glory of God and not your own requests. It is when you have learned to praise and glorify God in your quiet time, that you become aware of His presence.

But you need not restrict your praise and worship to your quiet time. You can praise Him everywhere. He is able to do much more than what you can pray for or imagine, and because He loves you, you are more than a conqueror (see Rom. 8:37).

Heavenly Father, I want to praise and glorify You, because to You belong the authority and the majesty and the power for evermore. Thank You that I know that You are on my side, and that I will be more than a conqueror. Amen.

Focus on things above

Read Colossians 3:1-5

Set your minds on things above, not on earthly things. For you died, and your life is now hidden with Christ in God (Col. 3:2-3).

The Message's interpretation of today's verse is crystal clear: *"Pursue the things over which Christ presides. Don't shuffle along, eyes to the ground, absorbed with the things right in front of you. Look up, and be alert to what is going on around Christ – that's where the action is. See things from his perspective."*

It is essential for Christians to get their priorities straight. Those things that take up most of your thoughts, will reveal to yourself, as well as to others, where your real interests lie.

What's really important to you? Before you answer, think of the things that you prefer to talk about, the things on which you spend most of your time and money.

Helen Keller said that to be able to see but to lack vision, is the one thing that is worse than being blind. Determine the things that are important to God, and make sure that you give priority to these things in your thoughts and in your life. Find a clear vision for yourself – know where you are heading and what the Lord's dream for you entails. Reflect upon it and do it!

Heavenly Father, please forgive me that those things that are unimportant to You still take priority in my thoughts. Help me to focus my thoughts on those things that are of value to You, to find a vision as a Christian, and to live like Your child every day. Amen.

God will be with you always

Read Matthew 28:16-20

Then Jesus came to them and said, "All authority in heaven and on earth has been given to me. And surely I am with you always, to the very end of the age" (Matt. 28:18, 20).

If you are sensitive to God's presence in your life, and spend enough time in the blessed shadows of His wings, you will experience Him with increasing intensity in your life, and you will become increasingly aware of His presence.

Then you will live with the knowledge that He enfolds you with His love, that He is in complete control, even during those times when it does not feel like it; that He only wants the best for you, even though He answers your prayers in ways that differ from your expectations. Then you will also discover that He, in the midst of times of suffering, never stops loving you and that you can depend on His miraculous power at all times.

God promises to be with you every day. Live in Him. "The kiss of God's presence is always there," writes Brenda Waggoner. "Our part is simply to abide, to stay with, to live in Him."[10]

The stronger your relationship with the Lord becomes, and the more time you spend in His presence, the more you will discover that you are intensely aware of His presence the whole day through.

Father, thank You for the glorious knowledge that I will never be alone again, because You are with me every hour of every day. Thank You that I can know that, regardless of what You allow to happen in my life, in the end it will be for my own good, because You love me. Amen.

Prayer

*H*eavenly Father, our Creator and Provider, the human mind cannot fathom Your majesty and mystery, but we know that Your presence spells joy and that it is wonderful for Your children to linger in the shadow of Your wings.

Lord Jesus, Our Savior and Friend, we want to kneel in Your presence and worship You as the King of kings.

Thank You that we can experience Your presence by spending time with You.

Holy Spirit, our Comforter and Guide, we ask that Your presence will characterize our lives every day and that You will teach and guide us; God in Three Persons, we pray that You will show us, day after day, and moment upon moment, exactly how You want to be worshiped.

Help us to make time for You, so that we will never again be without Your presence and so that we can linger in the shadow of Your wings all day long.

Amen.

February

Growing in faith

Faith is precious because, by believing in Jesus, we have the hope of eternal life.

When Christians do not grow in faith and become stronger spiritually, something is seriously wrong.

But growing in faith is not something that happens automatically.

It always involves a choice.

It requires commitment and effort from you.

If you want to grow in faith, you need to take responsibility for your own spiritual progress.

Growing in faith is not a goal that can be reached by a select few only.

It is God's will that each of His children will become spiritually stronger every day, that we reach spiritual maturity in Him, in the same way that we, as parents, want our children to eventually become independent adults who can pull their weight in life.

In Hebrews 6:1 we are urged to leave the elementary teachings about Christ and go on to maturity.

This month you are going to learn to do exactly that.

Faith in a nutshell

Read Revelation 22

I warn everyone who hears the words of the prophecy of this book: If anyone adds anything to them, God will add to him the plagues described in this book. And if anyone takes words away from this book of prophecy, God will take away from him his share in the tree of life and of the holy city, which are described in this book (Rev. 22:18-19).

My husband and I attended a World Book Exhibition in New Orleans in 2000. The congress was opened with a declaration of faith and the presentation of the book, *This I Believe.* This book requests people to return to the fundamental truths of the Word, with prominent American theologians declaring that the Bible should be the only standard for our faith. Everything that God wants to tell us has already been chronicled in His Word. Therefore, we do not need to add to it or take anything away.

It seems to me as though some present-day theologians are doing exactly that. While endeavoring to make the Bible more accessible to modern man, they adapt it to suit our current circumstances, instead of obeying the Word of God unconditionally.

The modern-day scenario reminds me so much of the text in Judges 21:25: *"Everyone did as he saw fit."*

Perhaps you are also in the process of diluting the Bible just a little, "rewriting" it to suit you better. Beware! It could become a dangerous game. God personally commands that nothing in the message of His Word is to be changed.

Heavenly Father, thank You for Your Word that is constant and true. Help me to obey it unconditionally and never try to change it or water it down. Amen.

Have childlike faith

Read Matthew 11:25-30

At that time Jesus said, "I praise you, Father, Lord of heaven and earth, because you have hidden these things from the wise and learned, and revealed them to little children" (Matt. 11:25).

The salvation that Christ offers cannot be gained by the wisdom of this world: it requires a simple, childlike willingness to believe.

Professor Jaap Kies wrote an interesting letter to a daily newspaper in which he said that ordinary believers are taught that certain passages of the Bible are not merely to be read, interpreted and accepted. Rather, the Bible should be 'interpreted in keeping with the life and world-views of the authors as well as the views of modern science.

Such divergent opinions regarding biblical truths could confuse Christians. I find it unsettling when modern-day theologians state that Jonah was never in the stomach of the fish. But it is even more upsetting when they argue that it does not really matter whether Jesus was born of a virgin or not.

Perhaps it is time to return to Matthew 18:3 and 19:14 and be willing to believe with childlike faith exactly what has been chronicled in the Word. Stop worrying about biblical facts that you cannot understand or explain, and believe with the faith of a child that your Bible contains the truth. *"I believe in everything that agrees with the Law and that is written in the Prophets"* (Acts 24:14). To this I say, 'Amen!'

Heavenly Father, forgive me because I so easily get confused by all the different interpretations of Your Word, and enable me to retain my childlike faith in You. Amen.

You lack solid food

Read Hebrews 5:11-6:1

Therefore let us leave the elementary teachings about Christ and go on to maturity (Heb. 6:1).

Milk is the only food a new-born baby can digest, but as the child becomes older, he needs solid food in order to grow. If you want to grow spiritually, you will have to ensure that you leave behind the elementary teachings about Christ and start partaking of solid food.

Spiritual maturity takes time. It is a way of life that must be maintained day after day and year after year. It requires of you to become more like Jesus every day, until you are as perfect and mature as Christ Himself.

Peter writes that we should enrich our faith and make every effort to add to it *"goodness; and to goodness, knowledge; and to knowledge, self-control; and to self-control, perseverance; and to perseverance, godliness; and to godliness, brotherly kindness; and to brotherly kindness, love"* (2 Pet. 1:5-7).

Have a good look at this list of characteristics. How many of these are present in your life and how many of them are you still lacking? Make certain now whether you have consumed sufficient solid food lately to grow spiritually, or whether you are still consuming only milk and are not experiencing spiritual growth.

Lord, please forgive me because I consume so little solid food that my spiritual growth is being stunted. Teach me how to enrich my faith and become more like You. Amen.

Return to the fundamental truths

Read 1 Corinthians 15:1-11

For what I received I passed on to you as of first importance: that Christ died for our sins, according to the Scriptures, that he was buried, that he was raised on the third day ... this is what we preach, and this is what you believed (1 Cor. 15:3-4, 11).

Hot, freshly baked bread spreads a lovely aroma through the house, but after four days, the same bread is old and moldy. The same can sometimes apply to Christians. When we first become Christians, we are enthusiastic and filled with zeal. But the longer we are believers, the greater the danger becomes that our earlier enthusiasm about our faith could wane. It might become necessary to once again return to the fundamental truths of our faith.

The faith of the people in Corinth started to wane. Paul described for them the cornerstones on which their faith was founded: Jesus' crucifixion and His resurrection. *"This is what we preach, and this is what you believed,"* he wrote.

Through this succinct confession of faith, Paul wants to focus the thoughts of the Corinthians on Jesus once again. Has your own faith, over time, become diluted? Then you must return to the fundamental truths of your faith. The resurrection of Jesus only becomes reality when Jesus becomes your life. Then you can declare with Paul, *"I no longer live, but Christ lives in me"* (Gal. 2:20).

God wants to make your faith new and fresh every day – like freshly baked bread. May this be your experience!

Heavenly Father, I confess that my faith has become diluted over the years. Let me regain my earlier enthusiasm for You by returning to the fundamental truths of my faith. Amen.

Assess yourself

Read 2 Corinthians 13:1-7

Examine yourselves to see whether you are in the faith; test yourselves. Do you not realize that Christ Jesus is in you? (2 Cor. 13:5).

Sometimes it becomes necessary to take stock of your faith. There are various things against which you can measure your own spiritual growth:

- Do you still enjoy your quiet time and going to church?
- What is the state of your relationships with other people?
- Do you obey the guidance of the Holy Spirit in your life?
- Are you guided by the Word of God – and does He speak to you personally when you are studying the Bible?
- Is the expansion of God's kingdom important to you?
- Are you doing something about the physical and spiritual needs of those who are less privileged than you?
- Are you still aware of the fact that you often sin?
- Are you willing to forgive those who have hurt you?
- Do you spend enough time every day preparing yourself for eternal life?

If you have answered these questions honestly, give yourself one mark for every affirmative answer. What have you learnt about your spiritual growth?

Heavenly Father, I am sorry that my progress on the road to sanctification is still so slow. Please help me to grow spiritually every day and to become stronger. Thank You for living in me. Amen.

February 6

Recipe for spiritual growth

> Read 2 Corinthians 13:8-11

Our prayer is for your perfection. Finally, brothers, good-by. Aim for perfection, listen to my appeal, be of one mind, live in peace. And the God of love and peace will be with you (2 Cor. 13:9, 11).

Paul sends a flop-proof recipe to the congregation in Corinth about how to become spiritually perfect. *"We pray hard that it will all come together in your lives. Be cheerful. Keep things in good repair. Keep your spirits up. Think in harmony. Be agreeable. Do all that and the God of love and peace will be with you for sure,"* says *The Message* translation of our text.

Spiritual growth is going to require of you to obey God and to live according to the way He sets out in His Word. Furthermore, you should always be filled with joy. The joy that comes from God is never dependent on your physical situation; it comes from within. The faithful should not fight with each other. We must be peace-makers who live in peace with one another, as well as with God.

If you are prepared to follow this recipe, you will soon be able to see it producing fruit in your spiritual life.

Heavenly Father, I pray that You will enable me to be obedient to You and to be joyful always. Help me to not live in discord with others. Please give me Your love and peace in my life so that I can become spiritually stronger every day. Amen.

Time for spring-cleaning!

Read 2 Corinthians 6:14-7:1

Let us purify ourselves from everything that contaminates body and spirit, perfecting holiness out of reverence for God (2 Cor. 7:1).

To be committed to God is an essential element of spiritual growth. Commitment requires that you be willing to give yourself wholly to God and to obey Him in all areas of your life. It also implies that you will make sufficient time for God: Time to study your Bible and time to pray. Commitment also requires that you live a life totally dedicated to God. *The Message* words it as follows, *"Let's make a clean break with everything that defiles or distracts us. Let's make our entire lives fit and holy temples for the worship of God."*

Before you can live a life totally committed to God, it is necessary to have a major spring-cleaning in your life. Sin in your life prevents God from hearing your prayers. *"But your iniquities have separated you from your God; your sins have hidden his face from you, so that he will not hear,"* the prophet Isaiah warns God's sinful people (Isa. 59:2).

This warning is personally addressed to you. Think carefully about the things in your life that are still causing estrangement between you and God. Pray about them and ask the Lord to specifically show you those things in your life. Confess your sins by name and then go and live differently by forsaking those sins.

Lord, I want to live a life of greater commitment to You. Please forgive all my sins and help me to forsake them so that, from now on, my entire life will glorify Your Name. Amen.

Return to the Word

Read Psalm 119:89-112

Your word, O Lord, is eternal; it stands firm in the heavens. Oh, how I love your law! I meditate on it all day long. Your command-ments make me wiser than my enemies, for they are ever with me Your word is a lamp to my feet and a light for my path (Ps. 119:89, 97-98, 105).

The psalmist finds God's Word and law very special. In today's text there are eight characteristics of the Word which stand out:

- ❧ God's Word is eternal (v. 89);
- ❧ It is something that we delight in (v. 92);
- ❧ It gives meaning to our lives (v. 93);
- ❧ It helps us to resist temptations and keeps us from every evil path (vv. 95, 101);
- ❧ It is boundless (v. 96);
- ❧ It gives us wisdom and insight (v. 98);
- ❧ It is a light and a lamp on our path through life (v. 105);
- ❧ It gives us joy (v. 111).

How important is your Bible to you? Are you as enthusiastic about it as the psalmist? One of the consequences of our busy schedules is that we read God's Word superficially. Diligently study your Bible and then go out and live as the Bible requires you to live.

Lord, I praise You for Your wonderful Word. Thank You for the important part it plays in my life. Help me to find sufficient time every day to study Your Word and please talk to me every day through Your Word. Amen.

A double-edged sword

Read Hebrews 4:12-16

For the word of God is living and active. Sharper than any double-edged sword, it penetrates even to dividing soul and spirit ... it judges the thoughts and attitudes of the heart (Heb. 4:12).

God gives us His Word as a sword – not a sword to use against others, but a sword that judges our thoughts and the attitudes of our hearts. A Christian can never be untouched by the Word – it changes your life if you are willing to obey it. Perhaps this is one of the reasons why we are hesitant to become quiet with the Word in the presence of God.

To become quiet with God's Word requires you to empty yourself, to get rid of your sins, to forsake wrong deeds and to nurture a different attitude toward the people you don't like. In other words, you are required to open yourself to the Word and to allow God's Word to change you into a new person.

When you are empty of yourself, God's Word can fill you with new wisdom and insight and inject hope and joy into your life. This hope and joy do not depend on your physical circumstances, will never be taken away from you and will fill you anew with courage for the road ahead.

Lord, empty me of myself so that I can open myself to Your Word. Let Your Word change me into the person that You intended me to be – as perfect and mature as You are. Amen.

The best weapon

Read Ephesians 6:10-18

Be strong in the Lord and in his mighty power. Put on the full armor of God so that you can take your stand against the devil's schemes. Take the helmet of salvation and the sword of the Spirit, which is the word of God (Eph. 6:10-11, 17).

Every day we are locked in a battle against evil. Christians need God's armor if they want to win the war against the devil. However, the armor of a soldier is not worth much if that soldier does not have weapons at hand as well. God's weapon is the sword of the Spirit, your Bible.

During the siege of Moscow in August 1991, Father Alexander Borisov gave each Russian soldier a small version of the New Testament. When the copies of the New Testament ran out, he gave one soldier a full-color children's Bible. The soldier realized that he would have to hide this Bible from his commanding officer. There was only one pocket in his uniform that was big enough for the Bible. He emptied his ammunition pocket and placed the Bible inside it. He then went to the battle front with a Bible in his pocket instead of bullets!

The Word of God is the best weapon with which to approach the battlefield of life. If you carry your Bible with you and let it point you in the right direction, you won't go wrong. Make sure that you carry your sword with you every day.

Heavenly Father, thank You for the sword of the Spirit with which I can successfully ward off all onslaughts from the devil. Help me never to be without the most important of all weapons. Amen.

The Word revives the soul

Read Psalm 19:8-15

The law of the LORD is perfect, reviving the soul. The statutes of the LORD are trustworthy, making wise the simple. The precepts of the LORD are right, giving joy to the heart (Ps. 19:7-8).

The psalmist found God's law of inestimable value. It is trustworthy and perfect. It gives wisdom and brings joy. It reveals God's will to the faithful.

Take a moment to decide for yourself what your Bible means to you. An American survey revealed disturbing, almost unbelievable statistics: churchgoers spend 30 seconds per day on average reading their Bibles, and 15 seconds in prayer. The preachers, however, fare somewhat better. They spend approximately one minute per day with their Bibles.

If this sounds rather far-fetched to you, work out how much time you spend with your Bible every day. If it is less than half an hour per day, the time has come for you to restructure your daily schedule. It is essential for you to make sufficient time for Bible study if you wish to grow spiritually. Without your Bible, you cannot become stronger as a Christian.

God's Word is the Word of life. See to it that you make your Bible part of your life every day.

Lord, I pray that You will once again reveal to me just how important Your Word should be in my life. Thank You for my Bible, which helps me to grow spiritually and in which my faith is anchored. Amen.

Study the Word

But as for you, continue in what you have learned and have become convinced of, because you know those from whom you learned it, and how from infancy you have known the Holy Scriptures, which are able make you wise for salvation through faith in Christ Jesus (2 Tim. 3:14-15).

Timothy learned to study the Scriptures in his childhood. Have you discovered a way to study the Bible so that it truly enriches you spiritually? The following method might help you to discover your Bible anew and make your quiet times delightful. This method is based on three things: The Bible reveals God to us, it discloses who man is, and it asks us certain questions. Apply this method to the Scripture passage that you are currently studying.

- The Word *reveals* God
  What does the text say about God? Who is He or what does He do? What is the good news contained in this passage? What, according to this passage, does God give to us?
- The Word *discloses* man
  What human behavior is disclosed here? What kind of sinful tendencies of man are disclosed? What part of life is revealed here?
- The Word *asks*:
  What does God ask of man? What does He command us to do? What does He require of us in response to the first two points?

Lord, thank You that the Holy Spirit explains Your Word to me. Please teach me who You are, teach me to know myself and reveal to me what You ask of me today. Amen.

The Word stands forever

Read Isaiah 40:1-8

All men are like grass, and all their glory is like the flowers of the field. Surely the people are grass. The grass withers and the flowers fall, but the word of our God stands forever (Isa. 40:6-8).

Isaiah prophesied that God would deliver the Israelites from exile and that their suffering would come to an end. God would liberate them and end their exile. The transience of man is emphasized here. All men are like grass, their glory is like the flowers of the field. When the breath of the Lord blows on them, they wither. In contrast with this transience is God and His Word, which stands forever. The message of salvation in the Word comes from God personally and the promises chronicled in His Word are constant and true.

Everything written in the Bible will endure for ever and you can count on every promise in the Bible. It is interesting that scientists have questioned the Bible over the ages, while excavations have, time and again, confirmed that the biblical facts are correct. We may not take anything away from God's Word, nor add anything to it. The Bible is God's letter to us. It was written through the Holy Spirit. *"For prophecy never had its origin in the will of man, but men spoke from God as they were carried along by the Holy Spirit"* (2 Pet. 1:21).

Lord, I praise You for Your Word that endures forever and for the promises contained in it, which are constant and true. Thank You for Your letter to me, which I may read unhindered so that I can once again receive confirmation of Your love for me. Amen.

Discover your Bible, and yourself

> *Read Psalm 119:161-168*

I rejoice in your promise like one who finds great spoil. Great peace have they who love your law, and nothing can make them stumble (Ps. 119:162, 165).

When you are alone, engaging with the Lord and His Word, you will discover that you can clearly hear Him talking to you. Bible study should never be relegated to the scraps of time that are left after a busy day. It is so important for your spiritual growth that it is essential for you to set aside a specific time and place for it. Diarize your time for Bible study. It is your most important appointment of the day. You cannot only listen to God's voice when it suits you. He is the most important Person in your life and He asks of you to find time for Him. He wants to reveal the treasures hidden in His Word to you personally.

Through regular Bible study you also get to know yourself better. God's Word is a mirror in which your sins are reflected as well as a light that shows you how you should live. You should never do Bible study simply out of a sense of duty; it should always be spontaneous communication with God.

If you open your Bible every day with expectancy, you will grow spiritually and become stronger. Then God will help you to apply the wisdom which you derive from His Word constructively in your own life.

Lord, please forgive me for sometimes rushing my time spent in Your Word and for just reading a verse here and there. Please teach me to set aside fixed times to study Your Word. Amen.

Group Bible study

Read Matthew 18:15-20

"For where two or three come together in my name, there I am with them" (Matt. 18:20).

It is essential for you to spend time alone in the Word of God, but you can also receive a great spiritual blessing when you gather around God's Word with other Christians.

My own Bible study group has been in existence for almost 18 years. We meet every Thursday and it remains a time of joy for all of us during which we experience God's presence. It is amazing how each woman in the group has different insights to share about a passage of Scripture and how all of us are enriched after the study. My own spiritual life has been enriched tremendously over the years through this Bible study group.

If you do not belong to such a Bible study group, you could start one in your area or congregation. Bible study material must be chosen carefully and good planning is essential. (Involve your minister in this, if possible.) Guard against your Bible study group becoming too exclusive. Give other women in the congregation the opportunity to join and split the group if it becomes too big.

Christ should always remain the center of your Bible study group. This is the condition for His presence. *"For where two or three come together in my name, there I am with them."* Become quiet before you start and consciously focus on God before opening His Word.

Heavenly Father, I praise You for a Bible study group that has brought me so much closer to You over the years. Thank You that each of us is intensely aware of Your presence every time we gather around Your Word. Amen.

The gift of being a child of God

Read Galatians 4:1-5

But when the time had fully come, God sent his Son to redeem those under law, that we might receive the full rights of sons (Gal. 4:4-5).

To be God's child is not your right and is not something you deserve. It always remains a gift of grace. Read again what Paul says in Galatians 4:4-5.

When parents adopt a child, they don't do so because that child deserves it, but because they have something to offer him: parental love, a home, nurturing. That is exactly what God does with you. He adopts you as His child, not on the basis of what you deserve, but because He loves you and because He wants to offer you eternal life.

Man is sinful by nature and far from God. But God loves sinners. He sent His only Son to be crucified so that our sins can be forgiven and we can become His children. Now you are no longer a slave to sin – you have been redeemed by God and are a child and heir of God.

God wants to offer you the undeserved gift of eternal life today – something that you can never deserve, but which you can accept gratefully. If you have not yet done so, do not hesitate any longer.

Father, time and again, the realization that You offer me heaven because You love me, leaves me totally amazed. Thank You that I could respond to Your invitation and that I now rest assured in the knowledge that I belong to You. Amen.

A prayer for a congregation

Read Colossians 4:10-13

[He is] a servant of Christ Jesus. He is always wrestling in prayer for you, that you may stand firm in all the will of God, mature and fully assured (Col. 4:12).

Epaphras's beautiful prayer is almost hidden amongst Paul's greetings to the congregation at Colosse. When he bids farewell to the congregation, Paul gives a beautiful testimonial of Epaphras. He conveys Epaphras's regards to the congregation and tells them that he is always wrestling in prayer for them. In his prayer, he asks that the congregation will stand firm in complete obedience to God's will and become spiritually mature and fully assured.

If you try to live according to this prayer, your spiritual life will benefit immensely from it. To stand firm means that you will persevere in your faith, that you will not only listen to God's Word in church on a Sunday, but that you will also live it in full during the remainder of the week. To live in complete obedience to God's will means that you will readily subject your own will to that of God.

We have already spoken about spiritual growth. It requires of you to move ahead in your Christianity, to become increasingly like Jesus every day. I pray that this beautiful prayer will find expression in your own life.

Lord, I pray that You help me live my faith to the full, both in word and deed. Help me to live in complete obedience to God's will, and to grow spiritually every day until I am as mature as Christ. Please turn this into reality for me. Amen.

Church attendance

Read Psalm 84

Blessed are those who dwell in your house. Blessed are those whose strength is in you, who have set their hearts on pilgrimage (Ps. 84:4-5).

On festive occasions the Israelites spared no money or effort to visit the temple in Jerusalem. They traveled great distances and braved dangerous roads to visit the house of the Lord regularly.

Our churches are within easy reach for most of us. And yet, many Christians make no effort to attend church every Sunday. We often come up with excuses for not going to church.

The church service provides a special opportunity for you to draw near to God. There are three things to focus on when attending a church service: Listen to the message from the Word, worship God and experience the fellowship of your fellow-believers. The gathering together of the congregation is not only about coming to God, but also fellowship with one another. Believers should care for one another by encouraging each other in love and good deeds (see Heb. 10:24-25).

Church attendance is important for your spiritual growth. Encourage your family to attend with you.

Heavenly Father, thank You that I have a church and a congregation where I can listen to Your Word and experience fellowship with You and other believers. Help me never to stay away from Your house without reason. Amen.

To celebrate

> *Read Nehemiah 8:10-12*

Nehemiah said, "Go and enjoy choice food and sweet drinks, and send some to those who have nothing prepared. This day is sacred to our Lord. Do not grieve, for the joy of the Lord is your strength." Then all the people went away to eat and drink, to send portions of food and to celebrate with great joy (Neh. 8:10, 12).

It is God's will for His children to be joyful. Today, celebrations have become a way of life. Many towns have at least one festival per year. There are arts festivals, cherry festivals and music festivals! The church calendar also includes important celebrations such as Christmas and Easter.

In our passage for today, we read that Nehemiah told the people to celebrate when the wall around Jerusalem had been completed. A description of the Feast of Tabernacles follows (see Neh. 8:13-18). They devoted this time to the Lord by reading and teaching from the Book of the Law of God.

However, we do not have to wait for a Feast of Tabernacles to receive teaching from the Word or to celebrate our faith. Every Sunday is a day of celebration as we celebrate the glory of the Lord by gathering in His house. Spend your Sundays in such a way that they are truly devoted to God. Remember that every church service is an occasion to celebrate and to glorify the Name of the Lord.

Heavenly Father, thank You that I have the opportunity every Sunday to celebrate Your love and grace towards me. Help me to put my Sundays aside for You, and turn my weekly church attendance into a celebration devoted to You. Amen.

Spiral of spiritual enrichment

Read 2 Peter 1:8-11

For this very reason, make every effort to add to your faith goodness; and to goodness, knowledge; and to knowledge, self-control; and to self-control, perseverance; and to perseverance, godliness; and to godliness, brotherly kindness; and to brotherly kindness, love (2 Pet. 1:5-7).

Peter's spiral of spiritual enrichment starts with your personal relationship with God, and gradually equips you to manifest God's love to the world. It establishes a process that should continue throughout your life, enriching you more each day.

The Message elucidates this process:

So don't lose a minute in building on what you've been given, complementing your basic faith with good character, spiritual understanding, alert discipline, passionate patience, reverent wonder, warm friendliness, and generous love, each dimension fitting into and developing the others. With these qualities active and growing in your lives, no grass will grow under your feet, no day will pass without its reward as you mature in your experience of our Master Jesus. Without these qualities you can't see what's right before you, oblivious that your old sinful life has been wiped off the books.

If you can succeed in doing this, you will live in the way that God expects of you every day.

Lord, please enable me to enrich my own faith according to Peter's religious spiral, so that I may live the way You want me to live. Amen.

Learn to lead a simple life

Read Luke 12:13-21

Then he said to them, "Watch out! Be on your guard against all kinds of greed; a man's life does not consist in the abundance of his possessions" (Luke 12:15).

One of our friends who regularly visits Mozambique told us that the Mozambicans think that the visitors have a lot of possessions even though they usually only have a small tent and some clothes. This makes one think about how little some people have to get by with and how much we have. Our houses are filled with appliances we seldom use; our cupboards are filled with clothes we haven't worn in years and we often buy things we don't really need.

Sometimes we buy things to impress other people. Perhaps we should decide to lead a more simple life; to learn to rid ourselves of those things that we no longer use; to buy only those things that we really need, and to give the things we don't need to those who really need them.

How attached are you to your worldly possessions? Always bear in mind that your life does not consist in the abundance of your possessions. Make sure that your treasures are in the right place – in heaven where moths and rust cannot destroy.

Lord, I stand guilty before You, because You know how many unnecessary possessions I have hoarded through the years. Please make me satisfied with what I have and teach me yet again that my life does not consist in the abundance of my possessions. Amen.

Faith strengthens you

Read Ephesians 3:14-21

I pray that out of his glorious riches he may strengthen you with power through his Spirit in your inner being, so that Christ may dwell in your hearts through faith. And I pray that you (will be) rooted and established in love (Eph. 3:16-17).

Jesus changes you when you invite Him into your heart and life. He makes you strong through the faith that He plants in your heart, and He personally makes His home in your heart through that faith. In *The Message* today's passage reads as follows, *"I ask him to strengthen you by his Spirit – not a brute strength but a glorious inner strength – that Christ will live in you as you open the door and invite him in. And I ask him that with both feet planted firmly on love, you'll be able to take in with all Christians the extravagant dimensions of Christ's love."*

When you feel weak and despondent, you can lean on the strength that God promises His children. *"The prayer of a righteous man is powerful and effective,"* writes James (James 5:16). When you are in need of strength, you can simply ask God for it. He will give it to you so that you are able to do those things you cannot do in your own strength.

Another thing that happens to you when Jesus enters your life, is that you are rooted and established in love.

When you go through crises in your life, you can remind yourself of the fact that you can never be outside the circle of God's love. With God's strength and love, you are more than a conqueror.

Lord, I praise You for Your infinite strength that You offer me every day, as well as for Your unconditional love in which I am rooted and established. Amen.

A glimpse of the glory of God

Read Exodus 33:17-23

Then Moses said, "Now show me your glory." And the LORD said, "When my glory passes by, I will put you in a cleft in the rock and cover you with my hand until I have passed by. Then I will remove my hand and you will see my back; but my face must not be seen" (Exod. 33:18-19, 22-23).

The relationship between God and Moses was very intimate. We read that God would speak to Moses face to face, as a man speaks with his friend (see Exod. 33:11). In our passage for today, Moses had just returned from Mount Sinai, where he spent forty days and forty nights in communion with God. He had just received the Ten Commandments. So special was this encounter with God that Moses' face was radiant (see Exod. 34:29).

This intimate communion with God changed Moses. He asked God to show him His glory. Yet, in spite of the close relationship between them, God refused. He is so holy that no one can see Him and live. However, He allowed Moses to see His back, as a sign that He would indeed go with His people.

We can also enter into a relationship with God. He still talks to us personally when we read His Word. God does even more for us than He did for Moses, because when Jesus returns to this world, we will be able to see God's glory. *"Anyone who has seen me has seen the Father,"* Jesus said to Philip (John 14:9).

Lord Jesus, thank You that You have come to show me the countenance of God. Help me to live in an intimate relationship with You. Amen.

God awaits your prayers

Read Isaiah 30:18-20

How gracious will [the Lord] be when you cry for help! As soon as he hears, he will answer you (Isa. 30:19).

Prayer is an act of drawing near to God. *"The LORD is near to all who call on him, to all who call to him in truth. He fulfils the desires of those who fear him"* writes the psalmist (Ps. 145:18-19). God is omnipotent. He does not need our prayers. He can do all the things that we want to ask of Him without our praying, because He already knows what we need, before we even ask. But when we pray, we prove to God that we want to communicate with Him.

"Prayer is a stepping stone that leads to a higher objective,"[1] writes Erwin Lutzer. Every time we pray to God in our distress, we realize that we need God more than we need our prayers to be answered. He allows distress in the lives of His children, because He knows that desperate people pray the most fervently.

Think about it. Your life is often difficult so that you can learn to have an unwavering trust in God. Unanswered prayers can also be a blessing if these prayers bring you closer to God. Therefore, continue to pray, since God longs to be gracious to you; He wants to show you compassion! (see Isa. 30:18).

Father, I now realize that You allow situations of distress in my life to draw me nearer to You. Thank You that I can talk to You and know that You are listening, even though You do not always answer me immediately. Amen.

Faith is a gift

Read Ephesians 2:1-9

For it is by grace you have been saved, through faith – and this is not from yourselves, it is the gift of God (Eph. 2:8).

The Christian religion is the only one of all the thousands of religions in the world where man does not have to achieve anything. Faith is a free gift from God. We do not have to do anything to earn it. We need not do good deeds, give a tenth of our entire income to the church, or fast and pray for weeks on end to earn God's grace. We have been saved by the grace of God, because we believe in God. Our salvation is not our own achievement.

"Saving is all his idea, and all his work. All we do is trust him enough to let him do it. We neither make nor save ourselves," explains *The Message*.

God presents you with faith as a gift of grace. It is free. All you have to do is to hold out your hand to God to receive that gift. Through His crucifixion, Jesus has already paid the price of your sins in full – once and for all. Because He has settled your debt of sin on your behalf, God forgives you your sins. All you have to do is to thank God and demonstrate your love for Him in a practical way every day by leading the kind of life He expects of you.

Lord Jesus, I glorify You that You, through Your crucifixion, gave me the gift of grace. From now on, please help me to demonstrate my gratefulness and joy for such a magnificent gift through my way of life. Amen.

Faith in desperate circumstances

Read Psalm 116:1-11

*I believed; therefore I said, "I am greatly afflicted." And in my dismay
I said, "All men are liars"* (Ps. 116:10-11).

The psalmist discovers, through his personal experiences, that
God is gracious and righteous, that He is full of compassion for
His children and that He protects the simplehearted. God helped
him in his distress and put an end to his tears (see Ps. 116:5-6, 8).
That's why the psalmist is able to keep on believing in God despite
his trying circumstances. He also realizes that God remains faithful
even when men prove unreliable.

It is easy to believe in God when things are going well. But it's
a different matter altogether when you are struck by a series of
disasters and you are unable to see even one of God's promises
being fulfilled.

Christians who are able to keep on believing in God, despite
negative circumstances, discover that God not only carries them
through difficult times, but ensures that everything works out best
for them. As a result, they can testify that they have become spiritually stronger because of their suffering. *"It was good for me to be
afflicted so that I might learn your decrees,"* the psalmist testifies
(Ps. 119:71).

If you are going through a crisis, just keep on believing – even if
all men are liars, God is completely dependable.

Heavenly Father, I glorify You for always being there for me, especially under the most difficult of circumstances. Thank You that I
can always trust in You and know that You will help me. Amen.

The God Whom you worship

Read Jeremiah 32:16-27

You have made the heavens and the earth by your great power and outstretched arm. "Nothing is too hard for you. I am the LORD, the God of all mankind. Is anything too hard for me?" (Jer. 32:17, 27).

God commanded Jeremiah to buy a piece of land. Through this, God wanted to let him know that He would show His people compassion again: houses, fields and vineyards would again be bought in that land. Jeremiah obeyed God's command, even though he did not fully understand it and the future prospects for God's people seemed bleak. It is faith that allows you to carry on with your life in times of trouble, trusting that God will continue His good work in you. God promised Jeremiah that He would allow His people to return from exile and ensured him that nothing was too difficult for Him to accomplish.

We must realize who God is. God can do everything. Nothing is too hard for Him. We can never judge God. He is omnipotent and eternal. God is still the same God as in the days of Jeremiah. *"You performed miraculous signs and wonders in Egypt and have continued them to this day,"* writes Jeremiah (Jer. 32:20).

The same holds true for us today. God's power is unchanging. He can still save and protect His children as He did in the times of the Old Testament. He is still ready to help you when you need Him.

Heavenly Father, thank You that I can continue to believe in You, even through difficult circumstances. Please help me to always remember that nothing is too hard for You. Amen.

God chose you

Read Isaiah 44:1-5

"But now listen, O Jacob, my servant, Israel, whom I have chosen. This is what the LORD says – he who made you, who formed you in the womb, and who will help you" (Isa. 44:1, 2).

God chose Israel out of all the nations to be His special people and to establish a covenant with them. He promised to be their God and to take care of them. All that He asked in return is that they keep the covenant and obey and love Him (Gen. 17:7-9). But they often failed to do so. Time and again they deserted God to worship idols, even though He remained faithful to them and forgave them every time.

When you become a Christian, it means that God destined you to be His child, even before He created the world. It is always God who takes the initiative: *"Before I was born the LORD called me; from my birth he has made mention of my name,"* the prophet Isaiah says (Isa. 49:1). Paul writes that God has chosen His children *"in him before the creation of the world to be holy and blameless in his sight"* (Eph. 1:4).

God chose you long ago, even before you were born, and invited you to belong to Him. Faith is believing God and accepting His invitation.

Heavenly Father, it is wonderful that You chose me to belong to You even before I was born, even though, like Your people of old, I have disappointed You so many times. Thank You that I was able to accept Your invitation. Amen.

Choose life!

Read Deuteronomy 30

Now choose life, so that you and your children may live and that you may love the LORD your God, listen to his voice, and hold fast to him. For the LORD is your life, and he will give you many years in the land he swore to give to your fathers (Deut. 30:19-20).

Deuteronomy 30 is Moses' farewell sermon to the people of Israel. In his final address, Moses concentrates on what is most important. *"Now choose life, so that you and your children may live,"* is his advice to them. Then he explains, *" … love the LORD your God, listen to his voice, and hold fast to him. For the LORD is your life."* To have faith means that you have chosen God and that you undertake to love Him, follow Him and obey Him.

To make the right choice is important. The wrong choice could mean the difference between success and failure. If you choose God, you can be certain that, for the rest of your life, you will have security and safety that no one will ever be able to take away from you. If you choose life, the Lord will always be by your side. He promises to help and carry you, to take care of you, to guide you and to protect you.

God has already chosen you. Are you willing, with your entire being, to choose Him? If you have been undecided up to now, do not hesitate any longer, choose life! You will definitely never regret this choice.

Heavenly Father, thank You that I can choose life, and that I now know for certain that You will always be by my side and that eternal life is awaiting me. Amen.

Prayer

Heavenly Father,

Thank You for the gift of faith that You came to offer me so freely, and which I do not deserve by any means.

I wish to accept this gift with open hands.

Give me childlike faith so that I may hold on to each of Your promises.

Please help me to grow daily in my faith, to make enough time for You, to devote my life to You and to show total obedience to You in all that I do.

Thank You for the sword of the Spirit, Your Word, which leads me to victory over the devil, and which shows me how to live so that I may strive to become as perfect and mature as Jesus.

I pray that You will make me aware of those things in my life that are wrong and make me willing to rid myself of them.

Give me the power to achieve inner strength so that my entire life will be built on the love that emanates from You.

Thank You that I could choose life and that I can know that heaven is awaiting me.

It is wonderful to know that You are eager to answer my prayers.

Amen.

March

The God that you worship

This month we are going to reflect on the characteristics of God. Who is the God we worship?

He is the triune God: the Father, the Son and the Holy Spirit. He is great and wonderful. We cannot fathom Him with our human minds. He is holy and without sin. Majesty and magnificence emanate from Him; power and glory fill His sanctuary. He is omnipotent and eternal. He forgives sins, listens to His children and knows all there is to know about us. He knows your name and loves you unconditionally.

The better you get to know Him, the more you will love Him, and the more important His role in your life will become.

Where were you?

Read Job 38:1-19

Then the LORD answered Job out of the storm: "Brace yourself like a man; I will question you, and you shall answer me. Where were you when I laid the earth's foundation? Tell me, if you understand" (Job 38:1, 3, 4).

Job had dozens of questions that He wanted to ask God. Why did God allow him to suffer? Why was he born at all, if only misery awaited him in the world? Job did not want to listen to the explanations of his three friends – he wanted answers from God.

Eventually, God had had enough of all Job's questions. *"I will question you, and you shall answer me,"* says the Lord to the rebellious Job. And then He presents Job with mind-boggling questions: *"Where were you when I laid the earth's foundation? Who shut up the sea behind doors? Have you ever given orders to the morning or shown the dawn its place?"* (Job 38:4, 8, 12).

When the Lord had finished speaking, Job was at a loss for words. Never before had he thought of God as the omnipotent Creator who made everything and who holds the world in His hands.

When the "why" questions in your life sometimes cause you to become discontented, think about how great and wonderful God really is. Try to answer the questions that God put to Job. God is so great and mighty that He does not owe you any explanations. Rather become quiet and allow Him to teach you, instead of trying to understand Him.

Father, forgive me all my "why" questions. I know that You are great and omnipotent, and do not owe me any explanations. Amen.

God is not bound by time

Read 2 Peter 3:8-15

But do not forget this one thing, dear friends: With the Lord a day is like a thousand years, and a thousand years are like a day (2 Pet. 3:8).

Peter warns believers that in the last days scoffers will come who will question the Second Coming of Christ (see 2 Pet. 3:3, 4). Peter explains that God's concept of time differs greatly from ours. To the Lord a day is like a thousand years, and a thousand years are like a day. Unlike us, He is not dependent on calendars and watches.

The scoffers in Peter's time thought Jesus would never come. They thought it was just a story. The truth is that God doesn't want one soul to be lost and is postponing Jesus' return till everyone has had the opportunity to be saved.

C. S. Lewis gave an interesting explanation for why God is not bound by time. God is like an author writing a story, he says. While the author is busy with the novel, he has all the time in the world for each of his characters. Similarly, God has all the time in the world for each of us.

Is God still waiting for you? The Lord wants to give you yet another opportunity to accept His gift of love. If you have accepted Him, make sure that you are prepared for the second coming of Christ by living a life completely committed to Him.

Heavenly Father, I know that You are not bound by time. Thank You that You want to give all people the opportunity to become Your children and that You have all the time in the world for me. Please help me to be prepared for the day of Christ's second coming. Amen.

God's thoughts

Read Isaiah 55:8-13

"For my thoughts are not your thoughts, neither are your ways my ways," declares the LORD. "As the heavens are higher than the earth, so are my ways higher than your ways and my thoughts than your thoughts" (Isa. 55:8-9).

There is often a vast difference between our expectations and how God arranges for things to turn out. God's thoughts are higher than our thoughts. His actions differ totally from ours. For this reason, it is impossible for us to explain God's actions. Unlike us, God can see the future. Often we find that the things that were most difficult to work through were used by God for our own good.

Joni Eareckson Tada was paralyzed by a diving accident when she was a teenager. She writes that she shudders at the thought of what might have happened to her if the Lord had answered her desperate prayers to be able to walk again. Through her life in a wheelchair, she learned valuable lessons such as dependency on God and absolute obedience. God could use her greatly because she was bound to a wheelchair.

Perhaps there are issues in your own life that you cannot understand. Remember: God's thoughts are higher than yours. You do not need to try to understand Him. All you need to know is that He always wants the best for you and He knows what's best.

Lord, sometimes I find it very difficult to make peace with the things You allow to cross my path. Help me to realize that You know best, that Your thoughts are higher than mine and that I will never be able to understand You with my human mind. Amen.

God performs miracles

Read Isaiah 25:1-9

O LORD, you are my God; I will exalt you and praise your name, for in perfect faithfulness you have done marvelous things. In that day they will say, "Surely this is our God; we trusted in him" (Isa. 25:1, 9).

A friend of mine, whose husband had cancer, said that the doctor told her that her husband needed a miracle. The following day she read the above Scripture verse. "Then I just knew that the Lord was going to perform a miracle," she said. Her husband recovered. We worship a God who can perform miracles!

In the Old Testament, God often delivered His people by performing miracles. Jesus also performed many miracles when He dwelt on earth. God is still perfectly able to perform miracles today. We witness so few miracles, not because God is powerless, but because we lack faith. In God's creation, you can encounter miracles every day without noticing them: the dry branches of a tree that are covered in delicate pink blossoms overnight; a caterpillar that turns into a brown cocoon and then becomes a multi-colored butterfly …

God also performs supernatural miracles. We all know of people who recovered from illness against all medical expectation; others who were protected in a supernatural way. The God whom you worship is a God of miracles! If your faith in Him is strong enough, you will experience these miracles in your own life.

Lord, You are my God! Today I want to praise You for the miracles You have performed in my life. Thank You that I know that I can always put my trust in You. Amen.

God created the galaxies

Read Job 38:31-38

Can you bind the beautiful Pleiades? Can you loose the cords of Orion? Can you bring forth the constellations in their seasons? Do you know the laws of the heavens? Can you set up [God's] dominion over the earth? (Job 38:31-33).

When we read scientific reports about the galaxies and the whole universe we realize how small we really are. It is only God who can control the movements of celestial bodies and only He who can determine their influence on our times, seasons and weather.

Even with the most advanced cameras and telescopes, we can see only a small part of the universe. Like God, the universe is far too big to be measured with our man-made instruments. The more we learn about the universe, the more we realize that man will never really be able to fathom it – not even with the best technology available to us.

When we realize this, we can only echo the words of the prophet Isaiah, *"Lift your eyes and look to the heavens: Who created all these? He who brings out the starry host one by one, and calls them each by name. Because of his great power and mighty strength, not one of them is missing"* (Isa. 40:26), and pray with the psalmist, *"O Lord, our Lord, how majestic is your name in all the earth! You have set your glory above the heavens"* (Ps. 8:1).

Father, I glorify You as the Creator of the stars. Your power and greatness is beyond comprehension. Thank You that You, who are so great and mighty, love me. Amen.

Glorify God, the Creator!

Read Nehemiah 9:5-8

You made the heavens, the earth and all that is on it, the seas and all that is in them. You give life to everything (Neh. 9:6).

When we read the story of creation in Genesis 1 and 2, we see the greatness of God in the process of creation. God created the world out of nothing – He spoke and the chaos and darkness disappeared; heaven and earth came into existence. During the first three days, God subdued the darkness, as well as the mass of water covering the earth. During the last three days He created the sun, moon and stars to banish the darkness; the birds and marine animals to fill the air and water, as well as man to inhabit the earth. Man was the crowning glory of God's creation. God instilled His own divine characteristics in man when He created us in His image.

The story of creation does not simply answer the question 'Where does everything come from?' Creation marks the beginning of God's interaction with the world. It is the proclamation of God's ownership of the world. It is also the event through which God introduces Himself in all His greatness and goodness.

When you see all the things God has made, remember to glorify Him for the wonder of His creation.

Lord, how great You are! I glorify You for creating such a beautiful world. Thank You for nature and for all life. Thank You that You have created man to tend and conserve Your creation. Thank You that we are blessed with the ability to worship You. Amen.

Our God is incomparable

Read Isaiah 40:12-18

Who has understood the mind of the LORD, or instructed him as his counselor? To whom, then, will you compare God? What image will you compare him to? (Isa. 40:13, 18).

Isaiah's beautiful song shows us exactly how powerful and incomparably great our Creator is. With this song, he wanted to convince Israel that God's message of redemption is true, that nothing is too difficult for Him.

God not only created everything, but He also maintains His creation every day. He measures the waters in the hollow of His hand; He marks off the heavens with the breadth of His hand; He weighs the mountains on His scales and the hills in a balance. God the Creator is so great that the nations are like a drop in a bucket to Him, and all the animals in the forests of Lebanon are not enough for burnt offerings to Him. He stretches out the heavens like a canopy and creates the stars one by one. There is nothing we can compare God to. He has no equal.

God also created you and me and He carries us day by day. He calls each of us by name. He loves us so much that He sent His Son to die for us. It is because He is so great and mighty that you and I can believe in the salvation He announced without any reservations.

Lord God, You are indeed incomparable in Your greatness. You have no equal. No one can do the things You do. I glorify You! I thank You that I can believe the message of redemption with all my heart. Amen.

Glory be to God!

Read Romans 11:33-36

Oh, the depth of the riches of the wisdom and knowledge of God! For from him and through him and to him are all things. To him be the glory forever! Amen (Rom. 11:33, 36).

Romans 11:33-36 is a beautiful song of praise. This doxology praises God's glory, wisdom and knowledge. With this description, the curtain is drawn back slightly so that we can get a glimpse of the greatness and majesty of God. For Paul, faith in God did not depend on understanding Him. He was able to keep on singing about God's greatness, regardless of his circumstances.

God is far too great for us to fathom with the human mind. His wisdom and knowledge are beyond our understanding. We will never be able to explain His actions, know His plans, or prescribe to Him what to do. There is no one that can do Him a favor. God is exalted far above us. *"From Him and through Him and to Him are all things, and only to Him be the glory forever."*

God does not owe you anything, but He gives you everything. He did not even hold back His Son. We read in *The Message*, *"Everything comes from him; everything happens through him; everything ends up in him. Always glory! Always praise!"*

Lord, I praise and glorify You with my entire being. Forgive me for sometimes being so arrogant that I attempt to understand You. To You be the glory forever. Amen.

Only one God

Read Daniel 6:24-29

For he is the living God and he endures forever; his kingdom will not be destroyed, his dominion will never end. He rescues and he saves; he performs signs and wonders in the heavens and on the earth (Dan. 6:26-27).

Many times in the Old Testament, God clearly says that He alone is God and that His people are not to worship other gods. *"See now that I myself am He! There is no god besides me. I put to death and I bring to life, I have wounded and I will heal,"* God says in Deuteronomy 32:39.

When the heathen nations came to know about the God of Israel, they quickly realized that He was not like the idols they worshiped. After God rescued Daniel from the lion's den, King Darius gave a beautiful description of this God who delivers His children. *"For he is the living God and he endures forever; his kingdom will not be destroyed, his dominion will never end. He rescues and he saves; he performs signs and wonders in the heavens and on the earth"* (Dan. 6:26). King Darius then decreed that, in every part of his kingdom, people must fear and revere the God of Daniel.

Our God is a jealous God. If you belong to Him, He will not tolerate idols in your life. He wants His children to remain committed to Him and that He be the top priority in their lives. Is this true in your life?

Lord, You are great and holy and omnipotent. Help me to be completely committed to You. Let nothing in my life be more important to me than You. Amen.

God keeps His promises

Read Psalm 119:9-16

I have hidden your word in my heart that I might not sin against you. I rejoice in following your statutes as one rejoices in great riches (Ps. 119:11, 14).

When someone promises you something and fails to keep that promise, it leaves you feeling discontent. Unfortunately, there are few people in this world who are completely trustworthy. I am sure that you too have made promises to people that you have not kept.

But, we can depend on God's promises. We can always count on His Word. There are hundreds of promises chronicled in the Bible. And each one of them is completely true. *"Every word of God is flawless,"* writes Solomon (Prov. 30:5). Twice Joshua reminds the people of Israel that the Lord has kept every one of the promises He made to them. Every promise has been fulfilled (see Josh. 21:45, and 23:14).

You can trust in God's promises to you – He will keep each one of them – even if it seems impossible to you right now. Sometimes God requires you to wait for the fulfillment of these promises. If this happens you may remind God of His promises: *"You who call on the LORD, give yourselves no rest, and give him no rest"* (Isa. 62:6-7). Be patient. God will fulfill each of the promises in His Word, in His own time.

Heavenly Father, thank You for being completely faithful and for fulfilling each of Your promises in the lives of Your children. Amen.

God, the Source of hope

Read Romans 15

May the God of hope fill you with all joy and peace as you trust in him, so that you may overflow with hope by the power of the Holy Spirit (Rom. 15:13).

There is little hope to be found in the world these days – even among Christians. We complain about the rising inflation rate and the increase of violence. In the process, we lose hope. This should not happen, because faith in God enables us to hope.

Hope always focuses on the future. And if you believe in Jesus, then you already know that heaven awaits you. Therefore, you can continue to hope, regardless of how bad your situation seems. *"For our light and momentary troubles are achieving for us an eternal glory that far outweighs them all,"* Paul promises the congregation at Corinth (2 Cor. 4:17).

No one can choose his circumstances, but each of us can choose how to respond to our circumstances. You can decide never to lose hope. Piet Naudé writes that hope works not because it is a cheap form of religious escapism. But because it looks at reality in the light of the One who is real. It does not consider my disposition or my chances. It considers God.[1]

Your faith fills you with the joy and peace of God, and enables your hope to become increasingly stronger through the power of the Holy Spirit.

Heavenly Father, thank You for being the source of my hope – I can hope because I believe in You. Please grant me peace and joy in my life, so that I may never lose hope again. Amen.

God takes care of His children

Read Psalm 105:1-9

Remember the wonders he had done, his miracles, and the judgments he pronounced. He is the LORD our God; his judgments are in all the earth (Ps. 105:5, 7).

The psalmist urges people to remember God's miracles and judgments. He assures them that God will keep His covenant with them for ever.

The prophet Ezekiel paints a beautiful picture of God as a caring Shepherd: *"'You my sheep, the sheep of my pasture, are people, and I am your God,' declares the Sovereign LORD"* (Ezek. 34:31). God promises to take care of His people like a shepherd takes care of his sheep. Although the people of Israel, because of their sins, were scattered amongst the nations, God promises to gather them together again and to provide for the needs of each and every one. He says, *"I myself will search for my sheep and look after them. I will tend them in a good pasture"* (Ezek. 34:11, 14).

History records many times when God, by way of a miracle, rescued His children from danger. God has faithfully cared for us. He will be there for us in the future, even though it may sometimes seem bleak.

If you stray from God, He will look for you like a shepherd looks for his stray sheep. He promises to take care of you and to protect you like a shepherd protects his flock.

Heavenly Father, thank You for the promise that You will take care of me and protect me from danger. I praise You for all the times that You have kept this promise in my life. Amen.

God is your Shepherd

Read Isaiah 40:8-11

He tends his flock like a shepherd: he gathers the lambs in his arms and carries them close to his heart; he gently leads those that have young (Isa. 40:11).

When I was still in elementary school, our neighbors' baby died suddenly. On her little grave her parents erected a beautiful tombstone of white marble. It was of a shepherd holding a little lamb in his arms. I was very sad about my friend's baby sister, but the tombstone of the shepherd with the little lamb comforted me. It made me realize that the baby was with Jesus and that there, in His arms, was by far the best place for her to be.

Isaiah assured the people of Israel that God still wanted to be a Shepherd to them even when they strayed from Him. In Psalm 23, David, who was himself a shepherd, writes about the Lord as his Shepherd. God is a Shepherd who cares for His sheep, and His sheep lack nothing. David's Shepherd provides food, water and security. Even when he walks through the valley of the shadow of death, his Shepherd will be there to carry him.

This Shepherd's promise is still valid for you today. God cares about you, as a shepherd cares about his sheep. He will walk with you every day of your life. In His arms you are safe, even if you are threatened by the worst possible dangers. He will carry you through the valley of the shadow of death. And one day He will welcome you into His house.

Heavenly Father, thank You for being my Shepherd. Thank you that I am not in want of anything; that You will carry me when I have to go through the valley of the shadow of death, and that You will welcome me into heaven one day. Amen.

God is eternal

Read Psalm 102:25-29

Your years go on through all generations. In the beginning you laid the foundations of the earth, and the heavens are the work of your hands. They will perish, but you remain; they will all wear out like a garment. But you remain the same, and your years will never end (Ps. 102:24-27).

The psalmist of Psalm 102 is distraught and turns to the Lord for help. He pleads with God not to be aloof, but to hear his prayers. At the end of the psalm, he is profoundly impressed by the fact that God is eternal, that although everything in creation will come to an end, God will remain. He has always existed – in the beginning He laid the foundations of the earth (v. 25) and He will remain, even though all else may perish (v. 26). Those people who trust in God can find comfort in the thought that He will always remain the same and that His years will never end (v. 27).

There is no real permanence in the world we live in. Everything is subject to change. Nothing looks much like it did even fifty years ago. Cities have been destroyed by earthquakes, share prices have dropped and prices have escalated. Only God has remained the same. He is the same yesterday, today and through all eternity.

God will always be there for you. His eternal arms support and carry you, just as He has supported and carried His children in the past. Of this you can be sure!

Lord, I praise You for being eternal – that You have always been there for me in the past and that You will also be there in the future. Thank You for helping and supporting me and for remaining the same for ever. Amen.

God has created you

Read Psalm 119:73-80

Your hands made me and formed me; give me understanding to learn your commands (Ps. 119:73).

I will never forget the first time I looked at a sonar of my unborn grandchild. The doctor explained to us in great detail where the little head, legs, arms, hands and feet appeared on the blurred image. We could clearly see the little baby's heartbeat. While looking at this miracle in front of me, I instinctively thought of Psalm 139:13-14: *"For you created my inmost being; you knit me together in my mother's womb. I praise you because I am fearfully and wonderfully made; your works are wonderful."*

Of all the wonderful things that God created, man is by far the most wonderful. It is amazing how intricately He has "knit us together". Through the years, scientists have succeeded in doing many wonderful things, but no one but God can create life. *"Know that the Lord is God. It is he who made us, and we are his; we are his people, the sheep of his pasture,"* says the psalmist (Ps. 100:3).

You are a creation of God – He is your Creator. All you have comes from Him. Because He created you, you belong to Him. Never forget to glorify Him for creating you so wonderfully. Also thank Him for all that He has done for you through the years.

Lord, I praise You for creating me so wonderfully. Thank You that my senses, my organs, and my nervous system function together so well. Thank You for all the things I receive from Your hand. Amen.

God knows you

Read Psalm 139:1-6; 16-17

O LORD, you have searched me and you know me. You know when I sit and when I rise; you perceive my thoughts from afar ... your eyes saw my unformed body. All the days ordained for me were written in your book before one of them came to be (Ps. 139:1-2, 16).

Even though God is great and omnipotent, He knows each one of us. He knows absolutely everything about us. He perceives our thoughts from afar, the psalmist writes. He saw us even before we were born, and then He wrote all the days ordained for us in His book before any of them came to be.

At first, I found the thought that God knows me so well rather disturbing. But the more I thought about it, the more I realized that it is indeed a very comforting thought!

God knows you inside-out. When you find yourself in the midst of a crisis, He knows about it, even though it may sometimes feel as though He is not listening to your prayers. He promises to help you.

God is aware of all your heartache and sorrow. He even knows how many hairs are on your head. Jesus says that not even a sparrow falls without His being aware of it. And you are worth more to God than many sparrows! (see Luke 12:7).

Lord, thank You for being so interested in me that You know everything about me. I praise You for numbering all the hairs on my head, for being aware of all my suffering and for surrounding me with Your love. Amen.

God knows everything about you

Read Hebrews 4:12-16

Nothing in all creation is hidden from God's sight. Everything is uncovered and laid bare before the eyes of him to whom we must give account (Heb. 4:13).

God knows everything about us. Yesterday, we read that God saw us even before we were born. It is easy to hide things from other people, but not from God. He even knows our thoughts. There is nowhere we can hide from God. *"Where can I go from your Spirit? Where can I flee from your presence?"* the psalmist asks. And then he answers his own question: *"If I go up to the heavens, you are there; if I make my bed in the depths, you are there. If I rise on the wings of the dawn, if I settle on the far side of the sea, even there your hand will guide me, your right hand will hold me fast"* (Ps. 139:7-10).

The Message says, *"His powerful Word is sharp as a surgeon's scalpel, cutting through everything, whether doubt or defense, laying us open to listen and obey. Nothing and no one is impervious to God's Word"* (Heb. 4:73).

It is amazing that God loves us despite our sins. However, today's Scripture verse carries a warning: God knows all there is to know about you and it is to Him that *"we must give account"*. Therefore live in such a way that you need not fear the day of reckoning!

Lord, I know that I cannot hide anything from You, nor is there anywhere that I could flee from You. Help me to live in such a way that I will not fear the day when I must give account to You. Amen.

God reveals Himself through His Son

> *Read John 14:6-14*

"If you really knew me, you would know my Father as well. From now on, you do know him and have seen him." Philip said, "Lord, show us the Father and that will be enough for us." Jesus answered: "Don't you know me, Philip, even after I have been among you such a long time? Anyone who has seen me has seen the Father" (John 14:7-9).

No one has ever seen God. He is too great and too holy for man to lay eyes on. *"You cannot see my face, for no one may see me and live,"* God explained to Moses (Exod. 33:20).

But when God sent His Son to this world, everything changed. Jesus is indeed God, but was also a human being. Therefore, people of His time could physically see and hear Him. *"That which was from the beginning, which we have heard, which we have seen with our eyes, which we have looked at and our hands have touched – this we proclaim concerning the Word of life,"* testifies John (1 John 1:1).

Jesus is the One who reveals the Father to us. Whoever knows Him, also knows God. In Jesus, the holy God came into our presence. He is Immanuel, God with us. He reflects the characteristics of His Father in all He says and does. *"Anyone who has seen me has seen the Father,"* He says to Philip. *"I and the Father are one,"* He tells His disciples (John 10:30).

If you get to know Jesus intimately by studying His words and deeds in the Bible, you will also come to know God better.

Lord Jesus, thank You so much for coming to show me what God is really like so that I can see His splendor in the things that You did and said when You dwelt on this earth. Amen.

God helps His children

Read 2 Chronicles 20:2-9; 24-25

[We] will cry out to you in our distress, and you will hear us and save us. We do not know what to do, but our eyes are upon you (2 Chron. 20:9, 12).

The Israelites had much practice in crying out for help to the God of the Covenant. When things went well, they strayed from God and worshiped pagan idols. But as soon as they found themselves in trouble, they knew where to run. They turned to God for help time and again, and He loved them so much that He delivered them from their predicament each time.

Therefore, when Jehoshaphat, King of Judah, heard that a large army was approaching to attack the people, he realized that only God would be able to help them. God did not disappoint him. He caused the enemy armies to fight each other, so that not a single man was left alive when Jehoshaphat and his soldiers reached the battlefield.

"My help comes from the LORD, the Maker of heaven and earth," testifies the psalmist. *"He who watches over you will not slumber"* (Ps. 121:2-3).

God is still ready to help His children when they need Him. But make sure that you do not follow in the footsteps of the Israelites who only acknowledged Him when they needed His help. Worship the Lord every day, then you can be assured on His help whenever you need it.

Lord, I praise You for all the times that You have helped me in the past. Thank You that I can know You as my Helper. Amen.

God is holy

Read Isaiah 6:1-8

"Holy, holy, holy is the LORD Almighty; the whole earth is full of his glory" (Isa. 6:3).

In a vision, the prophet Isaiah saw God sitting on His throne. Around this throne were seraphs, each with six wings, and they called out to one another, *"Holy, holy, holy is the Lord Almighty."* God is so holy that the creatures dared not look at Him. They had to cover their faces with their wings. When he saw this vision, Isaiah was convicted of his own sinfulness. *"Woe to me! I am ruined! For I am a man of unclean lips,"* he cried out (v. 5). Then one of the seraphs touched his lips with a live coal and assured him that his sins were atoned for.

To be holy means to be without sin. God is completely without sin and for this reason He does not tolerate sin, but punishes it with death. All people are sinful from the day they are born. Therefore, you can never come before the holy God in your own strength. But Jesus, through His crucifixion, made it possible for you to approach God. On the cross, He settled your debt of sin in full. God will forgive your sins, because of His Son's death on the cross. Jesus' blood cleanses you from all sin.

Because God is holy, He expects His children to be holy as well. *"Be holy, because I am holy,"* (1 Pet. 1:16). If you truly love God, the Holy Spirit will help you to lead a holy life.

Father, I worship You as the holy God who is without sin. Thank You that, through the intercession of Jesus, You enabled me to become holy, and that You forgive my sins. Amen.

God's Name

Read Exodus 3:13-16

Moses said to God, "Suppose I go to the Israelites and they ask me, 'What is his name?' Then what shall I tell them?" God said to Moses, "I am who I am. This is what you are to say to the Israelites: 'I AM has sent me to you'" (Exod. 3:13-14).

When Moses wanted to know God's Name, God revealed Himself as *"I am who I am"*. This name reflects something of God's nature. The Hebrew for God's first name can also be translated as "I shall be what I shall be". God's Hebrew name was written using four consonants: YHWH. This was pronounced as "Yahweh", as the original Hebrew did not make use of any vowels.

The Jews had such a deep reverence for the name of God that they did not say it out loud, but rather used the Hebrew word for Lord, "Adonai", when the name Yahweh appeared in the Scriptures.

The names of pagan gods usually revealed something about their characteristics. God differs from all other gods. When God revealed this Name to Moses, He proclaimed how great He is. He distinguishes Himself from the lifeless idols as the living God, the God who is.

"The name of the Lord is a strong tower; the righteous run to it and are safe" (Prov. 18:10). If you worship the living God, the God who is, you can be sure that His Name will also be a place of safety for you.

Heavenly Father, how great You are! Thank You for being the great I AM. Thank You that You are the living God and that I can be Your child. Amen.

God forgives

Read Psalm 103:8-14

He will not always accuse, nor will he harbor his anger forever; he does not treat us as our sins deserve or repay us according to our iniquities. As far as the east is from the west, so far has he removed our transgressions from us (Ps. 103:9-10, 12).

In God's eyes, every man deserves the death penalty, because of his inherent sinfulness. God is however merciful and loving. He does not hold the wrongs that we commit every day against us. He does not punish us the way we deserve to be punished – He loves us far too much for that. Instead, God sent His Son to pay the debt for our sins. God removed our sins from us, as far as the east is from the west. All we need to do is to identify and confess our sins and accept His gift of forgiveness.

In the Bible, we are often reminded that God is gracious and forgiving. *"But you are a forgiving God, gracious and compassionate, slow to anger and abounding in love,"* writes Nehemiah (Neh. 9:17). You, too, can depend on God's love and grace. God is willing to forgive you your sins time and again – provided you confess your sins and are willing to rid yourself of them. You should not ask the Lord for forgiveness, and then continue in your wrong-doing.

Father, forgive me my many sins and help me to rid myself of them. Thank You for always being willing to forgive me and for removing my sins from me as far as the east is from the west. Amen.

God's love is everlasting

> Read Psalm 103:11-22

For as high as the heavens are above the earth, so great is his love for those who fear him. But from everlasting to everlasting the LORD's love is with those who fear him (Ps. 103:11, 17).

One person's love for another is often subject to change. Many marriages fail because the love between marriage partners wanes as time goes by. The high divorce rate indicates that human love is inconstant.

God's love for His children is different. It is unchanging and eternal. Although God knows how sinful we are, He does not want us to perish. That is why He sent a Savior. All who believe in Jesus can be children of God and share in His covenant of love: *"For God so loved the world that he gave his one and only Son, that whoever believes in him shall not perish but have eternal life"* (John 3:16).

However, God expects His children to obey Him and to live as He requires, not in order to be saved, but out of gratitude because we have been saved.

Isaiah 54:10 says, *"Though the mountains be shaken and the hills be removed, yet my unfailing love for you will not be shaken"* says the LORD, who has compassion on you. Memorize this verse and recite it to yourself if you ever doubt God's love for you.

Father, I find it incomprehensible that You, who are so great and wonderful, can love me in this way. I glorify You for Your constant and everlasting love. Help me to live as You require of me. Amen.

A God who sees

Read Genesis 16:7-14

Hagar gave this name to the LORD who spoke to her: "You are the God who sees me," for she said, "I have now seen the One who sees me" (Gen. 16:13).

Hagar was mistreated by Sarai, so she fled. In the desert, God met her at a spring and asked her, *"Hagar, where have you come from, and where are you going?"* (v. 8) When Hagar replied that she was running away from her mistress, He asked her to go back. Hagar called the spring where she met the Angel of God Beer Lahai Roi, which means "well of the living One who sees me". God saw Hagar in the desert and He was willing to help her, provided she was willing to obey – to turn back and go home.

Sometimes, when times are tough, you might think that God no longer sees you. *"Why do you hide yourself in times of trouble?"* David asks God at the start of Psalm 10. Yet, at the end of the psalm, he testifies, *"But you, O God, do see trouble and grief; you consider it to take it in hand"* (v. 14).

"For the eyes of the LORD range throughout the earth to strengthen those whose hearts are fully committed to him," Hanani assures King Asa (2 Chron. 16:9). God is watching you today. He is ready to help you when you need His help.

Lord, thank You for being a God who sees Your children and their needs. I praise You for knowing about all the things that cause me heartache and make me worry, and that You are ready to help me. Amen.

A God who provides

> *Read Genesis 22:8-18*

Abraham looked up and there in a thicket he saw a ram caught by its horns. He went over and took the ram and sacrificed it as a burnt offering instead of his son. So Abraham called that place "The LORD Will Provide" (Gen. 22:13-14).

God gave Abraham an incomprehensible command to sacrifice his only son as a burnt offering (Gen. 22:2). Abraham did what the Lord asked, although he must have found it very difficult and probably did not understand why God had given him such a command. He was willing to sacrifice his son, but in the back of his mind he still counted on God's promise – he continued to believe that God would provide.

The Lord rewarded Abraham's faith and obedience. He provided a sacrificial ram in the place of Isaac. Abraham called the place where he would have sacrificed Isaac *The LORD Will Provide.*

Abraham's faith nearly cost him his only son. Faith can sometimes be very costly and make unexpected demands on us. After all, a cheap sacrifice is not really a sacrifice. You can measure your faith by what you are willing to give up.

God was willing to give up His Son on the cross, to sacrifice Jesus so that the price for your sins could be paid and so that you could be His child. Are you willing to pay the price for your faith by being obedient to God?

Heavenly Father, thank You for being willing to give up Your only Son so that I can have eternal life. Make me willing to pay the price for my faith by being obedient to You. Amen.

A God who hears

Read Isaiah 65:17-25

"Before they call I will answer; while they are still speaking I will hear" (Isa. 65:24).

In Isaiah 65, God renews His commitment to His people. In the new Jerusalem that He is preparing for them there will be no sorrow and death. The people will be able to enjoy the fruits of their labors. They will build houses and dwell in them, plant vineyards and eat their fruit. Everyone will experience unprecedented prosperity and abundance. God also promises to be so near to His children, that He will hear their prayers while they are still speaking.

The promise that God is near to listen to you, that He is a God who hears your prayers, is also for you. God loves us so much that He always listens to His children. When we pray, He hears our prayers. In situations of distress, He is always willing to help.

"In my distress I called to the Lord*; I cried to my God for help. From his temple he heard my voice; my cry came before him, into his ears,"* David testifies in Psalm 18:6. We can experience this too. When His children call, God listens and answers. He longs to be gracious to us and He wants to show us compassion. The prophet Isaiah promises, *"You will weep no more. How gracious he will be when you cry for help! As soon as he hears, he will answer you"* (Isa. 30:19).

Heavenly Father, thank You for the assurance that You hear me when I call to You, and that You are willing to intervene and help me. Amen.

Nothing is impossible for God

Read Genesis 18:9-15

Then the LORD said to Abraham, "Why did Sarah laugh? Is anything too hard for the LORD? I will return to you at the appointed time next year and Sarah will have a son" (Gen. 18:13-14).

The Bible is filled with "impossible" stories. If they were newspaper headlines they would definitely cause a stir: "Woman becomes a mother at 90!", "A talking donkey!", "Walking through the sea on dry ground!" In the history of His people God regularly does the impossible. Things that seem totally impossible to us, are possible for Him.

We cannot really blame the ninety-year-old Sarah, who had tried in vain to fall pregnant, for laughing when she heard that she would give birth to a son in a year's time. For Abraham and Sarah, children were out of the question, as they were both too old. It was indeed unrealistic, as well as impossible, to promise them a child in a year's time. Sarah's laugh was a laugh of disbelief – and yet God fulfilled His promise. She fell pregnant and bore Abraham a son. Clear proof that God can do anything!

Nothing in the world is impossible for God. He can do everything, even that which is humanly impossible. Be steadfast in your faith and you will find that He can also make the impossible possible in your life.

Heavenly Father, I believe that You are capable of anything, that nothing is impossible for You. Help me to steadfastly believe in You so that You can perform miracles in my life. Amen.

God knows you by name

> *Read Isaiah 45:1-7*

For the sake of Jacob my servant, of Israel my chosen, I summon you by name and bestow on you a title of honor, though you do not acknowledge me (Isa. 45:4).

Speaking through the prophet Isaiah, the Lord assured Cyrus that, for the sake of Israel, He had summoned him by name, even though Cyrus did not acknowledge Him. This is the only time in the Bible that a Gentile is called the anointed of the Lord. Cyrus was a heathen king who did not worship God, and yet, God singled him out to become His instrument, He summoned him by name. God does something unheard of here: He creates a unique event through which a heathen is used to deliver His people.

When God summons the children of man by name, pure grace is always involved. Through Jesus' crucifixion, He enabled you and me (who, by birth, are not God's people) to become His people. He knows each of us by name. He knows everything about us.

God promises to be there for you always. Even though a woman might forget the baby at her breast, God will never forget you. *"I will not forget you! See, I have engraved you on the palms of my hands,"* He promises in Isaiah 49:15-16. God invites you by name to be His child and offers you His mercy. Have you replied to His invitation yet?

Heavenly Father, thank You for knowing me by name. Thank You that I can be certain that You will never forget me, and for giving me the opportunity to become Your child. Amen.

God is trustworthy

Read Jeremiah 14:20-22

Do any of the worthless idols of the nations bring rain? Do the skies themselves send down showers? No, it is you, O LORD our God. Therefore our hope is in you, for you are the one who does all this (Jer. 14:22).

In the Bible we often read about idols. Every nation worshiped different gods. Today there are many religions in the world. The New Age movement and some religions claim that all these different gods are basically one and the same. Whether you pray to Buddah, Allah or whoever else, you end up at the same place.

But we know this is not true! There are millions of people who are praying to gods, hoping that those gods will be able to do something for them – but to no avail. There is only one true God. The triune God – the Father, the Son and the Holy Spirit. The faith of all those who do not believe in the crucifixion and resurrection of Jesus is worthless. Jesus said, *"I am the way and the truth and the life. No one comes to the Father except through me"* (John 14:6). God is the only true God. He is the only one who gives life, who sends rain and who can control nature. He is omnipotent and, therefore, you can trust in Him. He will never disappoint you.

If you do not believe in Jesus, you will never get to heaven. But for all who believe in Him, He makes it possible to be children of God and to be in heaven with Him for ever.

Heavenly Father, thank You for being omnipotent, for sending the rain and for holding nature in Your hand. Thank You that I can trust in You. Amen.

God is everywhere

Read Jeremiah 23:23-29

"Can anyone hide in secret places so that I cannot see him?" declares the LORD. "Do not I fill heaven and earth?" declares the LORD (Jer. 23:24).

There is no place on earth where we can hide from God. He is everywhere. For this reason, God's children can be certain that He will always be by their side. While Jesus dwelt on this earth, He could only be in one place at a time, because He was a human being like us. But God cannot be confined. He is everywhere simultaneously.

"So do not fear, for I am with you; do not be dismayed, for I am your God. I will strengthen you and help you; I will uphold you with my righteous right hand," God promises in Isaiah 41:10. *"Do not be terrified; do not be discouraged, for the LORD your God will be with you wherever you go,"* God says to Joshua (Josh. 1:9).

God promises to be near you too. God can never be far away, because He lives within you through His Holy Spirit. You always have Him by your side. He promises never to forsake you. He takes care of you and protects you every day. The fact that God is everywhere means that His children have absolutely nothing to fear. God is by your side, every day, to protect you.

Heavenly Father, thank You for the promise that You are everywhere, that You are by my side every day to assist, support, and protect me. I praise You that I never have to be without You, because through Your Spirit, You live within me. Amen.

God is interested in you

Why do you say, O Jacob, and complain, O Israel, "My way is hidden from the LORD; my cause is disregarded by my God"? (Isa. 40:27).

God's people were despondent and thought God no longer cared about them. But God assured them that he had perfect insight into their affairs, and was already in the process of bringing about their deliverance.

While I was writing this devotion, my gynecologist's secretary phoned to confirm the venue for my check-up. I had not realized until then that the check-up would take place elsewhere. The secretary was definitely not in the habit of telephoning each patient before every appointment, and if she had not phoned me on this particular day, I would have waited the entire morning at the wrong doctor's rooms.

This incident made me realize that nothing is a coincidence and that it was the Lord who saw to it that the secretary telephoned me on that specific day. How amazing! God knows everything about me – also that I would have missed the appointment with my gynecologist because I had the wrong venue in mind! God takes a personal interest in me – so much so that He made sure that I ended up at the correct place!

God also has a personal interest in you. If you believe in Him, He will ensure that everything will work out for you.

Lord, it goes beyond my understanding that You take such a personal interest in me and that You know about every small thing in my life, and that You organize my life in such a way that, in the end, everything works out for me. I want to glorify You for the love that You have for me! Amen.

Prayer

Heavenly Father,

I worship You as the Almighty Creator God, the only God who is holy, eternal and constant, the incomparable God, whose years will never end, the God from whom and through whom and to whom are all things.

I praise You for the unconditional love You show me, for Your great mercy and Your willingness to forgive, for the fact that You know me by name and care about me personally, that You see me and hear my prayers.

Thank You for Your promise to help and support me, for giving me hope for the future, for providing in every need and for caring for me every day, like a shepherd takes care of his flock.

It is wonderful that You are by my side every day, that You know me inside out and that You love me.

You are great and wonderful, filled with majesty and grandeur – to You be the glory for ever!

Amen.

April

With Jesus on the Via Dolorosa

Max Lucado wrote an exceptional book, titled *Six Hours One Friday*.

In this book the reader experiences the crucifixion of Jesus step by step.

While reading it, I realized for the first time exactly what Jesus had to suffer on my behalf. What that Friday really means to me personally.

"For every life clouded by failure, that Friday spells forgiveness. For every heart scarred by senselessness, that Friday spells the aim of life. And for every soul peering in from this side of the tunnel of death, that Friday spells salvation and life," writes Lucado.[1]

This month, we are going to walk the Via Dolorosa with Jesus – and at the end of the month, you will be able to answer this question: What does that Friday mean to you?

The message of the Gospel

Read 1 Corinthians 15:1-11

For what I received I passed on to you as of first importance: that Christ died for our sins according to the Scriptures, that he was buried, that he was raised on the third day (1 Cor. 15:3-4).

In his book, *No Wonder They Call Him the Savior*, Max Lucado tells of a student who asked him: "All I want to know is what counts. Do not speak to me about religion – I have walked that path and I steer clear of theology – I have a degree in it. Just get to the crux of the matter." Lucado writes that at that moment he did not know what to say to the student, but later realized that he should have read him 1 Corinthians 15:3-4.

In this Scripture verse we find the essence of our faith. *"For what I received I passed on to you as of first importance: that Christ died for our sins according to the Scriptures, that he was buried, that he was raised on the third day."*

Paul addressed this message to the congregation in Corinth, because some of them thought that Jesus' resurrection was only a myth. Paul wanted to tell them what being a believer is all about: Jesus died on your behalf and conquered death, so that you can have everlasting life.

Do you believe this with your whole heart?

Lord Jesus, thank You for dying on my behalf, so that God can forgive my sins. Thank You that You rose from the dead, so that I can live with You forever. Amen.

The reason for Jesus' suffering

Read 1 Peter 3:18-24

For Christ died for sins once for all, the righteous for the unrighteous, to bring you to God (1 Pet. 3:18).

When Jesus suffered on the cross for our sins, He was completely innocent. He did not deserve such suffering, to be forsaken even by His Father. He is completely free of all sin, but He endured the suffering on the cross on our behalf. He chose to suffer even though He was innocent, so that we can have access to the holy God.

Your sins are the reason why Jesus suffered on the cross. On the cross, He endured God's wrath against the sin of mankind, so that we, who are guilty, can be freed from sin. When the blood of Jesus flowed on the cross, He paid our debt in full, and God forgave us our sins on grounds of His Son's atonement.

All of us experience tribulation at one time or another. However, if you have to suffer undeservedly, remember how Jesus also had to suffer. Let that be your strength.

Lord Jesus, how can I thank You for the fact that You were willing to suffer undeservedly on the cross so that God could forgive my sins. Make me willing to accept undeserved suffering in my own life. Amen.

God gives His Son

Read Romans 8:31-39

He who did not spare his own Son, but gave him up for us all –
how will he not also, along with him, graciously give us all things?
(Rom. 8:32).

The omnipotent Creator God, who brought the world into existence, gave His own Son to be crucified so that we can experience salvation. He allowed His only Son to be put to death so that you and I can have eternal life. That is amazing. It is a miracle that we can only accept with gratitude and faith.

When parents allow their children to leave home, they hope and pray that all will go well for them and that they will be happy and successful. But we don't really know what will become of them. But God is omniscient. When He sent Jesus to the world, He knew full well how His Son would have to suffer; what Jesus would have to endure before His worldly mission would be completed. Yet God did not hesitate for one moment. He sent Jesus to this world to be crucified so that whoever believes in Him shall not perish but have everlasting life.

If you have not yet invited Jesus into your life, remember that God's gift was also meant for you. Jesus suffered so that you could be forgiven. God gave His Son so that you can experience salvation. Do not hesitate to accept His gift of grace.

Heavenly Father, I do not understand how You could bear to see Your Son suffer so that I could come into Your presence. However, I accept Your gift with gratitude. Thank You that I can be Your child because Jesus paid for my salvation. Amen.

Jesus in Gethsemane

Read Luke 22:39-46

He knelt down and prayed, "Father, if you are willing, take this cup from me; yet not my will, but yours be done" (Luke 22:41-42).

Just as God knew that His Son would have to suffer for the sins of mankind, Jesus knew that a terrible cup of sorrow awaited Him. *"Yet it was the LORD's will to crush him and cause him to suffer"* writes Isaiah (Isa. 53:10). Jesus knew that He could not escape the Way of the Cross, and yet, because He was also human, He asked whether His Father would not take his cup from Him.

In Mark 14:34, we find Jesus' heart-rending confession, *"My soul is overwhelmed with sorrow to the point of death."* Jesus knew that His heavenly Father could change His circumstances but chose not to do so. Jesus abided by the will of His Father.

We too become distressed and anxious at times when God does not respond to our prayers even though we know that everything is possible for Him. Sometimes God says "no" to His children (as He did to His Son), because He has a greater purpose for us. If God had agreed to Jesus' request, His coming into this world would have been in vain. Whenever God says "no", we often realize afterwards that He indeed knew best.

After Jesus had accepted God's will, God sent an angel to strengthen Him. God will also give you strength in times of suffering, provided that, like Jesus, you are willing to place His will first.

Lord Jesus, it breaks my heart when I think of how You had to suffer in Gethsemane and yet You were willing to abide by the will of Your Father. Please make me willing to abide by God's will in my own life. Amen.

Watch and pray

Read Mark 14:32-43

"Watch and pray so that you will not fall into temptation" (Mark 14:38).

In Jesus' hour of distress, He took three of His friends with Him to Gethsemane for support. But they failed miserably. They failed to stay awake and pray with Jesus and kept falling asleep until Jesus had to tell them that His hour had come. Directly afterwards, the soldiers came to take Him captive.

"Just as he was speaking, Judas appeared. With him was a crowd armed with swords and clubs" (v. 43). The disciples could not even succeed in staying awake with the Master for one hour. They did not follow Jesus' advice: to watch and pray so that they would not fall into temptation.

It is also necessary for us to watch and pray if we want to resist worldly temptation. To *watch*, means to be on our guard. *"Your enemy the devil prowls around like a roaring lion looking for someone to devour"* (1 Pet. 5:8). He knows exactly where to find the weak spots in your spiritual armor. Be alert so that he will not catch you unawares and cause you to fall into his trap.

To *pray* implies that you will turn to God for help. Ask Him to deliver you from evil. He promises that He will not let you be tempted beyond what you can bear. When you feel tempted, He will provide a way out (see 1 Cor. 10:13).

Lord Jesus, I regret that I am often asleep when You expect me to be alert and praying. Please deliver me from evil. Amen.

One of the Twelve

Read Mark 14:43-51

Just as he was speaking, Judas, one of the Twelve, appeared. With him was a crowd armed with swords and clubs. Going at once to Jesus, Judas said, "Rabbi!" and kissed him (Mark 14:43, 45).

Not only did Jesus' three friends fall asleep in the garden, one of the twelve disciples, whom Jesus had carefully chosen to work with Him for three years and to continue spreading the Gospel after His death, betrayed Him. And he did so with a kiss, which should be a sign of affection.

Judas betrayed His Master for thirty silver coins. Afterwards he did show some remorse and tried to undo his betrayal, but it was too late. Judas could not live with his guilt and killed himself after throwing the money on the temple floor (Matt. 27:3, 5).

Jesus willingly allowed Himself to be taken captive because He knew that it was part of God's plan. It must have caused Him much sorrow when His friends who had followed Him for so long all deserted Him. Jesus would have to walk the path of suffering alone.

Should you suffer greatly, you always have the assurance that you are not alone. God is always by your side to help and comfort you.

Lord Jesus, You were so alone during Your suffering. Thank You that, because You were willing to walk the path to the Cross alone, I never have to be alone again, and that I can now always have God by my side during times of suffering. Amen.

Jesus' disciples run away

Read Mark 14:47-52

Then everyone deserted him and fled. A young man, wearing nothing but a linen garment, was following Jesus. When they seized him, he fled naked, leaving his garment behind (Mark 14:50-52).

Judas betrayed Jesus. All of Jesus' disciples, who had sworn that they would never desert Him, abandoned Him and ran away when He was taken captive. Before Peter ran away he drew his sword and cut off the ear of the unfortunate Malchus (John 18:10).

A young man wearing nothing but a linen garment was the last one left with Jesus, but he dropped his garment and fled naked when the soldiers tried to seize him. Biblical scholars are of the opinion that this young man could have been Mark himself, but we do not know for sure. What is important is that this young man at least tried to assist Jesus. But when his own life was in danger, he too fled for safety. For him too, the cost of following Jesus was too high.

Jesus was now totally alone. He had no one to support Him on His way to the cross. Would you have done any better than the first disciples of Jesus?

Lord Jesus, I come to confess that I also often let You down, that I sometimes hesitate to follow You and that I am often a poor disciple. Make me willing to take up my cross and follow You. Amen.

Pilate washes his hands in innocence

Read Luke 23:1-4; 20-25

For the third time he spoke to them: "Why? What crime has this man committed? I have found in him no grounds for the death penalty. But they insistently demanded that he be crucified. So Pilate decided to grant their demand (Luke 23:22-24).

When Jesus appeared before Pilate, charged with inciting the people to rebellion by proclaiming a new kingdom, Pilate soon realized that Jesus was innocent. He half-heartedly tried to set Jesus free, but eventually gave in to the demands of the incensed crowd and handed Jesus over to be crucified.

Pilate had the power to set Jesus free. Even his wife warned him during the trial that Jesus was innocent. Against his better judgment, Pilate did the wrong thing because he was not brave enough to go against the riotous crowd. He questioned Jesus three times and then washed his hands of the matter. But his guilt was not washed away by this hand washing ceremony. He would have to live for the rest of his life with the knowledge of what he had done.

Sometimes we also do things that we know are wrong because we are afraid to stand up for our Christian principles. We remain silent when people take the name of the Lord in vain. We keep a low profile when people criticize others. To wash your own hands does not work. You must make a decision to follow Jesus, then have the courage to make a stand for Him.

Lord Jesus, I regret that I also sometimes wash my hands of important issues and allow things to happen around me that I know are wrong. Please forgive me and help me in future to make a stand for You. Amen.

Crucify Him!

Read Galatians 3:10-14

Christ redeemed us from the curse of the law by becoming a curse for us, for it is written: "Cursed is everyone who is hanged on a tree" (Gal. 3:13).

For the Jews, crucifixion was the most humiliating way to die. It was a cruel and slow death. The condemned were flogged beforehand, making them weak. They then had to carry their own cross-beam to the place of execution.

When Pilate wanted to set Jesus free, the crowd loudly demanded that He must be crucified. The fact that the crowd insisted that Jesus be crucified is a clear indication that they completely rejected Him. In the eyes of the Jewish people, all those who were hanged on a tree were cursed by God.

During Jesus' time, only criminals were crucified. Jesus was completely willing to die this painful, violent death, as this was why He came to earth – to redeem sinners by dying in their place. Jesus took the curse, which we deserve, upon Himself and, in so doing, redeemed us from the curse of the law. The law requires us to acquit ourselves – something which we are unable to do, because we have been guilty since birth and we will never be able to uphold the law.

When Jesus was innocently crucified, He answered to the law on your behalf. You, who have been guilty since birth, are forgiven by God, because His blood has flowed for you, cleansing you of all your sins.

Lord Jesus, thank You that You died the most painful death imaginable on my behalf, so that my sins can be forgiven by God. Amen.

Free access to God

Read Hebrews 10:19-25

Therefore, brothers, since we have confidence to enter the Most Holy Place by the blood of Jesus, by a new and living way opened for us through the curtain, that is, his body (Heb. 10:19-20).

The Most Holy Place in the temple was indeed so holy to the Jews that only the High Priest had access to it once a year. Just as it was impossible for an ordinary Jew to enter into the Most Holy Place, it is impossible for sinners to find their way to the holy God. However, Jesus' crucifixion makes it possible. When He died, the curtain separating the Most Holy Place from the Holy Place, was torn in two (see Matt. 27:51).

Through this symbolic event the holy God came within reach of sinners. It also declares that the dispensation of the Old Testament is now something of the past. The temple is no longer the only place where God can be worshiped. Through Jesus' crucifixion, all believers have access to God. *"The 'curtain' into God's presence is his body,"* we read in *The Message*.

Because Jesus' body was broken on the cross for you and because His blood flowed to cleanse you from all your sins, you can have the confidence to approach God. You can talk to Him in prayer knowing that He listens and hears and that He will forgive your sins.

Lord Jesus, I glorify You because Your body was broken on the cross so that I might have free access to God's throne of grace. Amen.

Jesus' crucifixion

Read Mark 15:21-32

They brought Jesus to the pace called Golgotha (which means The Place of the Skull). Then they offered him wine mixed with myrrh, but he did not take it. And they crucified him. Dividing up his clothes, they cast lots to see what each would get. It was the third hour when they crucified him (Mark 15:22-25).

Mark chronicles the time of Jesus' crucifixion as the third hour, which is nine o'clock in the morning. Darkness came over the entire world from twelve o'clock until three o'clock and shortly afterwards, Jesus died. He hung on the cross for approximately six hours before He died.

As we have already heard, crucifixion was one of the cruelest methods of executing a criminal. The condemned person's hands and feet were fixed to the cross with nails. When the cross was hoisted, the condemned person hung from his pierced hands. To get sufficient air, he had to pull himself up by his hands in order to be able to breathe. Every movement worsened the intense pain. Jesus had to endure unbearable suffering for six hours.

Mark reports that Jesus was offered wine mixed with myrrh to drink, which He refused. Perhaps it was because He wanted to remain conscious until the end. Jesus' suffering was worsened by the slander and insults of those surrounding Him. In addition, the appalling suffering He had to bear was completely unjust. It is good to reflect again during this Easter season on the price Jesus had to pay to redeem you.

Lord Jesus, until now I have never truly realized how unbearable the suffering on the cross was. Please help me never to forget how dearly my salvation cost You. Amen.

Undeserved grace

Read Luke 23:38-43

But the other criminal rebuked him. "Don't you fear God," he said, "since you are under the same sentence? We are punished justly, for we are getting what our deeds deserve. But this man has done nothing wrong." Then he said, "Jesus, remember me when you come into your kingdom" (Luke 23:40-42).

Two criminals were crucified on either side of Jesus. The one derided Him, but the second one sought His grace. He asked Jesus to remember him when He came into His kingdom. Jesus did not hesitate. *"I tell you the truth, today you will be with me in paradise,"* He promised (Luke 23:43).

The condemned criminal truly believed that Jesus could save him, although he had nothing whatsoever to offer in return. He did not have any time left to demonstrate remorse through his way of life either. In the eyes of man, he was a worthless criminal, someone who was getting what he deserved. But for Jesus, he was precious enough to inherit salvation. With his last breath, the criminal seized Jesus' grace. And he received a promise from Jesus personally, that his request had been granted.

Jesus' love for you does not depend on the things that you can do for Him. You need not offer anything in return for your salvation. Only a prayer is required to unlock the gates of heaven for you: "Father, remember me". Then you too can lay claim to Jesus' reply to the condemned criminal, *"You will be with me in paradise."*

Lord Jesus, we are so undeserving of the grace You show toward us. Please forgive me my sins, so that I can be with You in heaven one day. Amen.

Without God

Read Matthew 27:45-50

From the sixth hour until the ninth hour darkness came over all the land. About the ninth hour Jesus cried out in a loud voice, "My God, my God, why have you forsaken me?" (Matt. 27:45-46).

During the time that He spent on earth, Jesus endured dreadful pain and suffering. He experienced the spiritual pain of being rejected by the people He came to save, and of being forsaken by His disciples. There was also the physical pain of torture before the crucifixion, as well as unbearable bodily pain when He was nailed to the cross.

Jesus was able to endure the pain because He had the support of His Father. *"But a time is coming, and has come, when you will leave me all alone,"* He predicted to His disciples. But then He added: *"Yet I am not alone, for my Father is with me"* (John 16:32). However, on the cross this comfort is taken away from Him. God forsook His beloved Son in the hour of His greatest need because of His loathing of the sins that Jesus was carrying on our behalf.

In every person's life there are times when God seems to be far away, when you are almost certain that He no longer takes any notice of you and does not hear your prayers. But we know this is not true. Because God forsook His Son on the cross, He can never forsake you. You have the assurance that your worst suffering will be made bearable because you know God is by your side and He will carry you.

Lord Jesus, I glorify You for braving God's wrath against sin, so that I need never be separated from God again. Amen.

Darkness over the world

> Read Luke 23:44-49

It was now about the sixth hour, and darkness came over the whole land until the ninth hour, for the sun stopped shining. Jesus called out with a loud voice, "Father, into your hands I commit my spirit" (Luke 23:44-46).

While Jesus hung on the cross, a darkness came over the land and the curtain of the temple was torn in two. Directly after this, Jesus spoke His last words, *"Father, into your hands I commit my spirit"*. These words come from Psalm 31:5. This clearly indicates to us that Jesus had fulfilled God's will. Then Jesus died, and His life of obedience to His Father here on earth came to an end.

The darkness that descended on the world with the death of Jesus, is a sign of God's divine judgment of the people who rejected Jesus. In Amos 5:18, it is predicted that the day of the Lord will bring woe and darkness. Mark indicates that Jesus' death already forms part of the last days. In effect, the last days started with the crucifixion of Jesus.

With the darkness that accompanied Jesus' crucifixion, it seemed as though the Light of the World had been extinguished. But the death of Jesus formed part of God's plan of salvation for the world. Because He died, you can live in His light, and you need no longer be lost in the darkness of sin.

Lord Jesus, thank You that Your crucifixion has enabled me to live in God's light for the rest of my life. Help me to shine my light among all people so that they may glorify Your Name. Amen.

Jesus' death is reality

Read John 19:30-34

But when they came to Jesus and found that he was already dead, they did not break his legs. Instead, one of the soldiers pierced Jesus' side with a spear, bringing a sudden flow of blood and water (Jn. 19:33-34).

After Jesus' crucifixion there were people who argued that His body was removed by His followers and that He did not really die. Matthew reports that the chief priests and elders gave the soldiers who were present at the cross a large sum of money to say that Jesus' disciples had come during the night and stolen His body, while they were asleep. This story was widely circulated among the Jews (see Matt. 28:12-15).

But Jesus really did die. Evidence of this is the sudden flow of blood and water when one of the soldiers pierced Jesus' side with a spear. This indicates that Jesus was physically really dead. When He rose from the dead, He conquered death, so that we who believe in Him may have everlasting life. With His resurrection, Jesus renders the fear of death unnecessary. Paul writes that death's victory and sting no longer exist (see 1 Cor. 15:54-55).

You need no longer fear death. Jesus conquered it on the cross once and for all. You can be certain that for you, death will now merely mean a crossing-over to real life – everlasting life with God.

Lord Jesus, thank You that I don't have to fear death, but that I can be certain that it is merely a crossing-over into eternal life with You. Amen.

Jesus' burial

> Read Luke 23:50-56

Going to Pilate, he asked for Jesus' body. Then he took it down, wrapped it in linen cloth and placed it in a tomb cut in the rock, one in which no one had yet been laid (Luke 23:52-53).

A number of people who loved Jesus were involved in His burial. After Mary had washed Jesus' feet with her tears and poured perfume over them, Jesus said that she had poured perfume on His body in preparation for His burial (see Mark 14:8). Joseph of Arimathea and Nicodemus laid Jesus' body in a new tomb (see John 19:38-39).

We see that Joseph of Arimathea was a sincere and devout man. Although he was a member of the Sanhedrin, he did not agree with the manner in which they treated Jesus. He also did not want Jesus' body to fall into the hands of the Jews. That would have meant that Jesus would be buried like a criminal in a mass grave. Therefore, he asked permission from Pilate to bury the body of Jesus. He took Jesus' body down from the cross himself, wrapped it in a linen cloth and arranged for Jesus' body to be placed in a new tomb.

Many people were eyewitnesses to the fact that Jesus really died. The fact that His body was placed in a tomb is further proof that He did die.

None of us can escape death but, if we believe in Jesus, we have the assurance of eternal life.

Lord Jesus, the fact that Your body was placed in a tomb fills me with joy because it means that, through the grave, You conquered death. Therefore, I will live forever one day. Amen.

Jesus' resurrection

Read Matthew 28:1-10

And if Christ has not been raised, our preaching is useless and so is your faith (1 Cor. 15:14).

Jesus really died. But then the miracle of miracles took place – Jesus was raised from the dead. We can either accept or reject this message, but we can not change it, says the theologian, Karl Barth.[2] It sounds totally impossible that someone who is already dead and buried can come alive again, but to God everything is possible. If we do not believe that Jesus has been raised from the dead, then our faith is useless, writes Paul to the congregation in Corinth. *The Message* says, *"And if Christ wasn't raised, then all you're doing is wandering about in the dark, as lost as ever."*

Jesus' resurrection cannot be explained, but you must believe it, otherwise your faith is worthless and without substance.

When the women who wanted to embalm the body of Jesus, reached the tomb, there was only an angel who told them not to look for the Living among the dead (see Luke 24:5). Jesus was no longer in the tomb, He had been raised to life!

Above the door-frame of the garden tomb in Jerusalem, an inscription reads: "Jesus is not here, He has risen from the dead!" Jesus conquered death, He rose from the dead and He will live for all eternity. Do you believe this? Then you can rest assured that, when you die, He will give you life everlasting.

Lord Jesus, with my human mind I cannot understand how it is possible that You could have risen from the dead, but I believe it with all my heart. Thank You that through Your resurrection death has been conquered. Amen.

Three women at an empty grave

Read Matthew 28:1-11

I know that you are looking for Jesus, who was crucified. He is not here; he has risen (Matt. 28:5-6).

All through Jesus' ministry there was a group of women who cared for Him by bringing Him food and support (see Luke 8:3). These women wanted to do something for Him after His burial – unlike His disciples who remained inactive. The three women went to the tomb to embalm the body of Jesus with perfume. At first they were alarmed when they discovered that the stone had been rolled away and the tomb was empty. But then two men in clothes that gleamed like lightning, stood beside them, giving them the message, *"Why do you look for the living among the dead?"* they asked, *"He is not here; he has risen!"* (Luke 24:5-6).

Only then did the women remember the words of Jesus – that the Son of Man would be handed over into the hands of sinful men, that He would be crucified and that, on the third day, He would be raised to life (see Luke 9:22). The women left the tomb filled with joy, and went to tell the disciples that Jesus had risen from the dead. Once again, the reaction of the disciples was disappointing. Whereas the women believed the message from the angels immediately, the apostles were rather skeptical: *"But they did not believe the women, because their words seemed to them like nonsense"* (Luke 24:11).

Do you believe that Jesus truly rose from the dead? Then, start living for Him.

Lord Jesus, thank You that I, just like the women of long ago, can do something for You by offering assistance to others who need my help. Make me aware of the needs surrounding me. Amen.

Mary Magdalene and Jesus

Read John 20:11-18

But Mary stood outside the tomb crying. "Woman," (Jesus) said, "why are you crying? Who is it you are looking for?" Thinking he was the gardener, she said, "Sir, if you have carried him away, tell me where you have put him and I will get him" (John 20:11, 15).

Jesus' tomb was empty and the disciples had received the message that He had risen from the dead. Mary remained alone at the tomb after Peter and John had left. A man dressed in white asked her why she was crying. A rather strange question to ask at a tomb, but Mary replied, *"They have taken my Lord away, and I don't know where they have put him"* (v. 13).

After Mary had finished speaking, an unknown man behind her asked her the same question, *"Woman, why are you crying?"* Once again Mary explained. Then Jesus called her name, *"Mary"*. Then she knew for sure that it was truly Him.

Mary must have been very glad to see Jesus alive. However, He warned her not to hold on to Him, because He had not yet returned to His Father. He also asked her to tell the believers that He would be returning to His Father (v. 17).

Because Jesus has really risen from the dead we need no longer be sad at the graveside of a loved one. *"I am the resurrection and the life. He who believes in me will live, even though he dies,"* Jesus promised Martha (John 11:25). You can accept this promise for yourself.

Lord Jesus, thank You that my faith in You guarantees that my loved ones and I will live, even though we die. Amen.

The disciples' reaction

Read Luke 24:8-12

But they did not believe the women, because their words seemed to them like nonsense. Peter, however, got up and ran to the tomb (Luke 24:11-12).

Thomas was not the only doubting disciple! Not one of the disciples believed the three women when they said that Jesus had risen from the dead. Luke reports that the story seemed like nonsense to them. Actually, we cannot blame them for their skeptical reaction because, even though Jesus told them on a number of occasions that He would rise from death, they never really understood what He meant.

However, there was one disciple who decided to go and see for himself. The impulsive Peter got up and ran to the tomb. All he found there were the linen burial cloths. Peter is yet another independent witness of Jesus' empty tomb. *"He went away, wondering to himself what had happened,"* says Luke (Luke 24:12). This "wondering" may not yet be faith, but it is nevertheless an acknowledgement that the hand of God was at work.

From a human perspective, Jesus' resurrection was a physical impossibility. In order to believe in the resurrection, you have to take God's word for it! He is the only one who can plant this faith in your heart. Do you believe that Jesus rose from the dead? Then thank God that He has given you the faith to believe.

Heavenly Father, I know that my faith in You is a personal gift from You and that, on my own, I am not capable of whole-heartedly believing the supernatural event of Jesus' resurrection. Thank You for planting faith in my heart. Amen.

Two travelers on the road to Emmaus

Read Luke 24:21-31

As they talked and discussed these things with each other, Jesus himself came up and walked along with them. When he was at the table with them, he took bread, gave thanks, broke it and began to give it to them. Then their eyes were opened and they recognized him (Luke 24:15, 30-31).

Two disappointed travelers, devoid of all hope, were on their way to Emmaus, a small town outside Jerusalem. They were followers of Jesus, and were engaged in a lively discussion about all the strange events that had been taking place in Jerusalem. They had really hoped that Jesus was the Messiah but it seemed that this hope now lay with Jesus in His grave.

The two men from Emmaus had the wrong expectations about Jesus. Like the rest of the people, they were hoping that He would rescue Israel from Roman oppression, but Jesus actually came to save them from eternal death. The women's testimony, that Jesus had risen from the dead, only served to disconcert them even more (vv. 22-23).

"How slow of heart (you are) to believe all that the prophets have spoken!" Jesus said to them (v. 25). He then explained the references to Himself in the Scriptures. When they reached their destination, they invited their fellow-traveler to join them for a meal. Only after Jesus had given thanks, did they recognize Him. They then immediately returned to Jerusalem to tell the other believers about their experience.

Lord Jesus, make me Your witness, like the two men of Emmaus, and give me the confidence to tell others what an important role You play in my life. Amen.

Jesus appears to His disciples

Read John 20:19-23

On the evening of that first day of the week, when the disciples were together, with the doors locked for fear of the Jews, Jesus came and stood among them and said, "Peace be with you!" (John 20:19).

A group of disappointed disciples gathered behind closed doors. They were of the opinion that three years of hard work had been fruitless. The Messiah, who was supposed to save them from Roman oppression, was dead. In spite of all His wonderful promises, He had left them in the lurch. Although the doors were locked for fear of the Jews, Jesus suddenly stood among them with His message of peace. He showed them His pierced hands and side. *"Peace be with you!"* He said. *"As the Father has sent me, I am sending you."* And with that He breathed on them and said, *"Receive the Holy Spirit"* (vv. 21-22).

This appearance and these words of Jesus changed a small group of faint-hearted disciples into inspired witnesses (see Acts 2:36). Now it was up to them to tell the Good News to the world.

God's children still ought to be witnesses, spreading His good news in the world. As Jesus sent His disciples, He also sends you today. The Holy Spirit enables you to be a forceful witness of the salvation that Jesus brings about. If you are willing to testify about Him, God will bring His peace into your life. Are you a witness for Jesus?

Lord Jesus, I pray that You will give me the confidence, through the workings of Your Holy Spirit, to spread the gospel message to all I come into contact with. Thank You that I can experience Your peace in my life. Amen.

Thomas struggles to believe

So the other disciples told him, "We have seen the Lord!" But he (Thomas) said to them, "Unless I see the nail marks in his hands and put my finger where the nails were, and put my hand into his side, I will not believe it" (John 20:25).

Thomas was absent the first time Jesus appeared to His disciples after His resurrection. When they later told him that they had seen Jesus, he stubbornly refused to believe their story. *"Unless I see the nail marks in His hands and put my finger where the nails were, and put my hand into His side, I will not believe it,"* said the doubting Thomas.

Not long afterwards, Jesus appeared to His disciples again, and this time Thomas was present. Jesus was aware of Thomas's doubts. *"Put your finger here; see my hands. Reach out your hand and put it into my side. Stop doubting and believe,"* Jesus said to him. The overwhelmed Thomas could only reply, *"My Lord and my God!"* (John 20:27, 28). *"Because you have seen me, you have believed; blessed are those who have not seen and yet have believed,"* Jesus replied (John 20:29).

There are many people who argue that seeing is believing. But faith is the willingness to believe without seeing (see Heb. 11:1). If you are willing to believe wholeheartedly without seeing, you will discover, like Thomas, that Jesus always keeps His promises.

Lord Jesus, I confess that I am often also filled with doubt. Please come to my rescue and help me to believe steadfastly in You – without needing to see the evidence. Amen.

Feed my sheep

Read John 21:15-19

The third time he (Jesus) said to him, "Simon son of John, do you love me?" Peter was hurt because Jesus asked him the third time. He said, "Lord, you know all things; you know that I love you." Jesus said, "Feed my sheep" (John 21:17).

Peter's denial must have hurt Jesus greatly, but Jesus gave him an opportunity to repent for his failure. After His resurrection, Jesus appeared to Peter and asked him three times whether he really loved Him. By love He meant complete loyalty and the willingness to sacrifice yourself for the sake of the one you love.

When Peter said he did love Jesus, Jesus commanded him three times to take care of His sheep. (It is rather interesting that Jesus' number of questions and commands agree exactly with the number of times Peter had disowned Him!)

Peter was reinstated in the presence of the other disciples. Once again He was assigned a role in Jesus' kingdom. He must take care of the sheep!

Jesus is the Good Shepherd, the door for the sheep. He takes care of His children like a shepherd takes care of his sheep and, without Him, we do not have access to God. And yet God uses His children to do His work here on earth. He needs shepherds to take care of His sheep. Peter accepted Jesus' challenge. He was willing to continue Jesus' work here on earth.

Are you willing to feed Jesus' sheep?

Lord Jesus, thank You for being my Shepherd and taking care of me. Make me willing to take care of other believers, to guide them onto the right path. Amen.

Jesus ascends into heaven

> *Read Acts 1:1-11*

While he was blessing them, he left them and was taken up into heaven (Luke 24:51).

Jesus promised His disciples that He was going to heaven to prepare a place for them there. *"In my Father's house are many rooms; if it were not so, I would have told you. I am going there to prepare a place for you. And if I go and prepare a place for you, I will come back and take you to be with me that you also may be where I am"* (John 14:2, 3).

While His disciples were watching Jesus being taken away from them on a cloud, two men dressed in white comforted them saying, *"This same Jesus, who has been taken from you into heaven, will come back the same way you have seen him go into heaven"* (Acts 1:11).

Jesus' ascension into heaven offers us a number of guarantees, writes Johan Cilliers. Firstly, it provides us with the guarantee that, if we die before the second coming of Christ, we will be safe with Him. Secondly, it provides us with the guarantee that Jesus will return one day. Thirdly, we can believe that our bodies will also rise from the dead one day.[3]

Because Jesus was crucified, rose from the dead and ascended into heaven, you can be certain that a special place is being prepared for you in heaven where you will be happy with Him for all eternity.

Lord Jesus, thank You that Your crucifixion, resurrection and ascension are my guarantee of eternal life and that I can know that You are already in the process of preparing my place in heaven. Amen.

The second coming of Jesus

Read Mark 13:24-37

They were looking intently up into the sky as he was going, when suddenly two men dressed in white stood beside them. They said, "why do you stand here looking into the sky? This same Jesus, who has been taken from you into heaven, will come back in the same way you have seen him go into heaven" (Acts 1:10-11).

Jesus will return! No one knows when, except the Father. There are two ways in which we can approach the Second Coming. We can, like some people, remain at ease, believing that there is still a lot of time left before Jesus' return. Or we can expect His second coming at any moment.

It does not help us in any way to speculate about the Second Coming because we do not know when it will be. We must instead keep ourselves busy with our work for the Kingdom. God is indeed postponing the second coming of Jesus because He does not want one person to be lost. Therefore, you should tell others about Jesus.

The fact that Jesus will return enables Christians to live with hope in their hearts because we know that our suffering in this life will eventually result in eternal glory for us.

"He has given us new birth into a living hope, and into an inheritance that can never perish, spoil or fade – kept in heaven for you. Therefore, prepare your minds for action; be self-controlled; set your hope fully on the grace to be given you when Jesus Christ is revealed," writes Peter (1 Pet. 1:3-4, 13).

Lord Jesus, I glorify You and thank You that I can live with hope in my heart because I know for certain that You will return one day so that I can receive the inheritance You are keeping in heaven for me. Amen.

Ready for heaven

Read Matthew 24:36-44

Therefore keep watch, because you do not know on what day your Lord will come. So you must be ready, because the Son of Man will come at an hour when you do not expect him (Matt. 24:42, 44).

The theme of one of Jesus' last sermons concerned being ready for His return. This readiness is of such importance to Jesus that He told various parables that emphasize the fact that we must be ready for His return every day. The parable of the ten virgins, the parable of the faithful and the unfaithful servant, as well as the parable of the servants and the talents all urge us to keep watch and to be ready for Jesus' second coming.

Therefore, do not fool yourself with the idea that there is still a lot of time left to prepare yourself for Jesus' return. Jesus will come at an hour when you do not expect Him, the Bible warns. For each of us, His second coming is as near as the day you will die. And just as none of us know when we are going to die, so no one knows when Jesus will return.

Watchfulness implies loyalty to the work that the Lord has entrusted to you here on earth. The knowledge that Jesus will return should influence your whole life. Make sure that you are ready.

Lord Jesus, make me ready for heaven, and to live as though I expect Your second coming every day. Help me not to be caught off guard, but to be prepared for when it happens. Amen.

You have been redeemed!

Read Colossians 2:9-15

He forgave us all our sins, having cancelled the written code, with its regulations, that was against us and that stood opposed to us; he took it away, nailing it to the cross (Col. 2:13-14).

In biblical times, debts incurred by people were noted down in the same way as they are today. But the law of those times said that an entire family could be sold as slaves to settle an outstanding debt, if the debtor could not pay.

Every person is a sinner by nature and not one of us can wipe out our debt of sin. Therefore, in the eyes of God, we deserve the death sentence because of our inherent sinfulness. But Jesus paid this sentence for us by His death on the cross. *The Message* says, *"All sins forgiven, the slate wiped clean, the old arrest warrant canceled and nailed to Christ's cross."*

Unlike the Old Testament sin offerings that had to be repeated every year, Jesus' sacrifice was sufficient for all eternity. Through Jesus' crucifixion, you are redeemed forever. It is His blood that redeems you (see 1 Pet. 1:18-19). Because Jesus has canceled God's written code that was against us by nailing it to the cross, you are rid of the guilt of your sins forever. What will you do to show your gratitude toward Him?

Lord Jesus, I glorify You for redeeming me from all sin forever, by nailing the ransom for those sins to the cross. Help me to show my gratitude for Your sacrifice by the way I live. Amen.

Surely the Son of God!

Read John 20:26-31

But these are written that you may believe that Jesus is the Christ, the Son of God, and that by believing you may have life in his name (John 20:31).

Three groups of people were present at the cross of Jesus: the teachers of the law and the Pharisees who wanted to have Him crucified, His small group of sorrowful followers, and a group of people who did not know Jesus at all, such as the Roman soldiers who guarded Him.

When this last group of people saw the darkness that covered the earth when Jesus died, the earthquake and the tombs that broke open, they knew without a doubt that Jesus was not just a man. Matthew reported, *"When the centurion and those with him who were guarding Jesus saw the earthquake and all that had happened, they were terrified, and exclaimed, 'Surely he was the son of God!'"* (Matt. 27:54).

In the past month, we have walked the Way of the Cross with Jesus. We have observed the people that surrounded Him, as well as His own response to events. At the end of the month, we cannot but agree with the Roman centurion that Jesus surely is the Son of God. This makes His willingness to suffer so much for our sins all the more amazing. Good Friday signifies the fact that His death means life for you. Because He was willing to die in your place, He gives you the assurance that you will enter heaven.

Lord Jesus, I worship You as the Son of God and I glorify You that Your crucifixion gives me life. Amen.

You also have a cross to bear!

Read Matthew 16:24-28

"If anyone would come after me, he must take up his cross and follow me. For whoever wants to save his life will lose it, but whoever loses his life for me will find it" (Matt. 16:24-25).

All Christians are cross-bearers. There is not a single one among us who can escape our personal cross in this world. Jesus does not say that we have to make a cross or look for a cross, writes Henri Nouwen. Each of us already has a cross to carry. We did not choose it and it won't help to ignore it, but we can take up these crosses and follow Jesus with them.[4]

The reason Peter overreacted when Jesus told His disciples that He must be killed (see Matt. 16:21-22), is probably because none of us likes to suffer. If you want to take up your cross and follow Jesus, you will have to renounce your own will and desires, and let Jesus be King in your life. Instead of being self-centered, a follower of Jesus should now be Christ-centered.

It will require courage to lose your life so that you can gain eternal life. It will also require courage not to cast off your cross, but to be willing to carry it as Jesus did. Are you willing to follow Him unconditionally?

Lord Jesus, I dearly long to follow You but, like Peter, I am scared of suffering. Make me willing to renounce my own will and desires, so that Your will may be done in my life. Help me carry my cross so that I can follow You. Amen.

Prayer

Lord Jesus, after walking the Way of the Cross with You day after day during the past month, and for the first time really catching a glimpse of the unbearable suffering that You had to endure on my behalf, I realize afresh that You truly died, were buried and arose from the dead on the third day. I can only kneel down before Your cross and offer my entire life to You.

Help me never to forget the terrible price that You had to pay so that I could be a child of God.

Thank You for being willing to leave heaven and come to dwell on this earth as an ordinary man, that You did not shy away from brutal suffering, that You even endured the pain of being forsaken by God in order for me to be granted the opportunity to rid myself, once and for all, of my debt of sin.

Lord, I pray that You will help me never to disown You by the things that I do and say, to watch and pray so that I will not fall into temptation, to love You unconditionally, to take up my cross and follow You.

Grant that I may be ready when You return one day to come and fetch me to be with You for all eternity.

Amen.

May

On the road with Peter

When we travel with Peter, we often catch glimpses of ourselves.

Peter is someone we can easily identify with because he demonstrates so many typically human characteristics, such as uncertainty, rashness, doubt and denial.

But Peter was also honest. He was not afraid to ask questions, but he was afraid to acknowledge that he was a follower of Jesus. He was an ordinary, middle-class person like most of us.

There is a very important lesson that we can learn from Peter: to acknowledge Jesus and to get to know Him better. We also notice a gradual process of growth in Peter himself. He slowly progressed from a scared disciple, who did not want to acknowledge that he knew Jesus, to a powerful preacher at Pentecost and a miracle-worker who even raised a woman from the dead.

A fisher of men

Read Matthew 4:18-22

As Jesus was walking beside the Sea of Galilee, he saw two brothers, Simon called Peter and his brother Andrew. They were casting a net into the lake, for they were fishermen. "Come, follow me," Jesus said, "and I will make you fishers of men" (Matt. 4:18-19).

Peter and his brother, Andrew, were fishermen at the Sea of Galilee. Andrew was a follower of John the Baptist and when he heard John say that Jesus was the Lamb of God, he investigated the matter further. After meeting Jesus, Andrew told Peter, *"We have found the Messiah"* (John 1:41).

While Peter and his brother were fishing in the lake, Jesus came past and invited them to follow Him. He promised to make them fishers of men if they followed Him. Peter and Andrew were prepared to follow Jesus immediately. They left their nets and families and followed Him.

When Peter met Jesus, he left his former life behind. He was willing to follow Jesus unconditionally and to be His disciple.

Jesus still calls upon people to follow Him. He wants to make us fishers of men too. One of our most important tasks as Christians is to tell others about Jesus' good news. Are you willing to sacrifice everything and follow Jesus so that you can be a witness for Him?

Lord, like Peter, make me willing to sacrifice all that is dear to me and follow You unconditionally. Help me to expand Your kingdom by winning people for You. Amen.

Peter walks on water

Read Matthew 14:22-33

"Lord, if it's you," Peter replied, "tell me to come to you on the water."
"Come," he said. Then Peter got down out of the boat, walked on
the water and came towards Jesus (Matt. 14:28-29).

This account gives us a glimpse of Peter's impulsive nature. He is someone who acts first and then thinks. When he saw someone on the water approaching the boat, he thought that it must be Jesus. However, he is not quite certain. *"Lord, if it's you, tell me to come to you on the water,"* Peter said. *"Come!"*, Jesus invited him.

And then a miracle happened. Peter actually walked toward Jesus on the water – until he saw how strong the wind was. When Peter got scared, he began to sink. In a moment, the brave Peter turned into a scared man who almost drowned. However, he knew where to turn for help and Jesus was close enough to put out His hand and catch hold of him.

"You of little faith, why did you doubt?" (v. 31) Jesus wanted to know when He got into the boat with Peter. Peter would probably never forget this encounter with Jesus. For the other disciples, it confirmed that Jesus was truly the Son of God. *"Then those who were in the boat worshiped him, saying, 'Truly you are the Son of God,'"* Matthew reports (v. 33).

Lord, I too, sometimes become afraid when observing the conditions surrounding me. Help me to continue believing in You and please deliver me from dangerous situations, as You rescued Peter. Amen.

Peter's credo

Read Matthew 16:13-20

"But what about you?" he asked. "Who do you say I am?" Simon Peter answered, "You are the Christ, the Son of the living God" (Matt. 16:15-16).

When Jesus asked the disciples who the people said He was, they replied that some thought He was John the Baptist and others thought He was Elijah or one of the prophets. Jesus then asked, *"Who do you say I am?"* Peter answered, *"You are the Christ, the Son of the living God."*

Jesus told Peter that His answer was a revelation from God. He then told Peter that this was the rock on which His church would be built, and that He would give him the keys to the kingdom of heaven.

Peter must have been pleased with himself when he heard Jesus' announcement, and that the keys to the kingdom of heaven would be given to him. But Peter's glory was not to last very long. In the verses that follow, he again rushed in where angels fear to tread.

Lord Jesus, thank You that, like Peter, I can confess that You are the Christ, the Son of the living God. Help me to avoid Peter's mistakes in my own life. Amen.

Peter, the stumbling block

Read Matthew 16:21-26

Peter took him aside and began to rebuke him. "Never, Lord!" he said. "This shall never happen to you!" Jesus turned and said to Peter, "Get behind me, Satan! You are a stumbling block to me; you do not have in mind the things of God, but the things of men" (Matt. 16:22-23).

Within a few minutes, Peter progressed from being the rock on which Jesus would build His church, to becoming a stumbling block! In his rashness he felt confident enough to rebuke Jesus when He told His disciples that, in Jerusalem, He would suffer many things, that He would be killed and that on the third day He would rise from the dead. Jesus called Peter Satan, shortly after praising him for being open to a revelation from God.

Peter must have been embarrassed by Jesus' response. All he wanted to do, was to give Jesus some good advice. Humanly speaking, it was, after all, impossible that the long-awaited Messiah was going to die and be resurrected three days later. But Peter learned a valuable lesson – one of self-denial and taking up your cross if you want to follow Jesus.

Sometimes we are just like Peter. We feel that we are not being treated fairly. But we must remember that Jesus cannot make mistakes. Trust in Him and be prepared to take up your cross and follow Him.

Lord, please forgive me that I, too, have sometimes thought that You treat me unfairly. Remind me once again that You know what is best for me and make me willing to take up my cross and follow You. Amen.

Peter and the question of taxes

Read Matthew 17:24-27

When Peter came into the house, Jesus was the first to speak. "What do you think, Simon?" he asked. "From whom do the kings of the earth collect duty and taxes – from their own sons or from others?" (Matt. 17:25).

When the temple tax collectors wanted to know from Peter whether Jesus paid tax, Peter said He did. Jesus, however, asked him whether the kings collect tax from their own sons or from others. *"From others,"* Peter answered. *"Then the sons are exempt,"* Jesus said. *"But so that we may not offend them, go to the lake and throw out your line. Take the first fish you catch; open its mouth and you will find a four-drachma coin. Take it and give it to them for my tax and yours"* (Matt. 17:26-27).

Peter experienced another of Jesus' miracles. When he responded to Jesus' command, he caught a fish with sufficient money in its mouth to pay his and Jesus' temple tax.

Many people have a problem when it comes to paying tax. Some ignore their conscience by cheating on their tax returns. Jesus expects honesty from His followers. Although, strictly speaking, He owed no temple tax, He still paid it.

When the Pharisees asked Jesus a trick question regarding the payment of taxes, Jesus replied, *"Give to Caesar what is Caesar's, and to God what is God's"* (Matt. 22:21). Therefore, see to it that you are honest when paying your taxes and that you fulfill your financial responsibilities.

Heavenly Father, I pray that You will help me to be honest in my conduct at all times – especially with regard to the completion and payment of my tax returns. I also want to give to You what is Yours. Amen.

Peter seeks a reward

> *Read Matthew 19:23-30*

Peter answered him, "We have left everything to follow you! What then will there be for us?" (Matt. 19:27).

Today's Scripture verse is Peter's response to Jesus' statement that it is easier for a camel to go through the eye of a needle than for a rich man to enter the kingdom of God. Jesus made it clear that wealth is a stumbling block in the way to eternal life. It seemed that He was suggesting that it is impossible for a rich man to go to heaven. The disciples were justly astonished at this statement.

Naturally, the impetuous Peter wanted to know what the disciples were going to gain because they had left everything to follow Him. Jesus replied that one day the twelve disciples would sit on twelve thrones, judging the twelve tribes of Israel. Then He added, *"And everyone who has left houses or brothers or sisters or father or mother or children or fields for my sake will receive a hundred times as much and will inherit eternal life"* (Matt. 19:29).

But the words of Jesus contain a warning, *"But many who are first will be last, and many who are last will be first"* (Matt. 19:30). Jesus wanted to teach Peter that eternal life is a gift of pure grace that no one can earn.

There are no calculations that can measure your merit in the eyes of God. You were redeemed through grace and, purely through grace, God enables you to be His child.

Lord Jesus, thank You for Your great grace in my life. Grant that my possessions will never be more important to me than You. Amen.

Peter's mountain-top experience

Read 2 Peter 1:16-20

For he received honor and glory from God the Father when the voice came to him from the Majestic Glory, saying, "This is my Son, whom I love; with him I am well pleased." We ourselves heard this voice that came from heaven when we were with him on the sacred mountain (2 Pet. 1:17-18).

Even the glorification of Jesus does not cause Peter to hold his tongue. Once again he speaks out of turn, *"Lord, it is good for us to be here. If you wish, I will put up three shelters – one for you, one for Moses and one for Elijah"* (Matt. 17:4). The mountain-top experience was a highlight in his life.

We all sometimes experience moments that are almost perfect: times when we experience the presence of God so intensely that we, like Peter, wish we could feel like that for ever; moments when God allows us to experience Him in all His glory and majesty. I experience such moments when I walk along the beach, when I watch the sun set in flaming clouds of color, and when I see the world in a new light through the eyes of my three-year-old granddaughter.

"These moments are given to us so that we can remember them when God seems far away and everything appears empty and worthless. These experiences are true moments of grace," writes Henri Nouwen.[1]

When you next experience mountain-top moments like these, store them in your memory for those days when you are feeling low.

Heavenly Father, thank You for moments when You are especially near to me. I glorify You for enabling the children of man to get a glimpse of Your glory. Amen.

Peter swears allegiance

> *Read Matthew 26:31-35*

Peter replied, "Even if all fall away on account of you, I never will" (Matt. 26:33).

Peter is one of three disciples that Jesus drew into His inner circle. He shared the mountain-top experience with them and He also invited them to pray with Him in Gethsemane. Peter was one of Jesus' confidants and his love for Jesus was genuine. However, Peter was only human. He just could not succeed in being truly loyal to his Master.

When Jesus told His disciples that His followers would be scattered, Peter was the first to swear eternal allegiance to Jesus. Peter promised that even if all forsook Jesus, he would never do so. But Peter could not keep this promise. Together with all the other disciples, he ran away when Jesus was taken captive in the Garden of Gethsemane by the chief priests and Pharisees.

When we hear about acquaintances who have disappointed the Lord, we think to ourselves that we would never do that. That we will remain true to our faith no matter what. But all people are fallible. All of us stumble in many ways, writes James (James 3:2).

If, on occasion, you have failed to keep your promises to God, you can count on this promise: *Even though we are faithless, God remains faithful. He cannot disown Himself* (2 Tim. 2:13). You can depend on God's faithfulness to you in times of trouble.

Lord Jesus, please forgive me that I condemn people like Peter while I often disown You in the things that I say and do. Thank You for the assurance that You will always remain faithful to me. Amen.

Peter experiences a miracle

Read Luke 8:40-42; 51-56

When he arrived at the house of Jairus, he did not let anyone go in with him except Peter, John and James, and the child's father and mother (Luke 8:51).

Peter was present when an important member of the synagogue council knelt before Jesus, pleading with Him to heal his terminally ill daughter. However, on the way to Jairus's house, Jesus first stopped to talk to a woman who had suffered from bleeding, but who was cured from her illness when she touched His cloak. While Jesus was still speaking to her, someone arrived with the news that Jairus's daughter had just died.

Perhaps Peter wondered why Jesus did not go more quickly to Jairus's house. He had often witnessed Jesus healing sick people. However, a dead person was a different story altogether. He was most probably surprised by Jesus' calm words that Jairus simply had to keep believing.

At Jairus's house, Peter heard Jesus say to the mourners that the little girl was not dead, but only sleeping. They laughed at Him because they knew that she was dead. Jesus sent all the people away. He only allowed Peter, John, James and the girl's parents to enter the room. Then Peter saw how Jesus took the dead little girl by the hand and commanded, *"My child, get up!"* (v. 8). Peter then knew beyond any doubt that nothing is impossible for Jesus.

Lord Jesus, I know that You can do everything, that to You nothing is impossible. I pray that You will strengthen my faith so that I can see the miracles You perform in my life. Amen.

At Passover

> ### Read Luke 22:7-23

Jesus sent Peter and John, saying, "Go and make preparations for us to eat the Passover" (Luke 22:8).

Peter and John were singled out again when Jesus asked them to prepare the venue for Passover. This would be the last time that Jesus ate with His disciples before the crucifixion and it was also the meal during which He instituted the sacrament of communion.

Jesus told them exactly where the communion meal was to be held. They had to follow a man carrying a jar of water until they reached a specific house where they had to ask the owner where Jesus could eat the Passover with His disciples. Jesus also said that the man would show them a large upper room, furnished in readiness for the feast. Everything happened as Jesus had said. Once again Peter must have been surprised about Jesus' knowledge of the events that were still to happen.

At this meal, Jesus used bread and wine to introduce the first communion service. Jesus told His disciples that the bread is His body that would be broken for them, and that the wine is His blood that would be poured out for them. He also announced that one of the disciples would betray Him. This announcement shocked the disciples. They began to ask one another who would do such a thing.

Every time you partake in communion, the sacrament should be a reminder of Jesus' love for you, of His crucifixion that enabled you to have a relationship of trust with God.

Lord Jesus, thank You for being willing to die on my behalf, and for instituting communion so that I can commemorate Your crucifixion with the bread and wine. Amen.

Jesus washed Peter's feet

Read John 13:3-10

He came to Simon Peter, who said to him, "Lord, are you going to wash my feet?" Jesus replied, "You do not realize now what I am doing, but later you will understand." "No," said Peter, "you shall never wash my feet" (John 13:6-8).

At Passover, Jesus took it upon Himself to wash the feet of the disciples, even though He was their Teacher. When Jesus started washing the disciples' feet, Peter was the first to protest, *"You shall never wash my feet"* (v. 8). When Jesus said that unless He washed his feet, he would have no part with Him, Peter jumped to the other extreme, *"Then, Lord, not just my feet but my hands and my head as well!"* he requested (v. 9).

Jesus realized that Peter did not understand what His act of washing the disciples' feet meant. *"A person who has had a bath needs only to wash his feet; his whole body is clean,"* Jesus explained to him (v. 10). Jesus used the ceremony of feet washing to demonstrate to His disciples that His love for them lay in service and sacrifice. Just as He was willing to wash their feet, they were to be willing to serve each other, doing the things expected of slaves.

Jesus also expects a willingness on your part to serve other people. Are you ready to demonstrate sacrificial love and service to others – just as He did?

Lord, I do not really enjoy serving other people. Please forgive me my selfishness and make me willing to follow Your example and perform sacrificial duties for Your kingdom. Amen.

Peter in Gethsemane

Read Matthew 26:36-46

He took Peter and the two sons of Zebedee along with him, and he began to be sorrowful and troubled. Then he said to them, "My soul is overwhelmed with sorrow to the point of death. Stay here and keep watch with me." Then he returned to his disciples and found them sleeping. "Could you men not keep watch with me for one hour?" he asked Peter (Matt. 26:37-38, 40).

Time and again, Jesus chose Peter, John and James when He only wanted a few of His disciples with Him. When Jesus went to the Garden of Gethsemane to pray before His crucifixion, Peter was one of those whom He asked to accompany Him.

In Gethsemane Peter failed Jesus again. He and his fellow disciples could not even succeed in keeping watch with Jesus for a few hours. Jesus told His followers how sorrowful and troubled He was, but even this was not sufficient to motivate them to stand by Him. Although Jesus asked them three times to pray and keep watch with Him, they fell asleep each time.

The three disciples who were closest to Jesus failed Him miserably when He needed them most. To make matters worse, these disciples also ran away when He was taken captive and, a short time later, Peter disowned Jesus three times.

Before you get too indignant with Peter and his companions, consider whether you, too, have not failed Jesus by the things you have said and done.

Lord Jesus, I apologize for all the times in the past when I have failed You. Teach me to watch and pray so that I will not fall into temptation. Amen.

Peter and the high priest's servant

Read John 18:1-11

Then Simon Peter, who had a sword, drew it and struck the high priest's servant, cutting off his right ear. (The servant's name was Malchus.) (John 18:10).

By now, we are so used to Peter's rashness and impulsiveness, that we are not in the least surprised that he was the one to draw his sword and cut off the ear of the high priest's slave when Jesus was taken captive. At least Peter tried to do something to prevent Jesus from being captured.

I am sure that Peter was quite taken aback by Jesus' conduct. Instead of thanking him, Jesus said, *"Put your sword away! Shall I not drink the cup the Father has given me?"* (v. 11). Once again Jesus gave Peter and the other disciples a demonstration of His divine omnipotence – He touched Malchus's ear and healed him.

Although Peter meant well and his deed seemed heroic, He tried to interfere with God's plan for His Son. Jesus had to die in order for our sins to be forgiven – and this is exactly what Peter tried to prevent with his impulsive actions.

Sometimes, we act on impulse too, without first ensuring that what we do is in accordance with God's will. Resolve to pray first and then act.

Lord, help me to live so close to You that I will always first check that what I do forms part of Your will for my life. Amen.

Peter disowns Jesus

Read Mark 14:66-72

Immediately the cock crowed the second time. Then Peter remembered the words Jesus had spoken to him: "Before the cock crows twice you will disown me three times." And he broke down and wept (Mark 14:72).

When Jesus told Peter that he would disown Him three times, he emphatically insisted, *"Even if I have to die with you, I will never disown you"* (v. 31). Peter who was so convinced that he would never forsake Jesus, followed at a distance after Jesus had been taken captive. At least Peter risked entering the courtyard of Caiaphas, but there three times he denied that he was a follower of Jesus. Peter even began to call down curses on himself and swore when he was questioned, *"I don't know this man you're talking about"* (v. 71).

After Peter had disowned Jesus three times, a cock crowed. *"The Lord turned and looked straight at Peter,"* Luke reports (Luke 22:61). Peter was devastated. He realized how his actions must have hurt Jesus. Peter went outside and wept bitterly.

It is very easy to condemn Peter for disowning Jesus. But we must think twice before doing so. Don't you sometimes disown Jesus by acting and talking in a way that is not what is expected of a Christian?

Lord Jesus, once again I stand accused before You. You know how often I have disowned You by acting and talking in a way that's contrary to what You expect of Your children. Please help me to lead a life that will testify that I am Your child. Amen.

Peter at the tomb

Read Luke 24:1-12

Peter, however, got up and ran to the tomb. Bending over, he saw the strips of linen lying by themselves, and he went away, wondering to himself what had happened (Luke 24:12).

When they heard from the angels at the empty tomb that Jesus was not there, but that He had risen from the dead, the excited women immediately returned to the village to share the news of Jesus' resurrection with the disciples. But they did not share in the women's excitement. To them, the story sounded too far-fetched to be true. But Peter believed the women. Perhaps he remembered what Jesus had said on the day he had dared to rebuke Him! He would not easily forget that Jesus had called him Satan and a stumbling block.

Although Peter believed the women's account, he wanted to go and see for himself. Once again, he took the lead and ran ahead to the tomb. When he arrived there, he only found the linen burial cloths. Although Peter did not see an angel at the tomb, he knew for certain that Jesus had truly risen from the dead. Luke wrote that he went away wondering to himself what had happened.

Jesus' resurrection and His victory over death fill His children with joy and wonder to this day. His resurrection enables us to have everlasting life.

This promise is for you too. If you belong to Jesus, you have eternal life.

Lord Jesus, Your resurrection remains a miracle to me. Thank You for the assurance that I, too, will rise from death one day to live with You for all eternity. Amen.

Peter's second chance

> *Read Mark 16:1-8*

But go, tell his disciples and Peter, "He is going ahead of you into Galilee. There you will see him, just as he told you" (Mark 16:7).

Mark reports that the angel instructed the women to go and tell the disciples that Jesus had risen from the dead. He mentioned Peter by name. The angel told them that Jesus had gone to Galilee and would see them there as He had predicted.

Jesus knew that Peter was going to disown Him – He told him so! In Galilee Jesus gave Peter a chance to repent of his denial. Peter eagerly responded to Jesus' offer of forgiveness. Peter was so eager to be with Jesus, that he jumped straight into the water and swam to shore to reach Him sooner (see John 21:7).

In the competitive world in which we live, people are not really inclined to give each other a second chance. But Jesus is not like other people. Not only does He give His children a second chance, but also a third, tenth and even a 490th (70 times 7) chance to rectify our mistakes. He is willing to forgive us every time we sin.

Have you, like Peter, blundered by disowning Jesus in one way or another? Do not hesitate to respond to Jesus' gift of grace. Ask Him to forgive your sins. He will gladly do so.

Lord Jesus, I apologize for disappointing You so often. Thank You that You are willing to give me another chance to rectify my mistakes. Amen.

Peter and the miraculous catch of fish

"I'm going out to fish," Simon Peter told them, and they said, "We'll go with you." So they went out and got into the boat, but that night they caught nothing (John 21:3).

Peter and the other disciples had been fishing all night without catching a single fish. Suddenly they saw Jesus standing on the shore. He asked them whether they had caught anything. *"Throw your net on the right side of the boat and you will find some,"* Jesus said (John 21:6). Peter probably wondered why Jesus was sending them for a second time to do something that was hopeless – and yet he obeyed Jesus' command. He threw out the net and, this time, there were so many fish that the net almost tore and they were unable to haul it in.

When he saw that the net was filled with fish, Peter knew that this was a miracle. Perhaps he thought about the first time he had met Jesus, when Jesus promised to make him a fisher of men. Jesus' promise was fulfilled when Peter radically changed after this. From being a fisherman filled with fear, who did not want to acknowledge that he was one of Jesus' followers, Peter became a forceful preacher who conveyed his message with so much conviction that about three thousand people repented on that first day of Pentecost.

If you are willing to unconditionally obey Jesus' commands, you will discover that He will also perform miracles in your life.

Lord Jesus, I apologize that I so often question the things that You ask of me. Make me like Peter – willing to obey Your commands unconditionally. Amen.

"Peter, do you love Me?"

Read John 21:15-19

The third time he said to him, "Simon son of John, do you love me?"
Peter was hurt because Jesus asked him the third time, "Do you love
me?" He said, "Lord, you know all things; you know that I love you."
Jesus said, "Feed my sheep" (John 21:17).

Three times Jesus asked Peter whether he truly loved Him – once
for each time Peter had denied Him. Peter answered yes every time,
and each time Jesus gave him a command, *"Feed my lambs", "Take*
care of my sheep", "Feed my sheep" (vv. 15; 16; 17).

When Jesus asked Peter for the third time whether he loved
Him, Peter was hurt. *"Lord, you know all things; you know that*
I love you," (v. 17) he answered. Each question of Jesus probably
reminded Peter anew of his earlier denial of Jesus.

Peter had learned his lesson. There is very little left of the
impetuous Peter who acted first and then thought. The new Peter
is indeed a rock, as his name indicates. He is someone that Jesus
could truly depend on to be a leader in the early church, someone
who accepted the responsibility of telling people about Jesus and
who guided new converts onto the right path.

Indeed, in his sermon on that first day of Pentecost, Peter did
not hesitate to give powerful testimony about Jesus. This "new"
Peter was so persuasive that approximately three thousand people
were added to the church on that day (Acts 2:41).

Lord, You know that I love You very much. Use me in Your kingdom and help me to be willing to take on a leading role in my
own congregation and to guide others into the faith. Amen.

Peter's sermon at Pentecost

Read Acts 2:14-17; 37-42

Then Peter stood up with the Eleven, raised his voice and addressed the crowd. Those who accepted his message were baptized, and about three thousand were added to their number that day (Acts 2:14, 41).

The frightened Peter, who forsook Jesus when He was taken captive, and who disowned Him in the courtyard, underwent a complete metamorphosis. He brought such a powerful message on the first day of Pentecost that three thousand people were converted. Peter told those gathered there about Jesus' crucifixion and resurrection. He also told them about the outpouring of the Holy Spirit, which Jesus had promised His disciples.

Peter's testimony touched all who were gathered there. When the people wanted to know from him what they had to do to be saved, Peter had an answer ready, *"Repent and be baptized, every one of you, in the name of Jesus Christ for the forgiveness of your sins. And you will receive the gift of the Holy Spirit"* (Acts 2:38). Peter went on to explain that this message was not only for the Jews, but for everyone whom God calls.

The Good News of Jesus is also for you today. Have you repented and invited Him into your life? Then you will also receive the Holy Spirit to guide and sustain you.

Lord Jesus, I thank You for dying on my behalf, for rising from the dead and for ascending into heaven so that I can be a child of God. Thank You for the gift of the Holy Spirit in my life. Amen.

A crippled beggar is healed

Read Acts 3:1-9

Then Peter said, "Silver or gold I do not have, but what I have I give you. In the name of Jesus Christ of Nazareth, walk." Taking him by the right hand, he helped him up, and instantly the man's feet and ankles became strong (Acts 3:6-7).

On their way to the temple, Peter and John met a man who had been crippled since birth. He earned a living by begging from the people going into the temple courts. In those days, disabled people were totally dependent upon the generosity of others because they could not take care of themselves. When the crippled man saw Peter and John entering the temple, he asked them for some money.

"Look at us!" (v. 4) Peter said to the crippled man. When the man looked at them in the hope that they would give him some money, Peter said to him, *"Silver or gold I do not have, but what I have I give you. In the name of Jesus Christ of Nazareth, walk"* (v. 6). Taking the man by the hand, he helped him up and instantly his feet and ankles became strong so that he could stand upright. Then the crippled man went with Peter and John to the temple and praised God. All the people were filled with wonder and amazement at what had happened to him.

The crippled man received much more than what he had hoped for. The healing power of Jesus flowed through Peter and restored his health. The gospel offers much more than temporary benefits. It offers a brand new understanding of God, hope, joy and recovery.

Lord Jesus, thank You that faith in You is much more precious than material things, that it guarantees me hope, joy and peace. Amen.

Peter's speech in the Colonnade

Read Acts 3:11-19

All the people came running to them. When Peter saw this, he said to them: "Repent, then, and turn to God, so that your sins may be wiped out." (Acts 3:11, 19).

When the people heard about the miraculous healing of the crippled beggar, they ran to the temple to see Peter. They were also curious to see the healed man with their own eyes. They were not disappointed when they saw the wonderful sight of the once crippled man dancing and jumping for joy!

Peter seized this opportunity to fulfill his calling to witness. *"Why are you surprised?"* (v. 12) he asked the crowds gathered at the temple. He told them that the healing of the crippled man was not the result of his own powers, but the power of God. He rebuked them again for having crucified Jesus, and also urged them, *"Repent, then, and turn to God, so that your sins may be wiped out."*

Jesus is still able to perform miracles today. He can heal the sick, as He did when He dwelt on earth, as well as forgive sins. If you want to experience His miraculous power in your own life, simply believe His Word and believe in Him.

Lord Jesus, I know that You have always been able to perform miracles and that You can heal me when I am ill, if it is in accordance with Your will. I pray that You will strengthen my faith in You every day. Amen.

Peter as witness

Read Acts 4:10-20

But Peter and John replied, "Judge for yourselves whether it is right in God's sight to obey you rather than God. For we cannot help speaking about what we have seen and heard" (Acts 4:19-20).

Peter was still talking to the crowds in front of the temple when the priests heard about it. They did not like Peter's testimony at all and had him and John seized and put into jail until the following day. Peter and John were then brought before the Sanhedrin. They wanted to know what power Peter had used when he had healed the crippled man.

Once again, Peter did not hesitate. He told them that the miracle had taken place in the name of Jesus whom they had crucified and that there was *"no other name under heaven given to men by which we must be saved"* (v. 12). The Sanhedrin discussed the matter amongst themselves, and commanded the two apostles not to speak or teach at all in the name of Jesus.

However, Peter and John did not allow this important group of people to deter them. *"Judge for yourselves whether it is right in God's sight to obey you rather than God. For we cannot help speaking about what we have seen and heard,"* they replied.

Follow Peter's example and do not allow other people to stop you from testifying about Jesus. You should find it impossible to remain silent about what Jesus has done for You and what He means to you.

Lord Jesus, thank You for Your grace in my life. Make it impossible for me to remain silent about what You have done in my life. Amen.

Peter performs miracles

Read Acts 5:12-16

As a result, people brought the sick into the streets and laid them on beds and mats so that at least Peter's shadow might fall on some of them as he passed by (Acts 5:15).

Peter's ministry went from strength to strength, as did the miracles he performed. God worked so powerfully through him that more and more people brought their sick to him. *"Crowds gathered also from the towns around Jerusalem, bringing their sick and those tormented by evil spirits, and all of them were healed,"* Luke reports (v. 16). The power that radiated from Peter was so strong that people brought their sick into the streets so that his shadow could fall on them and they could be healed.

Jesus' earlier promise to His disciples, *"I tell you the truth, anyone who has faith in me will do what I have been doing. He will do even greater things than these"* (John 14:12) was indeed realized in the life of Peter. Peter possessed these supernatural powers not because he was so wonderful, but because he lived in close contact with God.

God still brings His miraculous power into the lives of His children today, if we pray for it. If you need strength, you can confidently call on God, asking Him to give you His power. With this strength, you will also succeed in doing great things in God's kingdom. Just be sure to always give the glory to God.

Heavenly Father, thank You for using people to work for You here on earth. Please strengthen me with Your power so that I, like Peter, can succeed in doing great things for You. Amen.

Peter raises Tabitha from the dead

Read Acts 9:36-43

Peter went with them, and when he arrived he was taken upstairs to the room. Peter sent them all out of the room; then he got down on his knees and prayed. Turning towards the dead woman, he said, "Tabitha, get up." (Acts 9:39-40).

In the little town of Joppa there lived a faithful woman whose heart went out to those who were less privileged than her. *"[She] was always doing good and helping the poor,"* Luke reports (Acts 9:36). This woman was herself a widow. Widows had no rights in those times, and were normally dependant on the care of their children. However, Tabitha was a very special woman. She took little notice of her own difficult situation. Instead of complaining, she reached out to the poor. She made clothes for them and did her best to help them.

This good woman fell ill and died. The widows to whom she had been so kind were inconsolable. They sent for Peter. When Peter arrived, they took him upstairs to the room where Tabitha lay. Peter sent them all out of the room and started to pray fervently.

Turning toward the dead woman, he said, *"Tabitha, get up."* Tabitha opened her eyes and sat up. Her friends were overjoyed to have their benefactor in their midst again. Many people who heard about this miracle believed in Jesus.

Lord, I still do so little for You. Help me, like Tabitha, to look away from my own problems, to notice those with big problems and to offer them assistance. Amen.

Peter learns a life lesson

Read Acts 10:9-20

"Surely not, Lord!" Peter replied. "I have never eaten anything im-pure or unclean." The voice spoke to him a second time, "Do not call anything impure that God has made clean" (Acts 10:14-15).

Peter was a Jew through and through. He never even considered eating food that God had declared unclean. But then something happened. While Peter was on the roof praying, he saw a vision of something like a large sheet, filled with unclean animals, and he heard a voice calling to him, *"Get up, Peter. Kill and eat"* (v. 13). Peter refused point blank. He had never eaten something that was unclean. He heard the voice speaking to him for a second time saying, *"Do not call anything impure that God has made clean"* (v. 15). After Peter had seen the vision for the third time, the sheet disappeared.

Peter must have been bewildered and he must have wondered what this strange vision meant. But God had already been work-ing in the heart of Cornelius, a centurion in the Italian Regiment. Cornelius was a God-fearing Gentile who prayed to God regularly. According to Jewish law, he was unclean and Peter was not allowed to enter his house.

But the vision God sent to Peter made it clear that the barriers between Jews and Gentiles were abolished with the advent of Jesus. All who believe in Jesus have access to heaven, whether Jew or Gentile.

Lord Jesus, I praise You for making no distinction between people, but that all who believe in You will be saved. Amen.

God does not show favoritism

Read Acts 10:17-35

I now realize how true it is that God does not show favoritism but accepts men from every nation who fear him and do what is right (Acts 10:34-35).

Before Peter had seen the vision of the sheet with the unclean animals, God had commanded Cornelius to fetch Peter from Joppa. Cornelius then sent two of his servants and a soldier to Joppa. *"While Peter was still thinking about the vision, the Spirit said to him, 'Simon, three men are looking for you. So get up and go downstairs. Do not hesitate to go with them, for I have sent them'"* (vv. 19-20).

The men told Peter that Cornelius wanted to hear what he had to say. After offering them accommodation for the night, he accompanied them to Cornelius's house the next day. He told all the people gathered there that God had shown him that no person is impure or unclean, because God does not show favoritism, but accepts men from every nation who fear him and do what is right (see vv. 34-35).

While Peter was still talking to the Gentiles about Jesus, the Holy Spirit came on all who were listening to him. Peter instructed them to be baptized in the name of Jesus Christ, and he stayed with them and taught them for a few more days.

In the church of Christ, the barriers between different people are being broken down. We are all equal in His eyes and each of us has access to heaven.

Lord Jesus, please teach me the same lesson that You taught Peter: that You do not show favoritism, but accept all who worship You. Amen.

Peter is freed from jail

Read Acts 12:5-16

Then Peter came to himself and said, "Now I know without a doubt that the Lord sent his angel and rescued me from Herod's clutches" (Acts 12:11).

When Herod saw that his persecution of the Christians pleased the Jews, he decided to take Peter captive. While he was in jail, an angel appeared to him. He ordered Peter to get up, put on his clothes and sandals, and wrap his cloak around him. When he obeyed the angel, the chains fell off Peter's wrists. He followed the angel and saw that the iron gates leading to the city were opening for him. Only then did Peter realize that God had sent an angel to free him from jail. He immediately went to Mary's house, where the Christians were gathered, praying for his release.

Peter's release from jail was not only a miracle but also a clear answer to prayer. Luke says, *"The church was earnestly praying to God for him"* (v. 5). It is ironic, however, that when the servant girl told the praying believers that Peter was standing at the door, they refused to believe it, and told her that she was out of her mind!

Sometimes we also pray for a miracle, but when it happens, we refuse to accept it. God can still perform miracles in your life. Make sure that your faith is stronger than that of the Christians in Judea!

Heavenly Father, I praise You for being able to do everything – even that which is humanly impossible. Thank You for still being able to free Your children and to protect them from danger. Amen.

Peter on suffering

Read 1 Peter 4:12-19

Dear friends, do not be surprised at the painful trial you are suffering, as though something strange were happening to you. But rejoice that you participate in the sufferings of Christ, so that you may be overjoyed when his glory is revealed (1 Pet. 4:12-13).

Peter faced much suffering in his own life. He had first-hand knowledge of this topic. Peter said that Christians should not be surprised when they encounter problems and suffering. All Christians face suffering. Even Jesus had to suffer much when He was in this world. Therefore, when we suffer for His sake, we should see it as a privilege, which will result in abundant joy when He returns one day.

There are very few people who succeed in rejoicing in times of suffering. But if you give some thought to the times of suffering in your own life, you will discover that your suffering was to your advantage, because it brought you closer to the Lord. God uses suffering in the lives of His children to draw us closer to Him and to provide us with a new revelation of His love for us and His grace toward us.

Therefore, do not be surprised when crises surface in your life. Remember that Jesus also suffered. You can look forward with joy to His second coming, when He will put an end to all suffering for ever.

Lord Jesus, I apologize for complaining when I experience difficulties. Help me to depend on You in times of suffering and to look forward to Your second coming. Amen.

Peter's warning

Read 1 Peter 5:8-11

Be self-controlled and alert. Your enemy the devil prowls around like a roaring lion looking for someone to devour. Resist him, standing firm in the faith (1 Pet. 5:8-9).

Peter writes that we should be self-controlled and alert, because we face a dangerous enemy who is out to destroy us. The devil never leaves God's children in peace. However, we have God on our side. If the devil attacks us, we should fight back with the strength God gives us.

When Jesus spoke to His disciples about His return to His Father, He said, *"I will not speak with you much longer, for the prince of this world is coming. He has no hold on me, but the world must learn that I love the Father and that I do exactly what my Father has commanded me"* (John 14:30-31).

With the strength that you get from Jesus, you will be able to ward off the attack of the devil successfully. Then the devil will have no power over you and, like Jesus, you will succeed in diligently obeying the commands of your heavenly Father.

Therefore, follow Peter's advice: Be alert and on your guard, so that you will know when the devil attacks you in an attempt to lure you away from God. Remain steadfast in your faith and resist him. Then he will be defeated.

Lord Jesus, thank You for siding with me in battle because with You, I will always be more than a conqueror in my battle against the devil. Amen.

Live holy and godly lives

> *Read 2 Peter 3:11-12*

Since everything will be destroyed in this way, what kind of people ought you to be? You ought to live holy and godly lives (2 Pet. 3:11).

In Peter's day, the people expected the Second Coming at any moment and they could not understand why Jesus was delaying His return. We have been waiting for two thousand years for the Second Coming. Peter suggested that God's children should examine their lives under a magnifying glass as Jesus' second coming approaches, and he calls on them to live holy and godly lives.

The word "holy" has a negative connotation for some people. They regard it as a synonym for hypocritical. The Greek word from which "holy" has been translated in today's Scripture verse, is *hagios* which means to be complete and perfect. It refers to a person of integrity. Thus holiness is actually a very positive concept.

For someone who is truly holy and godly, nothing is of greater importance than God. *"These have come so that your faith – of greater worth than gold, which perishes even though refined by fire – may be proved genuine and may result in praise, glory and honor when Jesus Christ is revealed,"* Peter writes at the beginning of his letter (1 Pet. 1:7).

Jesus' second coming is as close or as far away as your death. Be prepared for it now and don't waste time calculating when "one day" will be. Are you already leading a holy and godly life? Or are there still many things in your life that are of greater importance to you than God?

Lord Jesus, make me holy and completely devoted to You, so that I will be prepared for Your second coming every day. Amen.

Peter and the Second Coming

Read 2 Peter 3:8-13

The Lord is not slow in keeping his promise, as some understand slowness. He is patient with you, not wanting anyone to perish, but everyone to come to repentance (2 Pet. 3:9).

Sometimes we become impatient because Jesus does not seem to be coming soon. Peter gives two interesting reasons why we should not become despondent if Jesus' second coming takes longer than we have anticipated.

We cannot apply our concept of time to God. To Him a day is like a thousand years. Secondly, the lapse of time between His first and second coming is not a postponement of a promise, but rather the merciful withholding of such a promise. It is God's will that *all* people should be saved. Therefore, He is mercifully giving people the chance to hear and respond to the gospel message. God knows what He is doing and His timing is perfect.

This time of grace should be a fruitful time of labor for those of us who look forward to Jesus' second coming, a time to testify to others about His redeeming love, a time to encourage those who do not yet know Him.

You can follow John's advice, *"And now, dear children, continue in him, so that when he appears we may be confident and unashamed before him at his coming"* (1 John 2:28). From now on live your life in such a way that Jesus will be satisfied with your life when He comes.

Lord Jesus, thank You for the promise that You will return one day to fetch Your children. Help me to be fruitful in Your service so that, on that day, You will be satisfied with me. Amen.

Prayer

Heavenly Father,

Thank You for the precious lessons I learned this month while walking in Peter's footsteps.

You know that I recognize so many of my own characteristics in his life: my impulsiveness and my tendency to speak before I think; the fact that I, too, often disappoint and even disown You, in spite of my good intentions.

I pray that You work in my life as You did in the life of Peter, that You will strengthen my love for You, that You will make me willing to follow You unconditionally, that You will give me a key role to play in my congregation, and that You will make me willing to guide and teach Your children.

I pray that You will change me too, from being a faint-hearted doubter to being a fisher of men, and a powerful witness to Your omnipotence.

Help me to be prepared for the devil's attacks.

Help me to live a holy and godly life and to expect Your second coming every day, so that I will not be caught unawares.

I ask this in Your name.

Amen.

June

The wisdom of Proverbs

When you read Proverbs, the incisive words and clear perspectives hit you time and again.

There is a treasure of wealth hidden in Proverbs. It is a "rich treasure house of short sentences drawn from long experiences," Charles Swindoll aptly writes.[1]

The book of Proverbs is filled with the wisdom of life. It teaches us how to serve God and how to be happy; it shows us what things are of lasting value and how to be successful in our relationships.

These proverbs, written so long ago, can still be of immense value to you today. If you apply the wisdom in Proverbs to your own life, you will steadily learn how to use God's wisdom in your everyday life and, in the process, you will gain a much better understanding of your faith.

In Proverbs you are taught how to walk the path of life according to God's will. This month we will focus on that path.

The fear of the Lord is true knowledge

Read Proverbs 1:1-7

The fear of the LORD is the beginning of knowledge, but fools despise wisdom and discipline (Prov. 1:7).

We all like to gain knowledge so that we will make fewer mistakes and achieve greater success. The book of Proverbs was written *"for attaining wisdom and discipline; for understanding words of insight, for giving prudence to the simple, knowledge and discretion to the young,"* Solomon assures us in the very first chapter of the book (Prov. 1:2, 4).

Man is in a relationship with everything that surrounds him. Throughout his life he must figure out his position with regard to other people, the natural world, objects and God. The person who succeeds in finding a recipe for this is someone who has been blessed with wisdom.

How can you become wise and prudent? By listening to what the book of Proverbs is teaching you and by making this knowledge a part of your life. True wisdom means to serve God and to obey Him, because true wisdom always begins with a fear of the Lord. He is the only One who can give you the insight and wisdom you need in your daily life, and He is the only One who can teach you correct conduct. Gladly ask Him for His Divine wisdom and for the necessary insight whenever you are in need of advice.

Heavenly Father, thank You for giving Your children wisdom and insight. Help me to serve You with devotion. Teach me how to deal with others wisely in my daily conduct, and to ask Your advice in everything. Amen.

Why don't you listen?

Read Proverbs 1:23-33

But you rejected me when I called. You ignored all my advice and would not accept my rebuke. (Prov. 1:24-25).

The description in today's Scripture verse is quite typical – not only of God's people in Old Testament times, but also of most people today. None of us like advice; we would much rather have our own way and do what we want. This is why we often ignore good advice and reap the fruit of our disobedience in our own lives. We refuse to obey the commands that the Lord gives in His Word because we enjoy doing wrong too much.

If you are walking this path of disobedience, beware! It is a dangerous road and there are bound to be negative consequences. *"I will mock when calamity overtakes you like a storm, when disaster sweeps over you like a whirlwind"* warns the writer of Proverbs (vv. 26-27). People who ignore Jesus' advice often discover that He will not listen to them when they are in distress.

But if you are willing to listen to Him, two things will happen to you: you will believe in the Lord and He will shield you with His hand, and give you the ability to distinguish between right and wrong.

Heavenly Father, please forgive me for often wanting my own way and refusing to listen to advice. Make me willing to listen to Your Word and to obey You in everything. Amen.

Learn to trust unconditionally

> Read Proverbs 3:1-10

Trust in the LORD with all your heart and lean not on your own understanding; in all your ways acknowledge him, and he will make your paths straight (Prov. 3:5-6).

Before surrendering yourself to God, you first have to be willing to sacrifice your own will and turn to God. There are three central verbs in today's Scripture passage: trust, acknowledge and fear. Here "to fear" also means "to serve". If you are prepared to trust God, to acknowledge Him in all you do and to serve Him faithfully, He will make your paths straight.

Don't focus on your own problems. Trust in God, get to know Him better daily, and serve Him with all your heart. Then He will take care of you – now, and in the future. The Hebrew word used here implies "to remove rocks or obstructions". The Lord will clear your path of all stumbling-blocks provided you are willing to trust Him to do so.

First and foremost, ask God what He expects of you and be willing to surrender your all to Him. Exchange your many anxieties for trust today, so that God's peace may become part of your life. Then you will discover the abundance of His grace in your life.

Heavenly Father, teach me to trust You in everything, to get to know You better every day, and to serve You with enthusiasm, so that I may always receive Your grace. Amen.

Give the Lord His share

Read Proverbs 3:1-12

Honor the LORD *with your wealth, with the first fruits of all your crops; then your barns will be filled to overflowing and your vats will brim over with new wine* (Prov. 3:9-10).

This is one of the indisputable principles in the Bible. If you are willing to give the Lord His share of your income, He will care for you and bless you far beyond your expectations.

When you calculate your contribution for God, remember that everything you have comes from the Lord. He is the One who gives you health, talents and the initiative that you use to earn money. But often the more you have, the more difficult it is to part with God's share of your income. It is dangerous to get too attached to your money and possessions. Your love of your possessions might just cause you, like the rich young man, to forsake Jesus because your money has become more important than Him. *"Do not wear yourself out to get rich,"* warns the writer of Proverbs. *"Cast but a glance at riches, and they are gone, for they will surely sprout wings and fly off to the sky like an eagle"* (Prov. 23:4-5).

Make sure that you are willing to put everything you have at God's disposal, then He will provide abundantly in all your needs and everything you undertake will carry His blessing.

Heavenly Father, teach me that everything I have comes from You, and make me willing to honor You with my possessions. Amen.

Be discerning!

> *Read Proverbs 3:21-26*

My son, preserve sound judgment and discernment, do not let them out of your sight; they will be life for you, an ornament to grace your neck (Prov. 3:21-22).

Some people are so forthrightly honest that, in the process, they hurt others deeply. God expects His children to act with discernment and with sound judgment at all times. You should keep your cool and think before you act. Always pay attention to your words as well as your deeds. Before saying or doing something, think carefully whether what you want to say or do might be offensive to someone else. Each of us is very different and something which you might find completely acceptable, might hurt your sensitive friend.

The writer of Proverbs warns us repeatedly against speaking too quickly. We have received two ears but only one mouth, the old saying goes. Let us listen twice before speaking once. From now on be extra careful of what you say. And remember: Words once spoken, can never be undone. *"Even a fool is thought wise if he keeps silent, and discerning if he holds his tongue,"* Solomon advises (Prov. 17:28). Apply this advice to your life, and don't get carried away by your own ideas.

Heavenly Father, I apologize for often having said and done things that, unknowingly, were hurtful to other people. I pray that You will give me the wisdom to be discerning and have sound judgment in my speech and actions. Amen.

Be kind to others

Read Proverbs 3:27-35

Do not withhold good from those who deserve it, when it is in your power to act (Prov. 3:27).

God despises selfishness. He expects us to reach out to others and to help them where we can. To love others with the same kind of love that He shows us. If we are willing to care for others, He will bless us.

There are so many people who need help these days that we often feel like giving up, and not offering help to anyone. After all, it's impossible to help everyone. But it is possible to make a difference in the life of *one* person. Decide who you are going to help and how you are going to do it. Then do something about it.

If you keep postponing the kindness you want to show others, it often comes to nothing. Do it now – tomorrow could be too late. *"Do not say to your neighbor, 'Come back later; I'll give it tomorrow' – when you now have it with you"* (Prov. 3:28).

You obey Jesus' command when you help someone. He came to the world to serve people – and He expects His children to do the same. "I tell you the truth, whatever you did for one of the least of these brothers of mine, you did for me," Jesus states in Matthew 25:40.

Heavenly Father, forgive me for being so slow to help others, because there are just so many who need help. Make me willing to reach out to them instead of delaying my efforts to help. Amen.

Be on your guard!

Read Proverbs 4:20-27

Above all else, guard your heart, for it is the wellspring of life. Do not swerve to the right or the left; keep your foot from evil (Prov. 4:23, 27).

The author of Proverbs warns that every person must guard his heart, because it is the wellspring of life – meaning that what is in your heart determines the course of your life. When the author of Proverbs talks about the "heart", he is not referring to the organ that regulates your blood flow, but rather to man's inner self, the center of our being where our emotions are located.

Sadly, that center is not always completely innocent, *"But the things that come out of the mouth come from the heart, and these make a man 'unclean'",* Jesus warns. *"For out of the heart come evil thoughts, murder, adultery, sexual immorality, theft, false testimony, slander"* (Matt. 15:18-19).

Ensure that your heart is clean and that it is sensitive to God's voice. The Lord wants you to be aware of His will in your heart. Only when your heart is ready, will you be willing to accept God's plan for you and to obey His will.

Every man is sinful by nature and only Jesus has the ability to cleanse your unclean heart with His blood (see Isa. 1:18). He wants to do this for you. Are you willing to open your heart to God's guidance so that your entire life may benefit from it?

Heavenly Father, You know how deceitful and sinful my heart can sometimes be. Help me to be careful of those things originating in my heart. Make me willing to listen to the thoughts that You plant in my heart. Amen.

God knows you

Read Proverbs 5:21-23

For a man's ways are in full view of the LORD, and he examines all his paths (Prov. 5:21).

God knows everything about us. We cannot hide anything from Him. He is aware of every thought we think, every decision we make and everything we do – including the things no one else knows about. He knows every person intimately because He made us all. He knows what awaits us in the future. He also knows exactly how bad and sinful we are, but He still loves us. He promises to help us whenever we are in need of help. *"For the eyes of the LORD range throughout the earth to strengthen those whose hearts are fully committed to him,"* Hanani, the seer, said to King Asa (2 Chron. 16:9).

God knows all there is to know about you. He knows all your fears, your joys, your dreams and your heart's desires. Your whole life is an open book to Him. *"He examines all your paths,"* is the reassurance we receive from today's Scripture verse. Regardless of what may be in store for you, God is already aware of it and He promises to stand by you and to help you.

He also wants to take care of you in the future. So when you have to face difficulties again, or if you are grappling with problems that no one else is aware of, You can rest assured in the knowledge that the Lord is aware of your problems and that He is willing to help you.

Heavenly Father, thank You for the comforting knowledge that You know all there is to know about me, that my entire life is an open book before You and that You see every step I take. Please guide me on the right path every day. Amen.

Learn from the ants!

Read Proverbs 6:6-10

Go to the ant, you sluggard; consider its ways and be wise! It has no commander, yet it stores its provisions in summer and gathers its food at harvest (Prov. 6:6-8).

Many people are inclined to postpone things and to be lax rather than to work hard every day. Successful people know the ant's secret of persevering in hard work. In *The Message* this passage reads as follows, *"You lazy fool, look at an ant. Watch it closely; let it teach you a thing or two. Nobody has to tell it what to do."*

There are two important lessons that you can learn from ants. Firstly, they work out of their own free will, without any supervision. See how diligently they run to and fro with heavy loads that look far too big for their small bodies.

Secondly, ants do the most important things first. They know when it is time to gather food and get on with the job. Laziness and procrastination are foreign concepts to them.

The ants show you how, by following their example, you can organize your life with the right kind of planning. This will enable you to do the right thing at the right time, and help you to finish everything on time!

Heavenly Father, make me as diligent and as willing to work hard like the ants, and show me how to plan my life so that I will be successful. Amen.

Don't be lazy!

Read Proverbs 6:9-11

A little sleep, a little slumber, a little folding of the hands to rest – and poverty will come on you like a bandit and scarcity like an armed man (Prov. 6:10-11).

There are so many people today who are unemployed. Having a job is a privilege that should be appreciated and made the most of. Someone once said that the definition of true happiness is to have somebody to love and something to do. But lets admit that sleeping in is also very nice! There is nothing wrong with times of relaxation, as long as you can afford to take the time off. If you battle to get up in the morning, you must be careful that you don't become a sluggard.

Guard against shirking your responsibilities at work. Do your work to the best of your ability and be as honest and punctual as you can. Proverbs 18:9 says, *"One who is slack in his work is brother to one who destroys".*

The advice Paul gave the slaves in Ephesus is appropriate to our work situation too, *"Obey (your masters) not only to win their favor when their eye is on you, but like slaves of Christ, doing the will of God from your heart. Serve wholeheartedly, as if you were serving the Lord, not men"* (Eph. 6:6-7). It is God's will for you to refrain from laziness and to do your work with enthusiasm – for Him.

Heavenly Father, thank You for the privilege of finding fulfillment in my job. Please help me not to be lazy and to do my work with enthusiasm. Help me to do my best for You and not for recognition from others. Amen.

Maintain the right values

Read Proverbs 6:20-24

My son, keep your father's commands and do not forsake your mother's teaching. Bind them upon your heart forever; fasten them around your neck. When you walk, they will guide you (Prov. 6:20-22).

Child psychologists have shown that what a child learns up to the age of seven, he will remember for the rest of his life. The values that we learned at our parent's knee are usually the right values and should set a standard for us for the rest of our lives.

The permissive, modern society in which we live often has other values. In all probability the things your parents taught you are nowadays regarded as obsolete and old-fashioned. If you get mixed up with the wrong friends, it is all too easy to cast away the values you were taught and to start acting like your friends.

The author of Proverbs advises us to hold on to the things our parents taught us. They should stick in our minds forever, providing us with guidance in whatever we do. When you are in doubt about something you are doing, think back to what your parents taught you. Also follow the advice of the author of Proverbs: *"Listen, my sons, to a father's instruction; pay attention and gain understanding. I give you sound learning"* (Prov. 4:1-2).

Lord, thank You for the Christian home I grew up in. Thank You that I could learn the right values in my home from an early age. Help me to hold on to these values so that I can pass them on to my children. Amen.

Beware of temptations

For these commands are a lamp, this teaching is a light, and the corrections of discipline are the way of life (Prov. 6:23).

If parents rear their children according to the right values, those standards will stay with them for the rest of their lives. They will show them how they should live and it will keep them on the right track, just as the Bible does.

It seems as though there are more temptations today than ever before. Apart from sexual temptations, we often face moral and financial temptations.

The values according to which you organize your life should not be measured against what others do, but against what the Bible teaches. If you are tempted to follow the values of our amoral society, consult your Bible first. The lamp of the Lord's Word always provides unerring guidance that you can follow in complete trust if you really want to be happy.

Sadly, later in his life Solomon was caught in the same trap he warned his readers against. He allowed wealth and pagan women to draw him away from the Lord. Make sure that temptations in your own life will not cause your relationship with the Lord to suffer. "I plead with you: run for your life from those flames of temptation. If you don't they are sure to grow hotter as the months pass and you will get burned. Remember, burn scars last a lifetime," writes Charles Swindoll.[2]

Heavenly Father, I pray that You will deliver me from temptation, and that You will help me to obey the commands in Your Word. Amen.

Make your Bible part of you

> *Read Proverbs 7:1-5*

My son, keep my words and store up my commands within you. Keep my commands and you will live. Bind them on your fingers; write them on the tablet of your heart (Prov. 7:1-3).

Binding God's words on your fingers and writing them on your heart will ensure that you will heed the words of wisdom that you have been taught so that you can build your entire life around Him. If we need additional wisdom, all we need to do is open our Bible. There is enough wisdom contained in the pages of your Bible to last you a lifetime, provided you are willing to follow the commands in it.

Reading your Bible regularly is not enough. You should also memorize verses in the Bible so that you will have God's commands at your fingertips. The better you know your Bible, the easier it will be to apply the guidelines it contains to your own life, and the more those things which you have learned from God, through His Word, will become part of you.

Do not put off memorizing your Bible. We remember Bible verses so much easier when we are still young. So start immediately and get to know your Bible better. Remember to reflect on those things that you read. Meditate on them until your Bible truly becomes part of you.

Heavenly Father, every time I read the Bible I am amazed by the wisdom contained in it. Help me to make Your Word inextricably part of my life. Amen.

Just how obedient are you?

Read Proverbs 12:22-28

In the way of righteousness there is life; along that path is immortality (Prov. 12:28).

Righteousness is of great importance to God. When Saul and his soldiers were disobedient to God and wanted to rectify their offence with sacrificial offerings, Samuel responded, *"Does the LORD delight in burnt offerings and sacrifices as much as in obeying the voice of the LORD? To obey is better than sacrifice, and to heed is better than the fat of rams"* (1 SAM. 15:22).

We learn an important life lesson from this account of Saul and his disobedient soldiers. Our outward behavior should reflect our inner attitude. To be obedient to God on the surface is useless if our attitude is questionable.

Those who are obedient to God, walk the path of life, the author of Proverbs states. God loves them and protects them on this path. But disobedient people are traveling the road of death.

Which road are you following? God demands obedience from His children. It is the criterion that He applies when determining our love for Him. God teaches you in the Bible how He wants you to live. In His Ten Commandments, He maps out the path of life that His children should follow if they want to be obedient to Him and if they want to get joy out of life. Are you willing to follow the guidelines that God gives in His Word?

Lord, forgive me for so often being disobedient to Your Word and commandments. Change my negative attitude and please guide me on the path of life so that I will live in complete obedience to You. Amen.

Be patient!

Read Proverbs 14:26-30

A patient man has great understanding, but a quick-tempered man displays folly (Prov. 14:29).

Some time ago, my three-year-old granddaughter was standing with me in the kitchen, watching me prepare a salad. "May I have some cold drink?" she asked. "In a moment," I said. "I just want to finish making the salad." Soon after she asked again and, when I told her again to wait, she said to herself, "Patience, patience!" I could clearly hear her mother's tone of voice in the little one's words!

Patience is a virtue which many people lack. We try hard to be patient, only to lose our temper and clearly display our impatience. *"Be completely humble and gentle; be patient, bearing with one another in love,"* Paul writes to the congregation in Ephesus (Eph. 4:2). Patience is also one of the fruit of the Spirit Paul lists in Galatians 5:22-23. In Greek the word "patience" implies to give someone a second chance.

Are you willing to give others a second chance? Are you able to tolerate things and wait without complaining? God is very patient with us. He is always willing to give us a second chance. Ask the Lord to give you more patience toward others and to make you willing to wait on Him. Remember to thank Him for the endless patience He shows you.

Heavenly Father, please forgive me for being so hurried and impatient. Give me greater patience and make me willing to give others a second chance. Thank You for the patience You show me. Amen.

Humor lightens life

Read Proverbs 15:13-18

All the days of the oppressed are wretched, but the cheerful heart has a continual feast (Prov. 15:15).

If you make a point of noticing the humorous side of life and of sharing it with others, it will be impossible for you to go through life with a long face. If there is one thing that can improve life, it is a healthy sense of humor. Of all the creatures God created only man has the ability to laugh. Therefore be cheerful and put a smile on the faces of those around you. You will soon discover how festive life becomes.

Scientists have confirmed that laughter is one of the world's best medicines, but the astute author of Proverbs knew this thousands of years ago. *"A cheerful heart is good medicine, but a crushed spirit dries up the bones,"* Solomon wrote in Proverbs 17:22.

When you laugh, your body releases hormones that combat stress and depression. That's why cheerful people are healthier than people who worry constantly.

Develop your sense of humor. Look at the lighter side of life. It might improve your health!

Heavenly Father, thank You for creating us with the ability to laugh. We are able to see the humorous side of life and share it with others. Make my heart cheerful and my life a continual feast. Amen.

Be content

Read Proverbs 15:16-17

Better a little with the fear of the LORD than great wealth with turmoil (Prov. 15:16).

Money and status have become very important to many people today. It is easy to become discontented and disgruntled if all your friends have more money than you have and if everyone you compare yourself with seems to be more intelligent, more beautiful and more popular than you. Discontented people not only make life unpleasant for themselves, but also for all those around them.

Stop comparing yourself to others. God created you. You are beautiful just as you are. He wants you to be contented with what He has given you. Money and possessions will only increase your anxieties – they cannot make you happy. But service to God can.

Stop focusing on the negative side of life and start counting your blessings. Look at all the things you receive by the grace of God. Look at yourself in a positive light and start showing gratitude. Stop coveting. *"Better what the eye sees than the roving of the appetite,"* we read in Ecclesiastes 6:9. From now on, be the person the Lord intended you to be by being content with what you have received from Him.

Heavenly Father, please forgive me for sometimes being so discontented with myself, my appearance, my talents and my bank balance. Show me all the positive things that You have given me and make me content with what I have. Amen.

A timely word

Read Proverbs 15:20-24

A man finds joy in giving an apt reply – and how good is a timely word! (Prov. 15:23).

Just as a bucket lowered into a well brings things to the surface, so a man's tongue brings out the things that are hidden in his heart. We all sometimes have thoughts that we will never express. If you catch yourself thinking things that you know are wrong, be careful not to allow these thoughts to escape from your mouth. Ask the Lord to place a guard before your mouth and to give you the right words to say.

Someone who can control his tongue is able to keep his whole body in check, writes James (see James 3:2). Most of us often stumble because of our words and only a few always have a timely word. Ask the Lord to provide you with the necessary wisdom so that you will always have an apt reply.

There is one reply that you should always be willing and able to give. *"Always be prepared to give an answer to everyone who asks you to give the reason for the hope that you have,"* writes Peter (1 Pet. 3:15). Make sure that you have exactly the right words ready when people question you about your faith.

Heavenly Father, You know that I often stumble with the replies that I give. Help me to reply aptly every time I am asked about my faith. Amen.

Do not be proud of heart!

Read Proverbs 16:1-5

The LORD detests all the proud of heart. Be sure of this: They will not go unpunished (Prov. 16:5).

Paul writes to the congregation in Rome that they should have a healthy self-esteem – neither too low, nor too high. If you have many talents, it is easy to become arrogant or proud of heart, or to feel that you are superior to the rest of the world.

Arrogant people conveniently forget that all they have comes from God. For a Christian, a healthy self-image is always characterized by modesty. Your talents come from God and you should always use them to glorify Him and to serve Him.

Arrogance can be dangerous. *"Do not think of yourself more highly than you ought, but rather think of yourself with sober judgment, in accordance with the measure of faith God has given you,"* Paul writes to the congregation in Rome (Rom. 12:3).

If you achieve success, remember to remain modest, and don't think too highly of yourself. Rather look toward Jesus – He is the King of the heavens and all power belongs to Him. Yet He is humble and gives all the glory for the things He does to His Father. If you can learn to do that, you will have the kind of self-image that God expects you to have.

Lord Jesus, forgive me for sometimes thinking too highly of myself and remind me that all that I have comes from You. Make me modest, humble and willing to serve, like You. Amen.

Count your words!

Read Proverbs 18:1-8, 20-21

The tongue has the power of life and death, and those who love it will eat its fruit (Prov. 18:21).

What you say reveals who you are. The wise Solomon had much to say about words: "*A fool delights in airing his own opinions* (v. 2); *The words of a man's mouth are deep waters, but the fountain of wisdom is a bubbling brook* (v. 4); *A fool's lips bring him strife* (v. 6); *A fool's mouth is his undoing* (v. 7); *The words of a gossip are like choice morsels; they go down to a man's inmost parts* (v. 8); and lastly, *The tongue has the power of life and death*" (v. 21). All of these are "great truths," as a minister I knew used to say.

Few people truly realize the enormously negative power in their words. James writes in detail about this in his letter: "*The tongue also is a fire,*" he says, "*a world of evil among the parts of the body. It corrupts the whole person, sets the whole course of his life on fire, and is itself set on fire by hell*" (James 3:6).

Your tongue truly has the power of life and death because what you say can destroy the lives of others. With your words you can distort the truth and demolish relationships between people. So think twice before making a negative remark about another person, or before repeating a juicy bit of gossip. Make sure that your words are a source of wisdom that will enrich others.

Heavenly Father, thank You for the gift of speech. Thank You for reminding me that my own words can do enormous damage. Please guard what I say so that I will not harm others with my words. Amen.

God is in control

Read Proverbs 19:16-21

Many are the plans in a man's heart, but it is the LORD's purpose that prevails (Prov. 19:21).

Every person has ideals, future plans, and dreams he wants to realize. However, *"Many are the plans in a man's heart, but it is the LORD's purpose that prevails,"* the author of Proverbs states.

If you are willing to measure your plans against the Word and the Lord's will, He will help you to execute them because He is in control of your life. His purpose prevails. Be careful of following your own desires. Putting your will first can cost you dearly.

If you are willing to place your plans in the Lord's hands, He will make them succeed. *"To man belong the plans of the heart, but from the LORD comes the reply of the tongue. Commit to the LORD whatever you do, and your plans will succeed,"* writes Solomon (Prov. 16:1, 3).

You often tend to think that you are in control of your life, but this is not the case. In the end you will gain nothing by trying to counteract God's perfect plan for your life. God is always on the winning side. You might as well surrender and obey His will, because if your actions and plans are not in line with His will you have no hope of them ever succeeding.

Heavenly Father, please forgive me for making my own plans before seeking Your advice. Teach me that Your plans will prevail, so that I can give You full control of my life. Amen.

Friends are precious

> *Read Proverbs 17:5-11, 17*

A friend loves at all times, and a brother is born for adversity (Prov. 17:17).

The Book of Proverbs has a lot to say about friends. Because your friends can make or break you, it is very important to choose the right kind of friends, friends with similar interests and values, Christian friends with whom you can go to church and worship, friends who will stand by you through thick and thin and who will love you no matter what. Friends who never disappoint you, and on whose assistance you can depend in times of crisis, friends who support you, listen to you and who will not hesitate to correct you when necessary.

Make sure that you realize the value of your friends. Take the trouble to make time for them, to share your thoughts with them and be sure to cherish their friendship for the rest of your life.

Heavenly Father, thank You for the joy of friends in my life. Make me a friend to my friends as You are a Friend to me – a Friend who was even willing to lay down His life for me. Amen.

Take care of your friends

Read Proverbs 27:9-17

Perfume and incense bring joy to the heart, and the pleasantness of one's friend springs from his earnest counsel (Prov. 27:9).

One of the most important aspects of true friendship is whether you are willing to rebuke your friends when necessary, even though you might find it very difficult and even though it might mean that you run the risk of that friend being angry or hurt.

If the tables are turned and some of your friends muster up the courage to tell you that you are in the wrong, accept their advice without feeling hurt. They are correcting you because they sincerely care about you. Johan Smit writes that criticism is the chisel with which friends can give your life a more beautiful shape and with which enemies can leave scars. Therefore, allow your friends to criticize you more often so there will be no need to hear it from your enemies.[3]

Sometimes your friends make mistakes that hurt you deeply. Unfortunately there are no perfect people in this world and, just like you, your friends also have their faults. When they hurt you, you must be willing to forgive them just as the Lord so often forgives you. You should not only forgive them, but also forget about feeling hurt. You will only be able to do this when you stop dwelling on the past. He who keeps harping on an issue causes estrangement between friends. So decide right now to forgive and forget.

Heavenly Father, thank You for friends who are courageous enough to give me advice. Make me willing to accept their advice and help me to wholeheartedly forgive those friends who have hurt me. Amen.

Refrain from gossiping!

Read Proverbs 26:18-28

The words of a gossip are like choice morsels; they go down to a man's inmost parts. Like a coating of glaze over earthenware are fervent lips with an evil heart (Prov. 26:22-23).

It is true that women love repeating juicy gossip about one another – the more sensational these stories, the better. As long as these negative things that we say about others are true, we are inclined to try and salve our conscience. We are quick to forget that other people are readily going to believe these stories and that we can harm those we gossip about.

We must watch out for scandalmongers. They are the professional saboteurs of human relationships. People are always so eager to gossip and this adds fuel to the fire.

History has shown that "innocent" gossip has been the cause of immeasurable harm to people's lives. And those people who have showed the greatest regret afterwards, are always those who have spread the stories. I am sure that you too have, at times, given in to the temptation of repeating a juicy piece of gossip with great satisfaction. If you like to gossip, put an end to it immediately! *"A man of knowledge uses words with restraint, and a man of understanding is even-tempered,"* writes Solomon in Proverbs 17:27.

From now on use words with restraint, resist the temptation to talk about others, and if you have nothing good to say about someone else, keep your peace!

Heavenly Father, please forgive me that I too have repeated stories on occasion without calculating the harm that these stories could cause others. Please help me to use words with restraint. Amen.

Refrain from jealousy

Read Proverbs 23:15-23

Do not let your heart envy sinners, but always be zealous for the fear of the Lord. There is surely a future hope for you, and your hope will not be cut off (Prov. 23:17-18).

*A*nger is cruel and fury overwhelming, but who can stand before jealousy?" the author of Proverbs warns (Prov. 27:4). Negative emotions, such as jealousy and anger, always make one unhappy. Christians should guard against these emotions and always strive to live a positive life. It is difficult to be happy when it seems as though all is well with people who have no time for the Lord, while you and your fellow-Christians have many problems. Many biblical characters wrestled with the same problems. *"Why does the way of the wicked prosper? Why do all the faithless live at ease?"* Jeremiah asks the Lord (Jer. 12:1). *"This is what the wicked are like – always carefree, they increase in wealth,"* Asaph laments (Ps. 73:12).

Yet God's children know that the wicked will suffer a dreadful end. *"Surely you know that the mirth of the wicked is brief, the joy of the godless lasts but a moment,"* Zophar comforts Job (Job 20:4-5).

Jealousy and envy are two of the most destructive enemies of spiritual growth. Make sure that you keep your distance from them. A sign of spiritual maturity is not begrudging others their talents or possessions and being content with those things that God has entrusted to you.

Heavenly Father, I apologize that I have sometimes been unhappy when the unrighteous have prospered. Forgive me and make me content with those things which You have given me. Amen.

The world of thought

Read Proverbs 27:19-27

As water reflects a face, so a man's heart reflects the man (Prov. 27:19).

Have you ever thought that it is just as well that others cannot read your thoughts? The thoughts that you harbor are of utmost importance and radically influence your life. Before doing something good or evil, the idea must first take shape in your mind. For this reason your thoughts play a very important role in your life.

People who think fearful thoughts all the time often find that it is exactly the things they fear that become a reality. After all the terrible disasters that came upon him, Job confessed to his three friends: *"What I feared has come upon me; what I dreaded has happened to me. I have no peace, no quietness; I have no rest, but only turmoil"* (Job 3:25, 26).

If you are inclined to harbor anxious, troubled thoughts, ask the Lord to help you to think differently – to transform your negative thoughts into positive ones. If you trust in the Lord, there is no need to fear the future. You can be certain that He will take care of you and put an end to all your fears.

From now on, try to think positive thoughts, and see to it that the reflection you see in the water is a positive and joyous one.

Heavenly Father, I confess that I sometimes have very pessimistic thoughts and that those things I have feared have also come over me. Help me to trust in You completely from now on, and renew my thoughts and make them positive so that everything will go well for me. Amen.

Unanswered prayers

Read Proverbs 28:9-14

If anyone turns a deaf ear to the law, even his prayers are detestable (Prov. 28:9).

When you pray and your prayers go unanswered, you should always first look at yourself before blaming the Lord for not listening to you. Sin forms a barrier between God and His children. *"But your iniquities have separated you from your God; your sins have hidden his face from you, so that he will not hear,"* writes the prophet, Isaiah (Isa. 59:2). When you are not prepared to obey the Lord, you must not expect Him to listen to your prayers.

We all have "petty sins" that we do not always want to give up. If the wrong things to which you still cling are the reason your prayers go unanswered, Solomon provides you with a solution to your problem: *"He who conceals his sins does not prosper, but whoever confesses and renounces them finds mercy"* (Prov. 28:13).

However, it is not sufficient to merely confess your sins. You should also be willing to renounce them and to obey the Lord. Read the above verse once again: *"Whoever confesses and renounces (his sins) finds mercy."* Are you prepared to bid your petty sins farewell? Only then will God be willing to forgive your sins.

Heavenly Father, I apologize that there are still so many things in my life that are wrong and that I do not want to renounce. Make me willing to confess my sins and to renounce them so that You can forgive me and answer my prayers. Amen.

Balance is important

Read Proverbs 30:7-9

Give me neither poverty nor riches, but give me only my daily bread. Otherwise, I may have too much and disown you and say, "Who is the LORD?" Or I may become poor and steal (Prov. 30:8-9).

I had a teacher at school who liked to say that anything that was 'too good' really wasn't good at all. One should neither be too poor nor too rich, neither too thin nor too fat, neither too clever nor too stupid. The author of Proverbs confirms the fact that balance is important. He asks God to keep him from the extremes. That he will not be so rich that he won't need God any longer, or so poor that he will be driven to theft.

It is not good to have too much or too little. When wealth becomes too important to you, or if your brilliant achievements have made you arrogant, it could create problems.

Be content if you have enough. Most of us have enough of the things that are really essential. It is mostly only unnecessary luxuries after which we hanker. Therefore, it is not necessary for you to be richer, cleverer, more beautiful or slimmer than you already are. You are just right the way the Lord has created you. You are His creation, and He is incapable of creating something that is not good. Pursue a healthy balance in your life.

Heavenly Father, forgive me that I always want more and teach me to be content and to maintain a healthy balance in my life. Thank You for giving me everything that I need. Amen.

Remain positive

Read Proverbs 31:18-25

She is clothed with strength and dignity; she can laugh at the days to come (Prov. 31:25).

The woman who is described in Proverbs 31, is a woman of so many excellent qualities that very few other women could equal her: she is a home-maker par excellence; her talents in the kitchen and with the sewing needle are exceptional; she is an excellent business woman and possesses great wisdom; she has a warm heart toward others and, to top it all, she doesn't know what it means to be idle. She can indeed turn her hand to anything. No wonder that her husband admires her and her children praise her!

There is one characteristic of this special woman that stands out: *"She is clothed with strength and dignity; she can laugh at the days to come"* (v. 25). The woman of Proverbs is a woman who faces the future with humor and a positive disposition in spite of all her chores, because she belongs to God. She is a woman who does not complain about all the things she has to do. She is also not concerned about what lies ahead, because she knows that God is in control of her and her family's future.

You may not necessarily reach the heights the woman of Proverbs reached, but you can teach yourself to live in a positive manner and, in doing so, make a world of difference in your own life, as well as in the lives of those around you.

Heavenly Father, I pray that You will make me a woman who laughs at the days to come, who trusts in You completely, and who is positive about the future. Amen.

Beauty is fleeting

Read Proverbs 31:25-31

Charm is deceptive, and beauty is fleeting; but a woman who fears the LORD is to be praised (Prov. 31:30).

When I was a teenager, I became very upset when my grandfather told me that "beauty is only skin-deep, but ugliness goes to the bone." All women want to be attractive. Our modern world places a very high premium on physical beauty: Young girls can never be too beautiful or too thin, is the message the media sends out. Perhaps you also think that thick, wavy hair, a beautiful face and a breathtaking figure will ensure lasting happiness.

In the world in which we live, our looks have become more important than who we are. The Bible teaches us differently: *"Charm is deceptive, and beauty is fleeting; but a woman who fears the LORD is to be praised,"* says the author of Proverbs. Integrity and character are qualities that are much more important than beauty. Instead of spending hours in front of the mirror, you should rather work on your relationship with the Lord. Ensure that your inner self becomes more beautiful as the years go by. You will reap far greater dividends from this than from a pretty face and a perfect figure.

On the other hand, you should not neglect yourself. Make the best of your good qualities and stop fretting about the ones you cannot change. Be cheerful and friendly so that no one will even notice the fact that you may not be breathtakingly beautiful.

Father, I confess that I still attach too much value to my looks. Thank You that You have shown me that who I am is of much greater importance. Make me a woman who knows You, who serves You and who loves You. Amen.

Prayer

Heavenly Father, thank You that I could make the wisdom of Proverbs my own this month.

Thank You for the precious things that I could learn: that to fear You is true knowledge; that I can trust You unconditionally because You are in complete control of my life; that You know all there is to know about me and that You examine all my paths.

Lord, I pray that You will help me to use the things that I have learned in my relationships with others: Help me to stop gossiping, to show kindness to others, to be tactful and to do my work as I would for You.

Make me hard working and humble, careful about what is hidden in my heart and make me patient toward others, always willing to give them a second chance.

Thank You for friends who are precious to me.

Help me to accept their advice and to find time for them.

I pray that You will enable me to apply the wisdom of Proverbs in my own life every day, so that, as from today, I will walk the road of life according to Your will.

Amen.

July

Reconciliation and forgiveness

Jesus died so that man could be reconciled with God and with his fellow man.

Reconciliation requires us to look at one another in a different light, to no longer live with our backs turned to each other, but to embrace one another, and to be willing to forgive one another as God forgives us.

Reconciliation is always the work of God.

He is the One who takes the initiative, but we are the ones who need to be willing to be reconciled.

Reconciliation is one of the most difficult concepts in the Bible but, at the same time, one of the most essential.

No progress is possible without reconciliation – with God, and with one another.

Jesus has already prepared the path to reconciliation for us – but you need to *be willing* to take the first step down this path.

The work of God

Read 2 Corinthians 5:18-20

All this is from God, who reconciled us to himself through Christ and gave us the ministry of reconciliation (2 Cor. 5:18).

Reconciliation is the work of God. The initiative for reconciliation always comes from Him. Following the Fall, God decided to give mankind another chance. He sent His Son into this world to pay the price for our sins on the cross, so that we could be reconciled with Him and with one another. *"But now he has reconciled you by Christ's physical body through death to present you holy in his sight, without blemish and free from accusation,"* Paul writes to the congregation in Colosse (Col. 1:22).

When sin entered the world, God and man became enemies. But God does not leave us in the lurch – He sent His Son so that we could be holy once again. When Jesus died physically on the cross, He established peace between human sinners and the holy God. Only because He was willing to lay down His life and pay the price of sin once and for all, was it possible for us to be reconciled with God. The advantage of reconciliation lies in the fact that believers gain free access to their one-time enemy, God, and that He accepts them.

Through His actions Jesus made it possible for you to become holy and, so be accepted by God. God who sent His Son into the world, which means that reconciliation always takes place at His initiative.

Heavenly Father, thank You for taking the initiative by sending Your Son to be crucified so that I could be redeemed from my sins and be reconciled with You. Amen.

The ministry of reconciliation

Read 2 Corinthians 5:18-20

[He] reconciled us to himself through Christ and gave us the ministry of reconciliation (2 Cor. 5:18).

The initiative for reconciliation comes from God, but He has a task for us in this process. He gave *us* the ministry of reconciliation. We are ministers of Christ. God sent us, you and me, to minister the reconciliation, which He brought about for us through Christ, to the whole world.

Reconciliation is always the portal to peace. The history of the world has left many people with a legacy of hatred, injustice and bitterness. This heavy burden often makes it difficult for us to accept God's message of reconciliation. But we must make an effort – reconciliation is not only essential if we want to obey God, but it is a command coming from God personally.

Hennie Symington uses changes in South Africa as an example when she says that people need to gain a different perspective on the situation in order for reconciliation to take place. They must finally accept that the old order has passed. It is not feasible to continue regarding themselves as separate from the rest of the country. They are not an island, entrenched by money and power, disinterested in what is happening around them. The time has come for them to realize that their welfare depends on the extent to which they are willing to reach out to the less privileged and the disadvantaged citizens of their country.[1]

Will you do your part in this ministry of reconciliation?

Heavenly Father, I realize that reconciliation between people is a major challenge. Help me to be willing to reach out to all and to become reconciled with them. Amen.

The message of reconciliation

Read 2 Corinthians 5:18-20

God was reconciling the world to himself in Christ, not counting men's sins against them (2 Cor. 5:19).

God sends each of His children to carry the message of reconciliation into the world. Reconciliation means healing broken relationships. When Adam and Eve first sinned in paradise, the perfect relationship between God and His creatures was broken. Not only was the relationship between God and man marred by sin, but so was the relationship between man and his fellow man. Adam accused his wife who, in turn, accused the serpent. Neither of them was willing to accept responsibility for their sins. But God has a solution for this breakdown of relationships – He sent Jesus into this world to heal the breach between God and man and between man and his fellow man.

God expects you to be willing to walk the road of reconciliation with others. Reconciliation never comes cheaply, it always demands something of you. It means that you have to be willing to sacrifice your interests for the sake of others. True reconciliation must take place, first and foremost, with God, and then with one another. Therefore, you must first turn to God and make amends with Him. Ask Him to forgive your sins before you attempt to forgive the transgressions of others against you.

The Message says, *"God has given us the task of telling everyone what he is doing. We're Christ's representatives. God uses us to persuade men and women to drop their differences."*

Heavenly Father, thank You for the wonderful work that You have entrusted to me – to tell people about Your reconciliation. Please help me to bring about reconciliation, and to convey the message in the right way. Amen.

Accept reconciliation!

Read 2 Corinthians 5:18-20

We implore you on Christ's behalf: Be reconciled to God
(2 Cor. 5:20).

Before we can be reconciled with God, we first have to repent of our sins. God is holy and does not tolerate sin, but punishes it with death. On the cross, Jesus bore the punishment for our sins in full. Now God can, on grounds of His Son's atoning sacrifice, forgive our sins so that we live in peace with Him and our fellow man. *"He gave himself for us to redeem us from all wickedness and to purify for himself a people that are his very own, eager to do what is good,"* Titus testifies (Titus 2:14).

Reconciliation always presupposes grace. We can never earn it. It is never based on our righteousness. If this were so, all of us would, most probably, have ended up in the wrong place! There is nothing in the world more unjust than the innocent, sinless Son of God crucified on our behalf, so that we can enter God's presence. On the cross, Jesus was forsaken by God, so that we may never again be forsaken by Him.

You can accept God's reconciliation by confessing and turning from your sins. This will require you to come to repentance anew, daily turning your back on sin, while turning toward God. You must also be prepared to be reconciled with those people with whom you are still at odds.

Lord Jesus, thank You for making it possible for me to be reconciled with God through Your crucifixion. Help me to turn my back on sin every day and to act in a reconciliatory manner in my relationships with others. Amen.

Atonement calls for blood

> *Read Leviticus 17:10-16*

For the life of a creature is in the blood, and I have given it to you to make atonement for yourselves on the altar (Lev. 17:11).

During Old Testament times a sacrificial lamb had to be offered once a year so that the sins of the people could be forgiven. *"This is to be a lasting ordinance for you: Atonement is to be made once a year for all the sins of the Israelites,"* the Lord commanded Moses (Lev. 16:34). The life of a creature is in its blood. When the animal's blood was offered, his life was sacrificed on behalf of the sinner who was sentenced to die for his sins. When the blood of this sacrificial animal flowed, God forgave His sinful people their sins.

A comprehensive picture of this custom is painted in the account of Hezekiah's reinstituting temple worship: *"The goats for the sin offering were brought before the king and the assembly, and they laid their hands on them. The priests then slaughtered the goats and presented their blood on the altar for a sin offering to atone for all Israel"* (2 Chron. 29:23-24). These sacrifices had to be offered every year.

Jesus' sacrifice differs from the Old Testament sacrifices, because it is a unique sacrifice. When the blood of Jesus flowed on the cross, He paid the ransom for our sins in full – such a sacrifice need never be repeated ever again. Through the sacrifice of His body and blood on the cross, it became possible for you and me to receive forgiveness of sins and atonement before God.

> Lord Jesus, I glorify You for Your blood that flowed on the cross so that my life could be saved, my sins forgiven, and so that I can be reconciled with God for ever. Amen.

The perfect Sacrificial Lamb

Read Hebrews 10:11-19

By one sacrifice he has made perfect forever those who are being made holy (Heb. 10:14).

The sacrificial offerings of the Old Testament had to be made every year in order for God to forgive His disobedient people. But Jesus is the perfect Sacrificial Lamb. *By one sacrifice He made perfect forever those who are being made holy.* When His blood was shed on the cross, no other sacrificial offerings were required ever again. Jesus' crucifixion settled the debt for our sins once and for all. It is valid for the sins we committed in the past, for the sins we commit today, as well as for the sins we will commit in future.

Because of Jesus' crucifixion you can have a new life. No further sacrificial offering is required for your sins. Because the blood of Jesus flowed on the cross for you, your burden of sin has been fully erased once and for all and God forgives your sins the moment you confess them. *"And where these have been forgiven, there is no longer any sacrifice for sin,"* the author of Hebrews writes (Heb. 10:18). Through Jesus, you and I now have the confidence to enter the presence of God (see Heb. 10:19).

The promise in 1 John 1:7 can be yours personally: *"If we walk in the light, as he is in the light, we have fellowship with one another, and the blood of Jesus, his Son, purifies us from all sin."*

Heavenly Father, thank You that You have forgiven each one of my sins completely, because the blood of Jesus purifies me forever. Amen.

Perfect atonement

> *Read 1 John 2:1-6*

He is the atoning sacrifice for our sins, and not only for ours but also for the sins of the whole world (1 John 2:2).

Jesus not only walks the road of reconciliation ahead of us, but He was also the atonement for our sins. To experience complete reconciliation, we have to believe in Him, know Him personally and obey His Word. If we should sin once again, He will intercede for us and He will act as our Advocate with His Father.

He is the One who bridges the chasm between sinners and a holy God through His crucifixion. And He not only brings about reconciliation for us with God, but for the entire world. The impact of the tiny stone of redemption that fell into the water at Golgotha, ripples outwards to such an extent that all who embrace Him in faith will receive forgiveness.

Through Jesus, God heals the relationships broken by sin in this world. Jesus makes peace between God and man a reality. *"For God was pleased to have all his fullness dwell in him, and through him to reconcile to himself all things,"* Paul states (Col. 1:19-20).

However, there is a condition attached: If you wish to partake of this atonement or reconciliation, you must be willing to obey God's commandments and express your love for Him through your obedience. The substance of these commandments is love for one another. Can people recognize your love for God by the way that you love others?

Lord Jesus, thank You for being my Advocate who pleads my case with God to bring about peace between God and me. Help me to demonstrate my love for You through my love for others. Amen.

All people need reconciliation

Read Romans 3:9-20

There is no one righteous, not even one. All have turned away, they have together become worthless (Rom. 3:10, 12).

In his letter to the Romans, Paul paints a rather harsh picture of man. There is not one among us who is righteous; we are all sinners, he declares. We have all turned away, we have all become degenerate. And God does not tolerate sin – because He is holy, He always punishes it with death. With the Fall, a wide chasm developed between God and human sinners, which could only be bridged by the cross of Jesus. Because Jesus has paid the ransom for our sins in full on the cross, God now absolves us by His grace, even though we do not deserve His mercy (see Rom. 3:24).

Ernest Hemmingway wrote a moving story, depicting man's inherent need for reconciliation. A Spanish father, who was estranged from his son, wanted to forgive him after many years. He placed an advertisement in a Madrid newspaper: "Paco, meet me at the Montana Hotel, Tuesday at twelve o'clock. All is forgiven, Papa." Paco, however, is a very common Spanish name. When the father arrived at the Montana Hotel on the Tuesday, more than 800 young men named Paco, were waiting in the hotel square – each one of them eager to be reconciled with their fathers!

You also need God's reconciliation. And Jesus wants to make your reconciliation with God a reality. If you have not yet done so, accept reconciliation in His name today.

Lord Jesus, thank You for making reconciliation between God and myself a reality through Your crucifixion. I accept the reconciliation that You have brought about for me. Amen.

Sinners – one and all!

Read 1 John 1:5-2:2

If we claim to be without sin, we deceive ourselves and the truth is not in us. But if anybody does sin, we have one who speaks to the Father in our defence – Jesus Christ, the Righteous One. He is the atoning sacrifice for our sins, and not only for ours but also for the sins of the whole world (1 John 1:8, 2:1-2).

We have already established that all people are sinners from the day they are born. Perhaps you are secretly of the opinion that you, at least, are a good person and therefore not implicated in the wrong deeds that others commit so regularly. Should you reason like this, you are deceiving yourself and you are calling God a liar, John writes. You are indeed a sinner and if God does not intervene personally, there is no possible way of dealing with your sinful condition.

John shows us how to deal with our inherent sinfulness: *"If we confess our sins, he is faithful and just and will forgive us our sins and purify us from all unrighteousness,"* he promises in verse 9. Should you really wish to rid yourself of your sins, confess them so that God can forgive you.

In chapter two John gives further comfort: Although you are a sinner, you have Jesus as your Advocate with the Father. He is the atoning sacrifice, not only for your sins, but also for the sins of the whole world (see 1 John 2:2).

Jesus is ready to defend your case with God – if you believe in Him, you can rest assured that you will receive forgiveness from God.

Lord Jesus, thank You for pleading my case with God and for being the atoning sacrifice, not only for my sins, but also for those of the whole world. Amen.

In the jail of hate

Read 1 John 2:7-12

But whoever hates his brother is in the darkness and walks around in the darkness; he does not know where he is going, because the darkness has blinded him (1 John 2:11).

If you love your brother, you live in the light, writes John (see 1 John 2:10), but if you do not love other people, you are still living in the darkness of sin, in the prison of hate. Jesus gave us a new commandment – that His disciples should love one another just as He loved us. We are, however, by nature inclined to mistrust one another, to hate one another, to live in discord with one another. We turn our backs on one another, while Jesus wants us to love one another.

Therefore, forgiveness is not a virtue that comes easily. It only becomes reality when Jesus' love enters our hearts. The door to the prison of hate can only be unlocked if we are willing to forgive one another and to love one another. Our lives in the darkness of sin can only be transformed through the light of Jesus if we know and love Him and if we are willing to love one another.

If you believe in Jesus, you can be freed from the dark prison of sin for ever. To know God means to live in Him and, to live in Him, means that you will live in the light from now on. Are you ready to forgive those who have offended you?

Lord Jesus, I wish to live in Your light, so that I may never again know the darkness of sin in my life. Please enable me to forgive others with all my heart. Amen.

Reconciliation and forgiveness

Read 2 Corinthians 5:16-20

God gave us the ministry of reconciliation: that God was reconciling the world to himself in Christ, not counting men's sins against them (2 Cor. 5:18-19).

Reconciliation can only be obtained through forgiveness. We are reconciled with God because Jesus took the punishment of our sins. For this reason, God can now forgive us our sins and we can become reconciled with Him and with our fellow man.

Many people are burdened by past events that require their forgiveness. Sometimes, it is even more difficult to forgive someone who has harmed one of your loved ones, than someone who has hurt you personally. But forgiveness is essential – God places a very high premium on forgiveness and He demands it of His children.

Interestingly enough, the Greek word from which "forgiveness" is translated, literally means to set free. Therefore, when you forgive others, you set yourself free from the prison of bitterness.

Therefore, if you are still carrying a grudge against someone, you are nothing but a prisoner! Ask God to set you free from the prison in which you are held captive and experience the wonderful freedom of His forgiveness in your own life.

Heavenly Father, You know that there are still people whom I simply cannot forgive. I now realize that my unforgiving attitude is nothing less than a prison. Please set me free. Amen.

Forgiveness is a command from God

> *Read Colossians 3:9-17*

Bear with each other and forgive whatever grievances you may have against one another. Forgive as the Lord forgave you (Col. 3:13).

Sometimes, we deliberately refuse to forgive someone. Perhaps you feel that the person who has hurt you so much does not deserve your forgiveness – and you are probably right. We have, however, already learned that forgiveness is not based on justness. Forgiveness is a command from God. He requires His children to forgive each other as He forgave us.

To be able to truly forgive, you first have to receive forgiveness. When someone else has forgiven you out of gratitude, in all probability you will, in turn, be able to forgive someone else.

"That which we have experienced ourselves with regard to forgiveness, should become immediately effective in our relationship with our fellow man," writes Helmut Thielicke. "If I am not personally a pardoned sinner who lives in the grace of forgiveness, I cannot forgive. I can only freely forgive as a child of God who, himself, has been set free."[2]

God is willing to forgive us anytime. Therefore, all Christians should find it in their hearts to forgive others. With God, you are always on the receiving end of forgiveness. If you still find it hard to forgive, ask God to enable you to forgive. He is eager to do so.

Lord, I apologize that I sometimes withhold my forgiveness deliberately from some people. Please forgive me and make me willing to forgive others like You are willing, time and again, to forgive me. Amen.

If you refuse to forgive ...

Read Matthew 6:7-15

For if you forgive men when they sin against you, your heavenly Father will also forgive you. But if you do not forgive men their sins, your Father will not forgive your sins (Matt. 6:14-15).

There is an account of a Jew who was held captive in a German concentration camp during the Second World War, where he suffered extreme hardship. After the war, he went to visit one of his fellow-prisoners. They talked for a long time about their horrendous experiences. The Jew asked his friend whether he had forgiven the Germans. When the friend replied that he had, the first man replied, "I will never forgive them. Every day I hate them anew." His friend looked at him in silence for a long time. Eventually he said, "If you refuse to forgive, then you are still a prisoner."

An unforgiving attitude is a prison from which we can only escape if we ask God to help us to be willing with all our hearts to forgive those who have wronged us. If you persist in refusing to forgive others, then you will spend the rest of your life in a prison of your own making.

God wants to set you free from that prison. Allow Him to do it for you – and remember: If you withhold your forgiveness, you do not yet understand the meaning of God's forgiveness toward you. You may only pray for God's forgiveness if you, in turn, are willing to forgive others.

Father, I pray for Your forgiveness. Thank You that You are willing, time and again, to forgive my sins. Please make me, in turn, willing to forgive other people their transgressions. Amen.

Seventy times seven

Read Matthew 18:21-35

Then Peter came to Jesus and asked, "Lord, how many times shall I forgive my brother when he sins against me? Up to seven times?" Jesus answered, "I tell you, not seven times, but seventy times seven" (Matt. 18:21-22).

To forgive is a duty of love that Jesus requires from His children. Like God, we should be willing to forgive time and again. Jewish Rabbinic teaching in the time of Jesus said that it was acceptable to forgive someone three times for the same offense. Therefore, Peter was rather magnanimous when he wanted to know whether one should forgive seven times. Jesus' reply must have taken the wind completely out of his sails: Not seven times, but seventy times seven.

The parable that Jesus then told illustrated what it means to forgive seventy times seven. A king was willing to cancel a debt of ten thousand talents, but when the man who received such mercy, was not willing to forgive someone who owed him a small amount of money, he was severely punished.

God is willing to cancel your massive debt of sin. Therefore, in turn and out of gratitude, you should be willing to show the same mercy to others.

God's forgiveness knows no bounds – and He expects you to do the same. Will you do so?

Heavenly Father, I praise You for canceling my debt of sin. Make me willing to show Your great mercy to others and to forgive them seventy times seven. Amen.

Joseph and his brothers

Read Genesis 45:1-10

And now, do not get distressed and do not be angry with yourselves for sending me here, because it was to save lives that God sent me ahead of you. So then, it was not you who sent me here, but God (Gen. 45:5, 8).

If there was one man who had a lot to forgive, it was Joseph. He was sold by his brothers. In Egypt, he had to work as a slave and he spent many years in jail even though he was innocent. And yet, the Lord was with him all the time, so that he was later set free and was appointed second-in-command of Egypt.

When his brothers came to buy food from him during a famine, he was in the ideal position to take revenge on them. But what did Joseph do? He immediately forgave his brothers. He recognized God's plan with his life and told his brothers that God sent him ahead of them to save their lives.

He invited his entire family to come and live with him in Egypt and promised to take care of them. Then he embraced his brothers and wept with them. With his brotherly embrace he emphasized his act of reconciliation.

We can learn a lot from Joseph. If there is something in your past that you have difficulty in coming to terms with, remember that God has a plan for your life. He will see to it that all things will work together for your good. Therefore, forgive those people who have hurt you.

Heavenly Father, please enable me to discover Your divine plan for my life – even in the unpleasant things that happen to me. Amen.

Collective forgiveness

Read Nehemiah 1:4-10

Hear the prayer your servant is praying before you day and night for your servants, the people of Israel. I confess the sins we Israelites, including myself and my father's house, have committed against you (Neh. 1:6).

In Nehemiah's beautiful prayer for forgiveness, he confesses his own sins as well as those of his people and his family, and asks the Lord to forgive them. He fasts and prays for days, asking that the Lord will grant him success with the major task that he wants to undertake.

Nehemiah very specifically confessed the sins that he and his people had committed: *"We have acted very wickedly towards you. We have not obeyed the commands, decrees and laws you gave your servant Moses"* (v. 7). Then he reminded God of His covenant promise.

God answered Nehemiah's prayer and blessed his rebuilding of the walls of Jerusalem. Once his task was successfully completed, Nehemiah declared a day of fasting: *"You have kept your promise because you are righteous. You are a forgiving God, gracious and compassionate, slow to anger and abounding in love"* (Neh. 9:8, 17).

God is still exactly the same as during the times of Nehemiah. If you confess your sins, as well as those of your family, He will still help you to achieve those things that you would like to do for Him. His promises still hold good for you – He is still willing to forgive your sins and have mercy upon you.

Heavenly Father, thank You for being the same merciful God as during the times of Nehemiah. I confess the sins of my people and my family to You. Please forgive us and have mercy upon us. Amen.

Be willing to make peace

Read Matthew 5:21-26

Therefore, if you are offering your gift at the altar and there remember that your brother has something against you, leave the gift there in front of the altar. First go and be reconciled to your brother; then come and offer your gift (Matt. 5:23-24).

Relationships depend on forgiveness. If we live in discord with one another, forgiveness becomes impossible. However, if we are willing to work at our relationships, and obey God's command to forgive and be reconciled, we will soon discover that forgiveness is not quite as impossible or difficult as we thought.

Lewis Smedes describes forgiveness as "a new beginning, a small miracle. It means that it is possible to start a new relationship with the one who has hurt you."[3] If you refuse to forgive, then you are disobedient to God's command. God expects you to forgive, even when the breach between you and the other person was no fault of yours.

We should be willing to make peace with the past in which we made so many mistakes – as well as with the present where many mistakes are still being made. You should be willing to forgive those who transgress against you. Because, if you earnestly desire to bring about reconciliation, you will have to be willing to start with yourself.

Father, please make me willing to make peace with those people who have something against me, even though the breach between us is no fault of mine. I ask this in Your name. Amen.

A forgiving God

> Read Psalm 130

If you, O LORD, kept a record of sins, O Lord, who could stand? But with you there is forgiveness; therefore you are feared (Ps. 130:3-4).

We worship a God who is so keen to forgive His children their sins, that He personally faced death on their behalf. With God's forgiving attitude toward sinners, He demonstrates His love for us in an unmistakable way. His Son died so that we can be forgiven. When we look at the crucified Jesus, we see an unforgettable picture of forgiveness. This is how much God loves us and how much He wants to forgive us.

"God's forgiveness enables us to live a meaningful life. God knows that forgiveness is the only way to maintain His relationship of love with fallen mankind," writes Lewis Smedes. "If God did not have the ability to forgive within Himself, there would have been no future for the likes of us. Forgiveness does not always take away the pain and it does not deny the existence of wounds. Forgiveness simply refuses to stand in the way of a new beginning."[4]

God's love for you is so great that He cannot but forgive you and start anew with you, time and again. You can put your hope in the Lord, for with Him there is full redemption! He will forgive your sins time and again (vv. 5, 7).

Father, how can I begin to thank You for being willing, time and again, to start anew with me, to forgive me anew. Thank You that I can put my hope in You, because You will redeem me from all my sins. Amen.

To forgive, as well as to forget

Read Micah 7:18-20

Who is a God like you, who pardons sin? You will again have compassion on us; you will tread our sins underfoot and hurl all our iniquities into the depths of the sea (Mic. 7:18-19).

In the history of Israel, we see time and again that God is not only willing to forgive the sins of His people, but to forget about them completely. *"Their sins and lawless acts I will remember no more,"* God promises in Hebrews 10:17. There is no other God like Him, the prophet Micah justifiably states. He is unique and without equal.

God is willing to hurl all your iniquities into the depths of the sea and to remember them no more. Therefore, you need no longer be burdened by guilt – if you have confessed your sins, then God has already forgiven you and forgotten your sins.

It is virtually impossible for us to do the same. We might succeed, with great difficulty, to forgive someone else, but to forget about an injustice is beyond our ability. Over and over, we rake up the sins committed against us. Sometimes we think that we have forgiven, only to wake up at night, drenched in sweat and filled with indignation, brooding once again about the injustices done to us.

If you truly want to forgive, ask God to enable you, not only to forgive, but also to forget the injustices committed against you.

Lord, please enable me, according to Your example, not only to forgive, but to forget completely about the injustices people have done to me. Amen.

Become more like Jesus

Read 1 John 2:1-6

This is how we know we are in him: Whoever claims to live in him must walk as Jesus did (1 John 2:5- 6).

Jesus is the great Cultivator of reconciliation. Through His crucifixion, He reconciled us with God. He also reconciles people with each other. In New Testament times, there was hostility between the Jews and other nations. The Jews referred to all Gentiles as "heathens" and, in addition, regarded them as unclean. They thought that they were the only people who could have access to God and His covenant promises.

When Jesus came into this world, He removed the barriers between Jews and Gentiles. *"His purpose was to reconcile both of them to God through the cross, by which he put to death their hostility,"* Paul writes to the congregation in Ephesus (Eph. 2:15- 16). All believers are now equal in Christ, and all share in God's covenant promises.

If you belong to Jesus, you are one of His people, and you should accept all Christians, even though there may be barriers, such as racial or political convictions, which separate you from each other. Jesus wants us to be reconciled with all Christians, so that we will become one in Him.

Only when you have a disposition similar to that of Jesus, will true reconciliation become a reality for you.

Lord Jesus, thank You that You have come to reconcile me with my fellow-Christians. Make me willing to accept them unconditionally and to live in the reconciliation that You require of me. Amen.

Be willing to forgive

Read Matthew 18:21-35

This is how my heavenly Father will treat each of you unless you forgive your brother from your heart (Matt. 18:35).

True reconciliation can only become reality if we are willing to become more like Jesus every day; if we can succeed in looking at other people through His eyes. Reconciliation allows us to judge others from a different perspective. We no longer judge others according to human criteria, but rather look at others in the way Jesus looks at us – with love and compassion, willing to forgive them and to become reconciled with them.

Jesus never condemned people, but was always willing to forgive them. When the Pharisees brought a woman to Him who had been caught in adultery, He did not condemn her (see John 8:11). Even on the cross, He prayed for forgiveness for those who had Him crucified: *"Father, forgive them, for they do not know what they are doing"* (Luke 23:34).

Once you have decided to follow in the footsteps of Jesus and forgive others, you will indeed become more like Him day by day until, in the words of Paul, you *"become mature, attaining to the whole measure of the fullness of Christ"* (Eph. 4:13).

If you refuse to forgive others, you will not be able to receive God's forgiveness because He will treat you in the same way as you treat your fellow man.

Lord, please forgive me for seeking Your forgiveness, while I am not always willing to forgive others. Please help me to be willing to forgive, so that I can confidently ask for Your forgiveness. Amen.

Jesus, our Mediator

Read Hebrews 9:11-15

For this reason Christ is the mediator of a new covenant, that those who are called may receive the promised eternal inheritance – now that he has died as a ransom to set them free from the sins committed under the first covenant (Heb. 9:15).

People who, through the course of history, interceded on behalf of God's people, were called mediators. Because God is holy and the people were sinners, someone who could stand between God and the people was needed – someone through whom God could talk to His people and, in turn, the people could talk to God. The priests usually took the role of mediator.

Today, there is still only one way to maintain a correct relationship with God, namely through the intercession of Jesus, the only Mediator between God and man, who gave Himself as a ransom for us. Through Jesus' death on the cross He became a Mediator of the new covenant. He is the perfect Mediator, sent by God to atone for man's sins with His own blood. *"For there is one God and one mediator between God and men, the man Christ Jesus, who gave himself as a ransom for all men"* (1 Tim. 2:5-6).

Without the shedding of blood, sins could not be forgiven. And yet, the rituals of the Old Testament, where atonement was brought about through the offering of a sacrificial lamb, only made people outwardly clean, while their hearts remained sinful. Jesus' blood was not only shed so that God could forgive your sins, but so that you could be cleansed on the inside. It radically changes your life and turns you into a brand new person.

Lord Jesus, I glorify You because You were willing to come and stand between God and me, so that my sins could be forgiven and I could become a new person. Amen.

Revenge and retribution

Read Deuteronomy 19:15-21

Show no pity: life for life, eye for eye, tooth for tooth, hand for hand, foot for foot (Deut. 19:21).

Phil Bosmans writes that nothing makes one as depressed as being powerless to forgive. And nothing is as tragic as living with the sharp stone of grudge and hate in your heart, day and night. In the end, you will stumble over that stone, and you will suffer the most hurt, because of your persistent unforgiving attitude.[5]

During Old Testament times, the saying, "an eye for an eye", was the accepted norm (see Deut. 19:21). It was acceptable to take revenge on a person who had caused you harm.

This chain reaction of revenge can only be prevented by forgiveness. In His Sermon on the Mount, Jesus therefore says: "*You have heard that it was said, 'Eye for eye, and tooth for tooth.' But I tell you, do not resist an evil person. If someone strikes you on the right cheek, turn to him the other also*" (Matt. 5:38-39).

Instead of revenge, however, Jesus preaches forgiveness and reconciliation. He asks His followers to combat violence with love, to renounce revenge and retribution.

If there is someone in your life toward whom you still harbor a grudge, discard the grudge and ask the Lord to enable you to show forgiveness instead.

Heavenly Father, help me to take the initiative and to live in love, instead of taking revenge on others and insisting on retribution. Amen.

Atonement is grace

Read Ezekiel 16:59-63

"So I will establish my covenant with you, and you will know that I am the LORD. Then, when I make atonement for you for all you have done, you will remember and be ashamed and never again open your mouth because of your humiliation" (Ezek. 16:62-63).

Even in the Old Testament, we see that God is willing to forgive the sins of His wicked people time and again, and to reconfirm His covenant with His disloyal people, even though they do not deserve it. In Ezekiel 16, there is a detailed description of exactly how wicked these people were. And yet, God always seeks to forgive them and to make atonement for them. But it took the crucifixion of Jesus to bring atonement to fulfilment.

It is only by grace that God has forgiven your sins, and made atonement for you through the intercession of Jesus. The fact that you can forgive others who have hurt you, is also grace, because you could never do so on your own. It is only God who can bring about this forgiveness in your heart.

Forgiveness and reconciliation are two things that are in direct contrast with our human nature. Johan Smit writes that forgiveness leads to reconciliation. Forgiveness not only creates the possibility of beginning a new life, it leads to a new life filled with loving deeds.[6] And it is only when you surrender control of your life to the Holy Spirit that He will plant God's love in your heart, enabling you to forgive completely.

Heavenly Father, I pray that You will help me to heal my relationship with You and with my fellow man, so that I may be able to live fully according to Your will. Amen.

Unconditional forgiveness

Read Ephesians 1:3-8

In him we have redemption through his blood, the forgiveness of sins, in accordance with the riches of God's grace (Eph. 1:7).

Jesus' crucifixion resulted in two wonderful things for believers, namely our redemption and the forgiveness of our sins. With His shed blood, Jesus paid the ransom for our sins and set us free for ever from slavery to sin. He opened the way for God to forgive us, because His blood was the perfect sacrifice for our sins. And because of this sacrifice, sinners can be reconciled with the holy God.

I. L. de Villiers writes that we cannot earn God's forgiveness. Forgiveness never depends on merit. Forgiveness is always an act of grace. Forgiveness that imposes conditions is not forgiveness. And perhaps our unforgiving nature is precisely one of the greatest things for which we need God's forgiveness.[7]

When God forgives us, He does not impose any conditions. He forgives unconditionally. All that we have to do in exchange for His forgiveness, is to believe in Jesus and confess our sins. *"If we confess our sins, he is faithful and just and will forgive us our sins and purify us from all unrighteousness,"* writes John (1 John 1:9).

If you are willing to confess your sins, you can rest assured that God will forgive you.

Father, please forgive my sins and help me to forsake sin. I ask this in the name of Jesus, who paid the price for my sins on the cross. Amen.

Atonement out of love

Read 1 John 4:7-21

This is love: not that we loved God, but that he loved us and sent his Son as an atoning sacrifice for our sins (1 John 4:10).

God sent His Son to be crucified because He loves people. He made atonement for you because He loves you. Jesus said that while love for God is the first and the greatest commandment, love for one's neighbor is so important that He likens it to the first. God requires us to love our neighbors and therefore be willing to be reconciled with them. *"Dear friends, since God so loved us, we also ought to love one another. And he has given us this command: Whoever loves God must also love his brother,"* John writes (vv. 11, 21). And then John goes one step further: *"Anyone who does not love his brother, whom he has seen, cannot love God, whom he has not seen"* (v. 20).

Love for one's neighbor, which means a willingness to forgive time and again, can be very demanding. It does not come naturally. Johan Smit writes that it is the kind of love that comes into conflict with the love of ourselves. We are only capable of such reconciliatory love through the power of the cross.[8]

Do your relationships with other people reflect your love for God?

Heavenly Father, I confess that I fall far short in my love for others. Please help me to love others with the same love that You show toward me. Amen.

Jesus and reconciliation

Read Ephesians 2:11-22

His purpose was to reconcile both of them to God through the cross, by which he put to death their hostility. He came and preached peace (Eph. 2:15-17).

Through His death, Jesus enabled people, who are hostile toward one another, to be reconciled with one another. *The Message* says, *"Christ brought us together through his death on the cross. The cross got us to embrace, and that was the end of the hostility. Christ came and preached peace to you outsiders and peace to us insiders. He treated us as equals, and so made us equals. Through him we both share the same spirit and have equal access to the Father."*

God wants His children to live in the fullness of the reconciliation, brought about by His Son. Johan Smit writes that in the true sense of the word, reconciliation is not merely a legal term or a theoretical agreement. Reconciliation is demonstrated in the warmth of an embrace.[9]

Jesus makes it possible for you to live in peace with God and with your fellow man. Biblical reconciliation is seen in healed relationships. But first, you need to be reconciled with God. Once you are truly reconciled with God, this reconciliation will have far-reaching and positive implications in your relationship with others. You will gradually learn to look at others through the cross of Jesus and, in this way, you will succeed in truly loving them, as well as forgiving them with all your heart.

Jesus gave His life in order for you to become reconciled with God and other people. Does your life reflect this reconciliation?

Father, help me to demonstrate the reconciliation that Jesus has brought about for me in the way in which I live and in my conduct toward You and others. Amen.

Forgiveness sets you free

Read Luke 1:76-79

To give his people the knowledge of salvation through the forgiveness of their sins, because of the tender mercy of our God (Luke 1:77-78).

The prophet Zechariah foretells that the child who is to be born will give His people the knowledge of salvation through the forgiveness of their sins. Jesus redeems us by forgiving our sins. Forgiveness is always an act of liberation. If you refuse to forgive, then you remain locked in a prison that you have built yourself, but the moment you choose to forgive, you are set free from that prison.

"Forgiving someone with all your heart, is doubling an act of liberation. We set the person who has harmed us free from the negative bonds which have entangled us. We also set ourselves free from the burden of being the victim. As long as we do not forgive those who have wounded us, we carry them with us or, worse, pull them as a heavy load," writes Henri Nouwen.[10]

If someone has offended you, it is rather tempting to see yourself as the aggrieved person. But sincere forgiveness not only sets free the person who has harmed and offended you, but sets you free as well.

If you refuse to forgive someone else, you harm yourself much more than you harm that person. Make a decision of the will right now to forgive the person against whom you harbor a grudge – then you will discover that you, too, will be set free in the process! Forgiveness, according to Nouwen, is first and foremost the healing of our own hearts.

Father, forgive me for staying locked up in the prison of my own unforgiving attitude for so long, and enable me to be liberated from it for ever. Amen.

On the receiving end of forgiveness

> *Read Matthew 9:1-8*

Some men brought to him a paralytic, lying on a mat. When Jesus saw their faith, he said to the paralytic, "Take heart, son; your sins are forgiven" (Matt. 9:2).

Four men brought their paralyzed friend to Jesus so that He could heal him. When Jesus saw the sincere faith of the paralyzed man's friends, He immediately told him that his sins were forgiven. When the teachers of the law heard this, they started grumbling among themselves saying that He was blaspheming. Jesus answered, *"But so that you may know that the Son of Man has authority on earth to forgive sins"* (v. 6). He then instructed the man to take up his mat and go home. The man got up, and walked out and the people gathered there praised God.

The paralyzed man first had to be willing to accept Jesus' forgiveness before he could be healed.

It is not always easy to accept forgiveness from someone else. We find it difficult to accept forgiveness, precisely because we find it so difficult to offer our forgiveness to someone else. "Only when we can receive forgiveness can we give it," writes Henri Nouwen. "To receive someone else's forgiveness requires not only a confession that we have hurt somebody, but also the humility to acknowledge our dependency on others."[11]

Heavenly Father, I apologize that I find it so difficult at times to accept forgiveness, precisely because I find it so difficult to forgive others. Help me to forgive and to be forgiven. Amen.

Jesus' model prayer

Read Matthew 6:7-15

"Forgive us our debts, as we also have forgiven our debtors" (Matt. 6:12).

Ten years after the end of the Second World War, German Christians requested a group of Poles to allow them to formally ask forgiveness for the war crimes against Poland. At first, the Poles did not want to agree. "It is impossible to forgive," they said. "Every stone in Warsaw is drenched in Polish blood." The Polish Christians ended the meeting with the Lord's Prayer. When they reached the line of our text: *"Forgive us our debts, as we also have forgiven our debtors,"* silence descended on the room. Then one of the Poles said, "We forgive you. We cannot continue saying the Lord's Prayer if we keep on refusing to forgive."

This moving story holds a lesson for all of us: If we are not willing to forgive others, we cannot ask God for His forgiveness. God's forgiveness is never subject to our forgiveness of others, but there is a link: If we refuse to forgive, we do not yet understand what God's forgiveness is all about.

It is only when we are willing to forgive that God makes His forgiveness available to us. If we ask God for forgiveness, we have already received that forgiveness, because we are His children. Johan Smit writes that the fact that he can forgive is grace. It is evidence of victory – the victory of the Spirit over the flesh. It is indeed an event in which he can rejoice!

Lord, I pray that You will make me willing to forgive all who have harmed me, so that I can have the confidence to ask for Your forgiveness. Amen.

Reconciliation, the road to peace

Read Colossians 1:15-20

God was pleased to have all his fullness dwell in him, and through him to reconcile to himself all things, whether things on earth or things in heaven, by making peace through his blood, shed on the cross (Col. 1:19-20).

If we are willing to forgive, we prepare the road to reconciliation and peace.

Phil Bosmans writes that we have never been in such need of Jesus' peace which transcends all human understanding, as in the present climate of violence and discord. Peace can only grow through forgiveness. Every word and every gesture that offers forgiveness is a contribution to peace! Through forgiveness the heart is disarmed.[13]

Let us conclude with the prayer of Saint Francis of Assisi:

Lord, make me an instrument of Your peace!
Where there is hatred let me sow love;
where there is injury, pardon;
where there is doubt, faith;
where there is despair, hope;
where there is darkness, light;
where there is sadness, joy.
O divine Master, grant that I may not so much seek
to be consoled as to console;
to be understood as to understand;
to be loved as to love.
For it is in giving that we receive;
it is in pardoning that we are pardoned;
and it is in dying that we are born to eternal life.
Amen.

Prayer

Heavenly Father, I praise You because You initiated forgiveness.

I acknowledge that I am a sinner.

Please forgive each of my sins, and thank You for being willing to cancel my massive debt of sin.

Help me, out of gratitude, to be willing to offer my forgiveness to others.

I want to accept the reconciliation that you have brought about for me, and become a minister of this reconciliation to others.

Lord Jesus, thank You for being willing to die, for allowing Your blood to flow on the cross, so that I can be reconciled with God and my fellow man.

I pray that You will help me not to harbor grudges against others, but to forgive those who have done me an injustice, with all my heart, as well as to forget the things that they did to me.

Thank You that Your blood not only cleanses me from sin, but also makes a brand new person out of me.

Amen.

August

Suffering

Suffering and pain form part of human existence.

Life is not always pleasant, nor is it always easy. But God uses suffering to bring about good in our lives.

In times of suffering, God is the only One to whom you can turn.

Many people struggle with God's goodness because He does not relieve their suffering.

"You need to exchange your soft religion for a hard cornerstone on which you can stand firm under all circumstances.

"If everything goes wrong and it feels as though God has forsaken you, your faith must be strong enough to keep you steadfast in the knowledge that your Helper is actively with you. Then you must savor the knowledge that you belong to God, your 'only consolation in life and death'.

"God has placed you in this world and He provides you with a faith that is strong enough for this life.

"With Him, you will find shelter against the bitterest cold and the deepest darkness," writes Willem Nicol.[1]

I pray that this will become your testimony too.

At the end of your tether

Read Job 6:1-13

What strength do I have, that I should still hope? What prospects, that I should be patient? Do I have any power to help myself, now that success has been driven from me? (Job 6:11, 13).

In this chapter, Job has reached the end of his tether. *"If only my anguish could be weighed and all my misery be placed on the scales! It would surely outweigh the sand of the seas,"* he laments in verses 2 and 3. Eventually he realizes that his own strength is spent and that he can do nothing about his desperate situation – that he is at the end of his tether.

Perhaps you, like Job, have sometimes felt that you could no longer carry on. If you have reached the end of your tether, remember that God is always there for you. When you have no idea how to continue you will find wisdom and counsel with Him. He offers you His wonderful strength when your strength is spent.

You can gladly make the beautiful promise in Psalm 32 your own: *"I will instruct you and teach you in the way you should go; I will counsel you and watch over you. Many are the woes of the wicked, but the Lord's unfailing love surrounds the man who trusts in him"* (Ps. 32:8, 10).

God is offering you His counsel and love today so you can banish your despondency. Allow Him to do this for you!

Heavenly Father, You know just how despondent I feel today. Thank You that I can rest assured in the knowledge that You are always there for me, that Your strength carries me when my own is spent, and that I can depend on Your counsel when I reach the end of my tether. Surround me now with Your love. Amen.

Please answer me!

Read Job 23:1-14

If only I knew where to find him; if only I could go to his dwelling! I would state my case before him and fill my mouth with arguments. I would find out what he would answer me, and consider what he would say (Job 23:3-5).

Job himself provides the answers to his despondent questions of chapter 6: If only he knew where to find God, he would have gone to His dwelling and tried to obtain an answer from Him, tried to understand what God was saying to him with this period of suffering.

Job lived before Jesus died on the cross. He could not find his way to God on his own. God seemed far away and inaccessible to him. Unlike Job, we know exactly where to find God. To us He is but a prayer away. On the cross, Jesus opened the way into the Holiest of Holies so we can draw near to His throne and lay claim to His grace.

I am sure that, on occasion, you have also sought answers from God. There are thousands of things in our lives that we fail to understand and to which we have no answer. Even though God does not always provide you with every answer that you seek, you can always rest assured in the knowledge that He loves you. That, in the end, He Himself is the Answer to each one of your "why" questions.

Therefore, you can gladly become still in His presence and share all your doubts with Him.

Heavenly Father, thank You that You are there for me, every moment of the day, should I wish to talk to You. Please teach me once again that I do not need answers to all my "why" questions, and help me to become still in Your presence. Amen.

God is eager to help you

Read Isaiah 59:1-9

So justice is far from us, and righteousness does not reach us. We look for light, but all is darkness; for brightness, but we walk in deep shadows. Surely the arm of the LORD is not too short to save, nor his ear too dull to hear (Is. 59:9, 1).

The prophet Isaiah lived during a time of great darkness in the lives of God's people. They were constantly disobedient to God, and so He caused many enemies to rise up against them. He also warned them that their country would be overrun and they would be sent into exile. But He would eventually have compassion on them and show them mercy by allowing them to return to their own country.

There are two ways in which we can respond when we are faced with difficulties. You could turn your back on God and try coping on your own. But we find, time and again, that God is the only One who can really help us in our crises.

God's covenant people know that He is always with them. They do not need to turn to things such as alcohol or drugs to alleviate their anxiety. Only God can come to your rescue when you are faced with a crisis. And He *wants* to do it for you!

His arm is never too short to save, nor His ear too dull to hear your complaints. Even though you are surrounded by darkness, He will eventually bring the light back into your life.

Lord, my life is filled with darkness and I can see no light. Thank You for the promise to which I can cling: that Your arm is never too short to save me, nor Your ear too dull to hear me. Amen.

To advance the kingdom

Read Philippians 1:12-21

Now I want you to know, brothers, that what has happened to me has really served to advance the gospel. As a result, it has become clear throughout the whole palace guard and to everyone else that I am in chains for Christ (Phil. 1:12-13).

Paul was often unjustly tortured and imprisoned. Yet his attitude was remarkable: he testifies that his unjust treatment has led to the advancement of God's kingdom. He regards his imprisonment as an opportunity to preach the Word of God. *"What has happened to me has really served to advance the gospel,"* he writes to the Christians in Philippi.

Precisely because Paul was imprisoned, the palace guard and everyone else who came into contact with him, had the opportunity to hear about Jesus. When they saw the unusual way in which Paul responded to his unjust treatment, their own faith was strengthened by it. Paul realized that it was not his circumstances but what he made of them that helped to spread the gospel.

How you respond to negative events in your life speaks volumes about your faith. None of us can choose our circumstances, but we can all choose to remain positive.

Do you manage to not become bitter when things go wrong? Do you use your negative circumstances in a positive way for the kingdom of God?

Heavenly Father, forgive me that, unlike Paul, I have so much to say when I am unjustly treated. Teach me to handle injustice like a child of Yours, so that the faith of others may be strengthened by my actions. Amen.

Can God refuse to listen?

Read Ezekiel 8:15-18

Therefore I will deal with them in anger; I will not look on them with pity or spare them. Although they shout in my ears, I will not listen to them (Ezek. 8:18).

God had finally reached the end of His patience with His disobedient people. Speaking through the prophet Ezekiel, He declares that He will no longer look on them with pity. Although they may shout in His ears, He will not listen to them. The people themselves brought about this apparent callousness on the side of God. They refused to accept His love and constantly turned their backs on Him to worship pagan idols.

Have you prayed when faced with a crisis, only to feel as though God was not listening to you? As though He no longer heard what you wanted to tell Him, nor brought about the things you requested of Him?

In times like these, you should do some soul-searching and take a good look at your own sins and shortcomings. If God does not respond, it is probably your own fault. But He loves you too much to forsake you. As soon as you confess your sins He will forgive them and accept your prayers once again.

"He fulfills the desires of those who fear him; he hears their cry and saves them," declares the psalmist (Ps. 145:19). Do not hesitate to receive God's love and grace for you!

Lord, I praise You because You listen, and You are always ready to help me. Help me never to try Your patience like Israel did, but to identify and confess my sins. Amen.

In times of suffering

Read Psalm 102:1-12; 27-29

Do not hide your face from me when I am in distress. Because of my loud groaning I am reduced to skin and bones. I am like a desert owl (Ps. 102:2, 5-6).

This psalm is the *"prayer of an afflicted man. When he is faint and pours out his lament before the Lord"* (introduction to Psalm 102). The psalmist is going through extremely difficult times. He pleads with the Lord not to hide His face from him when he is in distress, to listen to him and hear his prayers. He has been reduced to skin and bones and feels that the end of his life is near. But what causes him the most suffering is the feeling that the Lord has forsaken him.

We do not know what had happened to the author of this psalm. But in spite of his perilous situation he clings to the fact that the Lord remains forever constant, that He will reign forever and that He responds to the prayers of the destitute (v. 17). Therefore, he has faith that the Lord will help him in his time of suffering just as He has always done in the past.

If you are going through a difficult time you might also feel as though God is far away. Although you may feel that way, remember that this is not the case. God loves you and stays close by your side. Through His Spirit, He dwells *in* you. God always remains constant. He listens to your prayers and is always ready to help you.

Heavenly Father, thank You that You are constant, that You are never far away from Your children, and are always willing to listen to their prayers and help them. Please hear my prayers today. Amen.

Darkness turning into light

Read Isaiah 42:10-16

I will lead the blind by ways they have not known, along unfamiliar paths I will guide them; I will turn the darkness into light before them and make the rough places smooth (Isa. 42:16).

God promises that He will turn the darkness into light and make the rough places smooth for His people. Throughout the Bible, times of suffering are likened to darkness. When Jeremiah is at his most despondent, he laments: *"He has driven me away and made me walk in darkness rather than light"* (Lam. 3:2).

When you face difficulties, it might feel at times as though you are surrounded by darkness and that the sun will never shine again. But even if you cannot see the sun on dark and cloudy days, it is still there. In the same way, God is your Light in times of darkness and He promises to turn the darkness into light again.

"Though I have fallen, I will rise. Though I sit in darkness, the Lord will be my light," says the prophet Micah. *"I will bear the Lord's wrath, until he pleads my case and establishes my right. He will bring me out into the light; I will see his righteousness"* (Mic. 7:8-9).

You can gladly hold onto God in times of darkness. He can change your situation or help you to work through it so that it works out for your good.

Heavenly Father, thank You that even when I am surrounded by darkness, I can know that You are still by my side and that You can turn my darkness into light once again. Amen.

August 8

God's favor lasts a lifetime

> Read Psalm 30

For his anger lasts only a moment, but his favor lasts a lifetime; weeping may remain for a night, but rejoicing comes in the morning (Ps. 30:5).

The suffering the psalmist experiences is the result of God's anger at sinfulness. But he knows that God's anger lasts only for a short while, and that God's favor lasts a lifetime.

God can turn our tears into joy. Praise and glorify Him! People who belong to God can hold onto this promise during times of suffering. God's grace and love for them last a lifetime. Although the night of suffering may endure for a short while, they can rest assured that joy will be awaiting them in the morning.

This psalm contains a beautiful message of comfort for all who are suffering: the God in whom we believe can change a dismal situation into a joyful one.

Remember, when darkness descends on you, then God is working in your life. You might feel the tremor of God's wrath, but His grace will soon transform life into a song of joy. "Do not fear the night, for it is in the night that the Lord comes to us," writes Heinrich Jung-Schilling.[2]

If you are facing relentless difficulties, begin to think of how God can be glorified in your circumstances.

Heavenly Father, I glorify You for Your love and grace that last a lifetime. Help me to hold onto this love when darkness descends on my life – and thank You that I can rest assured in the knowledge that joy awaits me in the morning. Amen.

Pray during times of suffering

Read Psalm 86

Hear my prayer, O LORD; listen to my cry for mercy. In the day of my trouble I will call to you, for you will answer me. Your are forgiving and good, O LORD, abounding in love to all who call to you (Ps. 86:6, 7, 5).

In this psalm, the psalmist pleads for God's help because he finds himself in great distress. He calls to God, confident in the knowledge that God will hear his prayer and help him because He abounds in love for those who call on Him. God inspires trust in His children because He has shown Himself to be a God who is able to deliver and help His children.

Therefore, you too can call on the Lord for help in times of trouble. He will hear your prayer and answer it; He will demonstrate His abundant love for you by helping you.

You can confidently ask God to help you in times of trial. If you stay close to God, He will ensure that you are not tempted beyond your ability to withstand, and He will deliver you from every tribulation.

In closing, the psalmist testifies to others about what the Lord has done for him. You too should testify to others about the goodness of the Lord in your life.

Heavenly Father, I praise You for always helping me when temptation and tribulation come against me. Thank You that I can pray to You, secure in the knowledge that You will listen to me and will answer my prayers. Amen.

Suffering puts you to the test

Read 1 Peter 1:6-9

In this you greatly rejoice, though now for a little while you may have had to suffer grief in all kinds of trials. These have come so that your faith may be proved genuine and may result in praise, glory and honor when Jesus Christ is revealed (1 Pet. 1:6-7).

Nobody enjoys suffering, but none of us can escape it. Believers are able to endure their suffering gladly, because we know that God is with us when we go through difficult times. The Lord can use suffering to put your faith in Him to the test. God purifies us so that our faith may be proved genuine, resulting in praise and honor when Jesus Christ is revealed.

Through our trials God teaches us to persevere in the faith. Before gold can be extracted from gold ore, it must first be purified. Tribulation forms part of God's process of purification for His children. Therefore, try to remain cheerful during times of suffering.

If you keep focusing on your own misery, your view will remain clouded. Rather look toward God. Think of all the times that He has helped you in the past. He is omnipotent and can do all things. He is able to help you with whatever problems you face. He will provide in your need at the right time.

Heavenly Father, thank You for this new insight that You use my suffering to test my level of faith. Please help me to pass this test of faith with flying colors! Amen.

Suffering has an added advantage

Read 2 Corinthians 7:11

See what this godly sorrow has produced in you: what earnestness, what eagerness to clear yourselves, what indignation, what alarm, what longing, what concern, what readiness to see justice done (2 Cor. 7:11).

The godly sorrow of the Corinthian Christians resulted in positive things. It made them aware of the indignation, alarm, longing, concern and readiness to see justice done.

The Message clarifies it even further:

And now, isn't it wonderful all the ways in which this distress has goaded you closer to God? You're more alive, more concerned, more sensitive, more reverent, more human, more passionate, more responsible. Looked at from any angle, you've come out of this with purity of heart.

This clearly proves that sorrow and suffering bring about positive results in the life of a Christian. Therefore, when you experience pain and suffering in your own life, reflect on the advantages that the pain has brought into your life. You may even succeed in thanking God for it!

Heavenly Father, none of us enjoys pain and suffering. You know that I find this time of sorrow extremely difficult. However, I have discovered that it is beneficial for me – and for that I wish to thank You. Amen.

The world suffers from birth pains

Read Matthew 24:4-14

"Nation will rise against nation, and kingdom against kingdom. There will be famines and earthquakes in various places. All these are the beginning of birth pains" (Matt. 24:7-8).

Jesus told His disciples that they would suffer trials and tribulations. And this suffering, He explained, will prepare them for the things awaiting them in the future. These things occur because the world is suffering from birth pains.

No one will deny that the world we live in is a mess. Violence, crime and fraud have become so commonplace that they no longer move us. When we listen to the news or read the newspapers, we cannot but wonder whether these evil things will ever come to an end.

Even though the world is imperfect, life is not meaningless for God's children. All the bad things occur precisely because the world is imperfect. But the promise of God's new world where everything will be good and whole again – like at the beginning of Creation – shines brightly in our imperfect world.

If your courage threatens to fail when you observe the current state of affairs in the world, go and read the beautiful picture of God's new world in Isaiah 11 and 65, and Revelation 21. Then go and live in such a way that you will be ready when this new world dawns.

Lord Jesus, thank You for the promise that a new heaven and a new earth are awaiting me, where all suffering will end. Help me to keep this promise in mind when my own little world suffers from birth pains. Amen.

Do not lose heart!

Read 2 Corinthians 4:16-18

Therefore we do not lose heart. Though outwardly we are wasting away, yet inwardly we are being renewed day by day. For our light and momentary troubles are achieving for us an eternal glory that far outweighs them all (2 Cor. 4:16-17).

Paul had firsthand experience of suffering. But even in the most difficult of circumstances he did not lose heart, because he knew the secret that motivates millions of Christians to persevere, regardless of their dreadful circumstances. We can endure suffering because we have the promise that it will pass, and that it will achieve an eternal glory for us.

The Message translates today's text wonderfully: *"So we're not giving up. How could we! Even though on the outside it often looks like things are falling apart on us, on the inside, where God is making new life, not a day goes by without his unfolding grace."*

You can hold on to this promise when you go through troublesome times. No suffering is completely unbearable if you know that God is with you. On your sickbed, beside an open grave, when you're retrenched or when people leave you in the lurch, He never forsakes you. And He wants to surround you with His loving presence – especially during troubled times.

Heavenly Father, I praise You that I can know that You are with me, even when things are very bad. Thank You that I can hold on to my hope, because I believe that today's suffering will, in the end, bring me eternal joy. Amen.

You have a future!

Read 2 Corinthians 4:18-5:6

So we fix our eyes not on what is seen, but on what is unseen. For what is seen is temporary, but what is unseen is eternal (2 Cor. 4:18).

There is a second reason why Christians do not allow suffering to get the better of them: they know that they have an eternal future in heaven in the presence of God. They can fix their eyes on the unseen glory that awaits them. Our earthly abode is like a tent, compared to the eternal house that God is building for us in heaven, writes Paul (see 2 Cor. 5:1).

Therefore, you do not need to be obsessed about your tribulations. With God's help you can look past your suffering, and see heaven waiting for you. When we know that a reward awaits us, we can remain positive through times of suffering. It is not difficult to study very hard for a while if you know that you will get good grades on your tests.

Even though things might be hard right now, you can focus on the eternal glory that awaits you in heaven – for God has promised this to all who believe in His Son (see 2 Cor. 5:8). Although you cannot yet see the new world that God has prepared for us, you know that your final destination will be with God in heaven. And knowing this helps you to make the best of things right now.

Heavenly Father, I glorify You for the promise that I have an eternal future with You. Help me to persevere for a little while, until I reach my true destination. Amen.

In times of wakefulness

Read Psalm 77

When I was in distress, I sought the LORD; at night I stretched out untiring hands and my soul refused to be comforted. You kept my eyes from closing; I was too troubled to speak (Ps. 77:2, 4).

This psalmist suffered from insomnia. Through the wakeful nights he prayed and called on the Lord for help, but God remained silent. He felt more and more dejected. What worried him most was that God seemed to be responding differently from how He had acted in the past (v. 10).

Perhaps you can identify with this cry of distress. Even though you might succeed in falling asleep while wrestling with major issues, if you wake up during the night, it is almost impossible to go back to sleep again. In these wakeful times it sometimes feels as though God is not answering your prayers in the same way as He did in the past.

But remember, God never changes. Sometimes He makes us wait for an answer, but He will answer each one of His children's prayers. In times of suffering you can hold onto this promise: God will deliver you once again. Perhaps He wants you to learn something about your life through your suffering. Therefore, try to look past your problem toward God and implicitly trust Him to deliver you.

Heavenly Father, at the moment I am finding it hard to recognize that You are the same merciful God You have always been. Forgive me and teach me to keep believing that You will deliver me once again. Amen.

God holds the reins!

Read Psalm 3

I lie down and sleep; I wake again, because the LORD sustains me (Ps. 3:5).

When he wrote this psalm, David was in a perilous situation: He was fleeing for his life and, to make matters worse, his own son wanted to kill him. His enemies were thrilled by this turn of events. They declared that the Lord had forsaken him. And to all intents and purposes, it seemed that they were right.

David however, knew better than that. Even though things were going so badly for him, he remained calm and slept peacefully at night. Under these difficult circumstances, David prayed to God and believed that the Lord would help him. He trusted in God implicitly. He knew that the Lord would help him once again, as He had always done in the past.

You, too, might feel as though the Lord does not hear you, as though He is delaying helping you, just when you need His help the most. Like David, you can trust steadfastly in the Lord and sleep peacefully, even though everything is going wrong.

If you love God, He holds the reins of your life firmly. He can use your suffering to His glory. Regardless of what may happen to you, the Lord is always in complete control of your circumstances.

Heavenly Father, thank You for the assurance that You will take care of me, that nothing will happen to me that You cannot use for Your glory. Help me to sleep peacefully, knowing that You are in control. Amen.

All's well that ends well

Read Romans 8:29-34

And we know that in all things God works for the good of those who love him, who have been called according to his purpose. What, then, shall we say in response to this? If God is for us, who can be against us? (Rom. 8:28, 31).

God uses suffering to mold the lives of His children. It is never the will of God that His children should suffer, but sometimes He allows it in order for us to grow closer to Him. Even suffering can be used by God for your good in His perfect plan for your life. If you belong to God you can be sure that He is on your side – and, therefore, there is nothing at all that can come against you and harm you.

When things go very badly for you, if you lose your job or fall seriously ill, you probably tend to pray more than you usually do and so the negative circumstances in your life bring you closer to God. God is always in complete control of your life. "God is not the Author of all events, but the Master of all events," the old saying goes.

God does not cause your suffering, but He does control it so that, in the end, it can be for your own good. If you are facing a crisis at the moment, you can gladly hold on to the promise in Psalm 138:8, *"The Lord will fulfill his purpose for me; your love, O Lord, endures forever."*

Father, how wonderful is Your master plan! Thank You for the promise that You do not cause my suffering, but that You control it and use it to bring me closer to You. Amen.

Surrounded by darkness

Read Isaiah 50:7-11

*Who among you fears the LORD and obeys the word of his servant?
Let him who walks in the dark, who has no light, trust in the name
of the LORD and rely on his God* (Isa. 50:10).

Things were going very badly for God's people. They thought that
God had forgotten about them. Everything around them was pitch
black. But Isaiah's words comforted them: *"Let him who walks in
the dark, who has no light, trust in the name of the LORD."* God will
always be there for them and He promises to help them once again,
as He has done so many times in the past.

In the Bible, darkness is often used to describe suffering. Even
children of the Lord, at times, have to contend with dark clouds
obscuring their path through life. And in this darkness it is easy
to bump your toe against a stone or to get lost, or even to go
completely astray at times. God promises to be with you when
darkness descends on you. *"Even though I walk through the valley
of the shadow of death, I will fear no evil, for you are with me; your
rod and your staff, they comfort me,"* David testifies in Psalm 23:4.

If your life is filled with darkness, allow God to be your light.
*"You, O LORD, keep my lamp burning; my God turns my darkness
into light,"* proclaims the psalmist (Ps. 18:28).

Trust Him to turn your darkness into light!

Heavenly Father, I praise You for being a Light to me, that You
are always by my side to guide me safely through the times of
darkness in my life. Thank You that I can rest assured in the
knowledge that You will never forsake me in that darkness.
Amen.

Steadfast in temptation

Read James 1:12-18

Blessed is the man who perseveres under trial, because when he has stood the test, he will receive the crown of life that God has promised to those who love him (James 1:12).

God is good and just – and He will never lead anyone into temptation. *"When tempted, no one should say, 'God is tempting me.' For God cannot be tempted by evil, nor does he tempt anyone,"* James warns in verse 13. It is usually our own sinful desires that cause us to succumb to temptation.

However, God can reverse the consequences of sin. He can turn the negative circumstances in your life around so that they will benefit you eventually. During a youth sermon, one of my husband's colleagues asked a group of young people what event in their lives they were the most grateful for. One girl replied that her father's illness had brought her so much closer to the Lord and that she had praised Him for it many a time.

When temptation confronts you on the path of life, take God at His Word. Persevere under trial and trust in Him, so that you will receive the crown of life that God has promised.

Heavenly Father, I pray that You will help me to persevere under trial, that You will turn my negative circumstances around so that they will be for my own good. Thank You that I can trust in You to help me. Amen.

Rejoice in your problems

> Read 2 Corinthians 11:23-31

If I must boast, I will boast of the things that show my weakness. The God and Father of the Lord Jesus, who is to be praised for ever, knows that I am not lying (2 Cor. 1:30-31).

Paul knew full well what it was to suffer because he had endured much of it in his own life. The list of disasters that he had to brave while he worked for the Lord reads like a nightmare: He was often in deadly peril, he was beaten and stoned, he was shipwrecked, on many a journey he feared for his life, and he was often hungry, thirsty and cold. But through all these things, he cared for his congregations (see vv. 23-28).

These negative experiences reminded Paul that in himself, he had nothing to boast about. He glorifies God for all his achievements.

In Romans 5:3-5 he outlines the positive results of suffering in his own life: *"We also rejoice in our sufferings, because we know that suffering produces perseverance; perseverance, character; and character, hope. And hope does not disappoint us, because God has poured out his love into our hearts by the Holy Spirit, whom he has given us."*

Like Paul, with God's help, you can rejoice in suffering, because it will guarantee you perseverance, character and hope.

Heavenly Father, help me, like Paul, to rejoice in those things that I would have preferred to be different because, in the end, these trials teach me to persevere, to believe in You and to place my hope in You. Amen.

Where is God when you are in trouble?

Read Exodus 1:8-14

The Egyptians came to dread the Israelites and worked them ruthlessly. They made their lives bitter with hard labor; in all their hard labor the Egyptians used them ruthlessly (Exod. 1:12-14).

At first, all went well with God's people in Egypt. The pharaoh was kindly toward them and they prospered in this foreign country. However, four hundred years on, the picture changed completely. The new pharaoh did not know the story of Joseph. Besides, the Israelites increased in numbers to such an extent that they became a threat to the Egyptians.

Pharaoh's solution was to kill all newborn Israelite boys and to use the people for slave labor. The people suffered greatly. It seemed to them as though God had forgotten about them. But God never forgets His children. He was already working to bring about their deliverance. He was preparing Moses to set them free from bondage in Egypt and to lead them to a land of great abundance.

If the things you face cause you to question God's caring love for you, remember the story of Israel. While they were wondering about God, and thought that He had forgotten about them, He was already bringing about their salvation.

Consider that while you are doubting God's love for you, in all probability He is already in the process of bringing about your deliverance.

Heavenly Father, forgive me for feeling as though You have forgotten about me. Thank You for the assurance that this could never happen – and that You are already in the process of bringing about my deliverance. Amen.

God knows your situation

Read Exodus 2:23-25

The Israelites groaned in their slavery and cried out, and their cry for help because of their slavery went up to God. God heard their groaning. So God looked on the Israelites and was concerned about them (Exod. 2:23-25).

Because the Israelites suffered as much as they did, they called on God for help. And God heard their groaning. He looked on them and was concerned about them. Although they could not see Him in their difficult circumstances, He was close to them, ready to help and to change their situation.

When circumstances turn against you, you might feel as though God has forgotten about you, as though He does not care what happens to you. Biblical figures like David, Job and Jeremiah, all at times questioned God's love for them. But they all discovered eventually that God was there for them and that He delivered them, as He had always done.

Even in your times of deepest despair, the Lord is by your side. He knows about your situation and He is already bringing about your deliverance. He is able to use even the most inexplicable things in your life to fulfill His master plan for your life. As a matter of fact, these inexplicable things often form a very important part of God's plan for you. God wants to use you – even in times of crisis.

Trust in Him to bring about your deliverance.

Heavenly Father, I glorify You for the assurance that You are by my side, that You are aware of my situation and that You co-ordinate the inexplicable disasters in my life in such a way that they form part of Your perfect plan. Amen.

Do not be afraid

Read Exodus 14:10-14

Moses answered the people, "Do not be afraid. Stand firm and you will see the deliverance the LORD will bring you today. The Egyptians you see today you will never see again. The LORD will fight for you; you need only to be still" (Exod. 14:13-14).

God chose Moses to set His people free from slavery in Egypt. But they had hardly left when they faced their first crisis. The Egyptians pursued them so that, almost literally, they found themselves between the devil and the deep blue sea. Before them lay the Red Sea and behind them, Pharaoh and his army. The people were terrified and unhappy. They reacted typically by blaming Moses. It would have been better for them to serve the Egyptians than to die in the desert, they muttered.

But Moses calmed them down and assured them that they had no reason to fear because the Lord would fight for them. And God saved His people by creating a path for them through the waters of the sea and by causing the Egyptians to drown.

This promise – that God fights for His children – is still valid today for the children of God. When you find yourself in a crisis, remember the two things that Moses said to the people: *"Do not be afraid – you only need to be still."* With God on your side, you do not need to fear. He is still able to help and save you, as He did long ago for His people. Therefore, let go of fear and be at peace!

Heavenly Father, I glorify You because You are able to save me from dangerous situations. Please help me to exchange my fear for trust and to remain calm, because I rest assured in the knowledge that You will help me. Amen.

A caring God

Read Deuteronomy 8:1-5

Remember how the LORD your God led you all the way in the desert these forty years, to humble you and to test you in order to know what was in your heart, whether or not you would keep his commands (Deut. 8:2).

In today's Scripture passage, Moses requests the people to be obedient to God and to always remember how He took care of them. God was with His people every day as they wandered through the desert. During the day as a pillar of cloud and during the night as a pillar of fire. He provided for all their needs. When their water was finished, He caused water to flow from a rock, and when their food was finished, He fed them with manna and quail.

God's people quickly learned that the God whom they worship, is a God of miracles. A God who never leaves His people in the lurch, a God who can be trusted completely.

And God is still the same today. When your road through life leads you into deserts, He will be there to take care of you. You can fully trust in Him to help you as He helped His people so many years ago. *"[In the desert] you saw how the LORD your God carried you, as a father carries his son, all the way until you reached this place"* (Deut. 1:31).

God still wants to carry you today – on that you can depend!

Heavenly Father, I glorify You for being a God who takes care of me, a God who carries me every day and a God who will always look after me. Thank You that I can trust in You completely. Amen.

Things that are inexplicable

Read Isaiah 55:8-13

For my thoughts are not your thoughts, neither are your ways my ways, declares the LORD. As the heavens are higher than the earth, so are my ways higher than your ways and my thoughts than your thoughts (Isa. 55:8-9).

God does not think in the same way that we do. There are events in our lives that we will never be able to understand. When your friend dies in a car accident, when your father falls seriously ill, when your husband loses his job – all these things make no sense to you at the time. You cannot understand why the Lord allows such pain. But after some time has passed and you look back on the events, you may discover that this specific period of darkness in your life was necessary so that the miracle of God's salvation could become even clearer to you.

When a child is born, the birth goes hand in hand with pain. *"A woman giving birth to a child has pain because her time has come; but when her baby is born she forgets the anguish because of her joy that a child is born into the world,"* Jesus explained to His disciples, assuring them that their sorrow will turn to joy (John 16:21).

Sometimes pain and suffering are necessary for a new birth to take place – a new revelation of God's plan for your life to come forth. God uses the suffering in your life to establish a new, more profound relationship with Him. Remember this when you are facing difficulties.

Heavenly Father, I know that, sometimes, Your plan for my life includes inexplicable events. Thank You for the assurance that You use the suffering in my life to strengthen my relationship with You. Amen.

God keeps you safe

Read Revelation 3:7-13

Since you have kept my command to endure patiently, I will also keep you from the hour of trial (Rev. 3:10).

The Lord warns the church in Philadelphia that a time of suffering will come upon them. Only those people who are submitted to God will be able to keep going during this oppression. God also gives the congregation a beautiful promise: because they have kept God's command to endure patiently, He will keep them safe in times of trouble.

To be held safely when you get hurt is a wonderful comfort. Just look at the toddler who hurts his knee in a fall, crying pitifully because of the pain. The moment his mother gathers him tightly in her arms, the hurt is eased.

God's children cannot avoid the pain of suffering. It is inevitable for all of us. Christians can be assured that they will never be alone in their suffering, because God promises to keep them safe in times of trouble.

This promise applies to you too. God will always be by your side in times of suffering, even though it may not seem like it, or even though God seems far away and uninvolved. God will never forsake you. He promises to keep you safe and to help you in times of trouble, provided that you promise to keep His command to endure. Are you prepared to do so?

Father, how comforting Your promise is – that You will keep me safe in times of suffering. Thank You that I can know that You will never forsake me in times of crisis. Amen.

God jealously guards over you

Read Nahum 1:2-7

The LORD is a jealous and avenging God. The LORD is slow to anger and great in power (Nah. 1:2-3).

The prophet Nahum emphasizes various facets of the nature of God. He jealously watches over His people, He loves them deeply and sincerely cares about them. The best explanation of the word jealous, as it is used in this context, is that God is like a mother who is constantly concerned about her children, who prays for them every moment of the day, who loves them unconditionally, regardless of what they may do.

Not only does God jealously watch over His children, He is also a God who takes revenge on His enemies. God is always angered by sin. But He is a God who is slow to anger – He is patient toward us and is willing to forgive us time and again. Moreover, He is great in power – and He wants to put this miraculous power at your disposal when you find yourself in a crisis.

When you are facing a crisis, remember that you worship a God who truly cares about you – just as a mother cares for her child. God is able to help and support you.

Heavenly Father, thank You that You, the great and mighty God, jealously watch over me. Thank You that I can know that You truly care about me and that You will come to my aid. Amen.

A refuge in times of trouble

Read Nahum 1:7-15

The LORD is good, a refuge in times of trouble. He cares for those who trust in him (Nah. 1:7).

Nahum brought the people of Judah a message of hope when the Assyrians reigned over them. He focuses on God and the assurance that God jealously watches over His children. Right at the beginning the prophet proclaims that God is good, that He is a refuge for His children in times of trouble, and that He cares for those who trust in Him.

These promises still hold true for God's children today. Therefore, you can take Nahum's promise for yourself. God is good to His children, even when it does not feel like that to you. You can find refuge in Him when you are in a crisis, and He will help you.

David agrees with Nahum's words: *"The LORD is a refuge for the oppressed, a stronghold in times of trouble. Those who know your name will trust in you, for you, LORD, have never forsaken those who seek you,"* (Ps. 9:10-11).

If ever you find yourself in a crisis situation, you can confidently find refuge in God. God promises to care for you. *"He cares for those who trust in him,"* writes Nahum. If you belong to Him, He will give you everything you need.

Heavenly Father, I glorify You as my refuge and secure stronghold. Thank You that I can seek shelter with You when I find myself in a crisis situation, and that I may trust in Your promise that You will care for me. Amen.

When God does not intervene

Read Habakkuk 1:12-17

You cannot tolerate wrong. Why then do you tolerate the treacherous?
Why are you silent while the wicked swallow up those more righteous
than themselves? (Hab. 1:13).

Like many people before and after him, the prophet Habakkuk
cannot understand why the Lord looks on while His people are
in distress, and seems to do nothing about it. We find it hard to
understand why the Lord does not immediately intervene to solve
our problems.

But by the end of the book of Habakkuk, the same prophet has
learned a very valuable lesson: God does not have to change our
circumstances in order to change our disposition. Although our
circumstances may remain unchanged, He can help us to rejoice
in Him, whatever those circumstances.

God can help you too to praise Him in your crisis. Then your
focus will shift from the intensity of your problems to God. You will
be reassured by His presence and His love. Like Habakkuk, you can
testify, *"Though the fig tree does not bud and there are no grapes on
the vines, though the olive crop fails and the fields produce no food,
though there are no sheep in the pen, yet I will rejoice in the LORD, I
will be joyful in God my Savior"* (Hab. 3:17-18).

Choose to praise God during your crisis, and to thank Him for
those things that you wish were different.

Lord, please teach me to glorify You, even though my circumstances are not to my liking. Amen.

Habakkuk's testimony

Read Habakkuk 3:1-11

LORD, *I have heard of your fame; I stand in awe of your deeds, O*
LORD. *Renew them in our day* (Hab. 3:2).

The prophet Habakkuk inundates God with "why" questions. "How
long, O Lord? Why has this happened to me? Why don't You hear
me when I call?" Many Christians ask the same questions when bad
things happen to them and it seems as though God is not hearing
their prayers, or that He does not want to intervene to help them.

However, after the prophet Habakkuk has become silent before
God (Hab. 2:20), his prayer changes. Instead of "why" questions,
he listens to everything that God says about what He has planned.
Habakkuk begins with questions of faith, but ends with a confession of faith. He is amazed at the deeds of God, and wants to show
us what it means to truly trust in God.

Perhaps you are wrestling today with as many "why" questions
as Habakkuk did. If so, follow the prophet's example. Become
silent in the presence of the Lord. Tell Him about your problems.
And reflect on how great and powerful He really is. Then you too
will stand in awe of God's great deeds. And if He does intervene in
your crisis situation, make sure that you glorify Him for it.

Heavenly Father, You are aware of all the "why" questions in my
heart. You also know that I cannot understand why You don't
always intervene to help me. I now choose to become silent in
Your presence, and focus anew on how great and glorious You
are. Glory be to You. Amen.

Habakkuk's testimony

Read Lamentations 3:18-33

So I say, "My splendor is gone and all that I had hoped from the LORD." Yet, this I call to mind and therefore I have hope: Because of the LORD's great love we are not consumed (Lam. 3:18, 21-22).

When Jeremiah's hope begins to dwindle, he remembers that God's compassion toward His children never fails, that His faithfulness is great, and that He is good to those whose hope is in Him. This helps Jeremiah to keep his hopes up.

God's children can confidently hold on to their hope. God is omnipotent and fully in control, even though things in your life may sometimes get out of hand. Even though you may not have any hope left, you can always hold on to God, and find hope in Him. He promises you eternal glory in heaven where all suffering and pain will pass away.

"If hope didn't whisper to us that tomorrow will be a better day, how would we have the courage to get through today?" writes Robert Burns.[3] As Christians we know that heaven awaits us one day.

If your hope is ebbing, I would like to offer you Paul's beautiful prayer for the church in Rome: *"May the God of hope fill you with all joy and peace as you trust in him, so that you may overflow with hope by the power of the Holy Spirit"* (Rom. 15:13).

Heavenly Father, I praise You because I can hope in You, even though my situation seems hopeless. Please help me to be filled with hope by the power of the Holy Spirit. Amen.

Prayer

Father, how good it is to know that, even though You do allow pain and suffering into my life, You will never forsake me in my distress.

Thank You for the assurance that You counsel me when I am at the end of my tether; that You are the answer to all my "why" questions; that I need not understand You, but nevertheless can steadfastly trust in You.

I know that You only want what is best for me, that You give me light in times of darkness, that You listen to my prayers and answer every one of them, even though sometimes it does not feel that way to me.

Lord, I want to glorify You because Your kindness toward me lasts for ever.

I have begun to understand the benefits of suffering: I now know that You are in complete control of my life, that tribulation teaches me to steadfastly believe in You, to persevere and to fix my hope on You, that You are with me in times of suffering, that You take care of me and that You will ensure that everything ends well for me.

Amen.

September

People who care

Most people today are very busy.

We do not even have time for ourselves and for those things that we would like to do, let alone time for others.

In the everyday rat race we forget to really notice one another, to really care for one another.

And yet, that is what God expects from His children – that we will carry each other's burdens and so fulfill the law of Christ (see Gal. 6:2).

"Care is being with, crying with, suffering with, feeling with others," writes Henri Nouwen.

"Care is compassion, grace and mercy. It is claiming the truth that the other person is my brother or sister, human, mortal, vulnerable, like I am. To care for others is to be human."[1]

This month, we are going to spend time with men and women from the Bible who really cared about others and from whose lives we can still learn lessons in caring, even today.

Abraham, an example of hospitality

> *Read Genesis 18:1-8*

He said, "If I have found favor in your eyes, my lord, do not pass your servant by. Let me get you something to eat, so you can be refreshed and then go on your way – now that you have come to your servant" (Gen. 18:3, 5).

Abraham was a very wealthy and important man. And yet his heart went out to others. When three strangers passed by his tent one day, he immediately invited them to join him for a meal. Abraham's "something to eat" became a feast. Three seahs of fine flour were used to bake bread and a calf was roasted. And all of that for strangers! Once the food had been prepared, Abraham served his guests in person.

It is a modern-day tendency for people to be far less hospitable than in the past. Because we are so busy, and perhaps because entertaining has become so expensive, we do not invite friends to dine with us as often as we used to – let alone strangers.

Perhaps you should remember Abraham's example when someone knocks on your door for food, or when you consider inviting a few friends for a meal. Joyfully follow the advice of the writer of Hebrews, *"Do not forget to entertain strangers, for by so doing some people have entertained angels without knowing it"* (Heb. 13:2). Which was indeed the case with Abraham!

Lord, I apologize for not being more hospitable. Help me to care more about acquaintances, as well as about those people who come knocking on my door for food. Amen.

Lot and his two visitors

Read Genesis 19:1-9

Lot went outside to meet them and shut the door behind him and said, "No, my friends. Don't do this wicked thing. Look, I have two daughters. Let me bring them out to you and you can do what you like with them. But don't do anything to these men, for they have come under the protection of my roof" (Gen. 19:6-8).

When two strangers arrived on Lot's doorstep, he offered them a place for the night. However, the sinful residents of Sodom demanded that Lot turn his visitors over to them so that they could have sex with them. Lot refused, he was even willing to give his two unmarried daughters to the men, if the people would leave his visitors alone.

When you read this, you tend to think that Lot was taking hospitality a bit too far. To be willing to sacrifice your own daughters for the sake of two strangers is outrageous. And yet the Lord took note of what Lot did and rewarded him for it. The strangers saved Lot by striking the residents of Sodom with blindness. When all the residents of Sodom and Gomorrah were later destroyed by fire, Lot and his family were spared.

The story of Lot holds both a lesson and a warning for us. God requires His children to care about others – including strangers in their midst. However, He warns us at the same time that we cannot live among infidels, taking no heed of God's standards, and expect to come off scot-free.

Lord, I pray that You will help me to really care about the people whom I come into contact with – including those whom I do not know. Teach me to obey You and not to seek my friends among infidels. Amen.

Rahab

Read Joshua 2:1-15

But she had taken them up to the roof and hidden them under the stalks of flax she had laid out on the roof (Josh. 2:6).

Rahab, a woman of loose morals, endangered her own life to save the lives of two Israelite spies whom she did not even know. She lied to the king, who was seeking to kill them and hid the two spies under the stalks of flax on her roof. When the king's men had gone, she let them down the city wall by a rope. In turn, the spies promised to spare the lives of Rahab and her family when they attacked the city.

Rahab knew that these spies worshiped the real God. *"The LORD your God is God in heaven above and on the earth below"*, she testifies (Josh. 2:11).

The spies kept their word and the lives of Rahab and her family were spared. The name of this pagan prostitute was later included in the Hebrews gallery of faith. *"By faith the prostitute Rahab, because she welcomed the spies, was not killed with those who were disobedient"* (Heb. 11:31).

Because she was willing to help two strangers, Rahab saved her own life, as well as the lives of her family. Even though her life was not perfect, God used her in His plans. Sometimes the Lord requires a caring disposition and courage from you so that His kingdom can be expanded here on earth. And you do not have to be perfect either in order to be used by Him.

Heavenly Father, thank You for using even sinful people in Your kingdom. Make me willing to help others, even though it may mean danger for me. Amen.

Ruth

Read Ruth 1:3-18

But Ruth replied, "Don't urge me to leave you or to turn back from you. Where you go I will go, and where you stay I will stay. Your people will be my people and your God my God" (Ruth 1:16).

Following the death of her husband and two sons, Naomi decides to return to Israel. She requests her two daughters-in-law to return to their families, but Ruth refuses. She will go where her mother-in-law goes, she states unequivocally.

The young Moabite woman is willing to leave her familiar surroundings and her family behind to travel to an unfamiliar country with her mother-in-law. She does this because she has learned to love Naomi's God, and also because she realizes that without her, her mother-in-law stands no real chance of survival in Israel.

When they arrive in Israel, she immediately starts looking for work in order to take care of Naomi and herself. And God blesses this brave woman. He sends Boaz to cross her path, they get married and, to Naomi's great delight, a son is born.

Ruth's new husband is impressed with the unselfish way in which she tends to her mother-in-law. *"I've been told all about what you have done for your mother-in-law. May the LORD repay you for what you have done,"* he says (Ruth 2:11-12).

Nowadays, it is becoming increasingly necessary for us to extend a helping hand to the members of our family. Are you, like Ruth, willing to put your own interests aside to help your family? Ask the Lord to open your heart to your family.

Lord, I apologize for not always being willing to extend a helping hand to my family. Make me unselfish, like Ruth, so that I will always be willing to help. Amen.

The widow of Zarephath

> Read 1 Kings 17:10-24

Elijah said to her, "Don't be afraid. For this is what the LORD, the God of Israel says: 'The jar of flour will not be used up and the jug of oil will not run dry until the day the LORD gives rain on the land'" (1 Kings 17:13-14).

During a famine in Israel, the Lord instructed the prophet Elijah to go to a widow in Zarephath so that she could take care of him. When he asked the widow for water and bread, she told him that she had only a handful of flour and a little oil left with which to prepare a meal for herself and her son. However, Elijah assured the widow that her flour and oil would last till the famine was over.

Everything happened as Elijah had predicted. The flour and the oil did not run out but, in the meantime, the widow's son fell ill and died. When his distraught mother complained to Elijah, he brought her son back to life. The widow then testified, *"Now I know that you are a man of God and that the word of the LORD from your mouth is the truth"* (1 Kings 17:24).

The widow obeyed the Lord's command, even though it could have meant that she and her son would have no food left to eat. And then she experienced miracles in her own house! Her oil and flour did not run out and her son rose from the dead.

If you are willing to obey God, if you are willing to share your possessions with others, you will also discover that He can perform miracles in your life.

Heavenly Father, thank You for the assurance that You will take care of me, should I be willing to be charitable and obedient. Teach me to trust in You to perform wonders for me as well. Amen.

Elisha's hostess

Read 2 Kings 4:1-10

One day Elisha went to Shunem. And a well-to-do woman was there, who urged him to stay for a meal. So whenever he came by, he stopped there to eat (2 Kings 4:8).

This Shunammite woman was a well-to-do woman who noticed the need of an simple prophet and did something to alleviate it. Every time Elisha passed by her house, she invited him to join her for a meal. And it did not end there either. Later on, she urged her husband to build a small room on the roof of their house, so that Elisha could stay there when he visited them. The plates of food and the room where he could rest must have been a great luxury for Elisha. He rewarded his hospitable friend for her good deeds by promising her a son. And indeed, a year later she gave birth to a son!

Many years later, when a famine broke out in Israel, the woman and her son traveled to the land of the Philistines (see 2 Kings 8). When she returned after seven years, Elisha requested the king to return her possessions to her, which he did.

This hospitable woman was richly rewarded for being willing to share her food and her home with Elisha.

How hospitable are you? Make it a priority from now on to notice the needs of others and to share your privileges with those who have less than you.

Heavenly Father, thank You for providing so abundantly for each of my needs. Make me willing to share my abundance with those who are less privileged than I am. Amen.

Naaman's servant girl

Read 2 Kings 5:1-15

Now bands from Aram had gone out and had taken captive a young girl from Israel, and she served Naaman's wife. She said to her mistress, "If only my master would see the prophet who is in Samaria! He would cure him of his leprosy" (2 Kings 5:2-3).

Despite the fact that the Arameans had taken the young girl captive from her parental home, and she had to work as a slave in a foreign country, she held no grudge against Naaman. When her employer fell ill with leprosy, she immediately wanted to help him. She told her mistress that the prophet from Samaria could cure her husband. Naaman was willing to listen to the young girl and he left for Samaria where, indeed, he was cured when he washed himself seven times in the Jordan River, as Elisha had instructed him to do.

The fact that the young girl really cared about the people for whom she worked not only led to Naaman's cure, but he also embraced the faith of his young servant girl. *"Now I know that there is no God in all the world except in Israel,"* he testified after being cured (v. 15).

Because a young girl was willing to ignore her own pain and reach out to her employers, an entire Assyrian family made contact with the God of Israel. From this young girl's example, you can learn not to become embittered when things do not turn out all that well for you, but rather to reach out to others and to remain a witness to the God in whom you trust.

Heavenly Father, help me to retain my faith in You, even though things do not always go well with me. Teach me to be a witness to You wherever I find myself. Amen.

A queen risks her life

Read Esther 4:12-17

Then Esther sent this reply to Mordecai: "Go, gather together all the Jews who are in Susa, and fast for me. When this is done, I will go to the king, even though it is against the law. And if I perish, I perish" (Esther 4: 15 -16).

When Queen Esther's uncle, Mordecai, heard of the evil Haman's plot to destroy all the Jews in Susa, he asked Hathatch, one of the king's eunuchs, to plead with her to ask the king to have mercy on her people. Esther agreed, although she had not been sent for by the king in thirty days, and this brave decision could cost her her life. She asked the Jews to pray for her for three days. Then she went to see the king, although she had not been invited.

The king received her kindly. When he heard about Haman's plot against the Jews, he ordered that Haman himself be hanged on the gallows that he had erected for Mordecai. Unfortunately, the king's decree, ordering the annihilation of the Jewish people, could not be revoked, but the king allowed the Jews to defend themselves against the Persians. With God's help, they succeeded in defeating the Persians. The result of Esther's courage was that her entire nation was saved.

Esther was willing to put her life at stake for her people, because she really cared about them. She was willing to risk her life for the sake of others. What would you have done had you been in her place?

Lord, thank You for still using people in Your master plan today. Make me willing to be used by You, even though it may mean that I myself would be put at risk. Amen.

Mary the obedient

Read Luke 1:30-38

But the angel said to her, "Do not be afraid, Mary, you have found favor with God. You will be with child and give birth to a son." "I am the Lord's servant," Mary answered. "May it be to me as you have said" (Luke 1:30, 31, 38).

When an angel appeared to the young, engaged Mary, telling her that she would fall pregnant and give birth to a son who would be the Son of the Most High, she must have been immensely frightened. She also knew for certain that not one of the residents of her little town (nor her betrothed, Joseph) would believe this story. And yet Mary did not hesitate for a moment – she immediately put herself at God's disposal.

Mary's obedience eventually resulted in all those believing in her Son, being able to become children of God. If it were not for her courage, you and I would never have known God. Jesus made it possible for our sins to be forgiven and for us to have eternal life.

God is still looking for women who will unconditionally obey Him and trust in Him. Usually we first think about our own comfort and convenience when we are asked to do things for the Lord. We usually put ourselves first, and then we think of other people.

Are you prepared to put yourself at God's disposal as did the young Mary? Then He will fulfill His master plan through your life.

Lord, I pray for the courage to put myself unconditionally at Your disposal, even though this decision could cost me dearly in future. Amen.

Jesus shows compassion

Read Matthew 20:29-34

Jesus had compassion on them and touched their eyes. Immediately they received their sight and followed him (Matt. 20:34).

When two blind men seated next to the road asked Jesus to have mercy on them, He listened immediately, although the crowd tried to keep the blind men quiet. "What do you want me to do for you?" Jesus wanted to know. "Lord, we want our sight," is the request of the two blind men. Jesus had compassion on them and touched their eyes. They received their sight immediately and followed Him.

Jesus truly showed sympathy toward others and always helped them. The more one reads about Jesus' life here on earth, the more one realizes that all people can receive Jesus' caring love. Including those (such as tax collectors and sinners) on whom the rest of the world looks down. When His disciples, on occasion, complained about this, He said: *"I have not come to call the righteous, but sinners to repentance"* (Luke 5:32).

Although Jesus is no longer physically with us, He still shows sympathy toward us. *"Christ Jesus, who died – more than that, who was raised to life – is at the right hand of God and is also interceding for us,"* Paul assures the Christians in Rome (Rom. 8:34). Jesus still cares about you. He intercedes for you with His Father!

Lord Jesus, thank You that You showed so much empathy toward people while You walked this earth. It is wonderful to know that You have sympathy and understanding with all my problems and want to help me solve them. I praise You for interceding for me. Amen.

Jesus at the wedding feast

> *Read John 2:1-11*

The master of the banquet tasted the water that had been turned into wine. Then he called the bridegroom aside and said, "You have saved the best till now." This, the first of his miraculous signs, Jesus performed at Cana in Galilee. He thus revealed his glory, and his disciples put their faith in him (John 2:9-11).

The very first miracle that Jesus performed to demonstrate His loving care for people took place at a wedding feast. When the wine ran out, Jesus' mother went to tell Him about it. But Jesus seemed unperturbed. *"Dear woman, why do you involve me? My time has not yet come,"* (v. 4) he said. However, His mother knew her Son. *"Do whatever he tells you,"* (v. 5) she told the servants. The rest is history.

Jesus asked the servants to fill six stone water jars, each holding approximately a hundred liters, with water and to draw some of it and take it to the master of the banquet. When the master tasted the water that had been turned into wine, he called the bridegroom aside and said to him: *"Everyone brings out the choice wine first; but you have saved the best till now"* (v. 10).

The time was not yet ripe for Jesus to perform miracles in public. However, He listened to His mother's request and turned water into wine, because He knew how embarrassing it would have been for the bridegroom if there had not been enough wine. Although it seemed to us like an unnecessary miracle, Jesus did not hesitate to help. He still shows an interest in the minor detail of our lives today.

Lord Jesus, thank You for still performing miracles in our lives today. Amen.

You give them something to eat

By this time it was late in the day, so his disciples came to him (and said), "Send the people away so they can go to the surrounding countryside and villages and buy themselves something to eat." But he answered, "You give them something to eat" (Mark 6:35-37).

When Jesus addressed the crowds in a remote place, the disciples became concerned that the people would not have anything to eat. They asked Jesus to send the people away to go and buy food. Jesus also cared about the hungry people, but He had something else in mind. *"You give them something to eat,"* He said. The disciples replied that it would take eight months' wages to buy food for so many people. *"How many loaves do you have?"* Jesus wanted to know. *"Five (loaves) and two fish,"* was their reply.

Jesus told them to have all the people sit down in groups of hundreds and fifties and, taking the five loaves and the two fish, He gave thanks. Then He broke the loaves and gave them to His disciples to give to the people. After everyone had had enough to eat, there were still twelve basketfuls of broken pieces left.

We often expect others to extend a helping hand to people in need. This is not how Jesus operates. He expects you to help. You should take note of the need of others and do something about it. How many loaves do you have to hand out?

Lord Jesus, thank You for caring about people, for noticing their hunger and feeding them. Please help me to do the same. Amen.

Five loaves and two fish

Read John 6:5-14

Another of his disciples, Andrew, Simon Peter's brother, spoke up, "Here is a boy with five small barley loaves and two small fish, but how far will they go among so many?" Jesus said, "Have the people sit down" (John 6:8-10).

In John's account of the miracle of the five loaves, he focused on the young boy who was willing to give up his lunch in order for others to get food. Young boys are normally very fond of eating! It is unusual that this little boy was so willing to offer his lunch box to Jesus. And then the day turned into one that he would probably never ever forget in his life. With his own eyes he saw Jesus praying, breaking his small loaves of bread and fish, and feeding thousands of people. To crown it all, there were still twelve baskets left over after everyone had had enough to eat.

The excited young boy definitely would have enjoyed telling this story at home.

If you truly care about others and, like the young boy in our story, are willing to part with your possessions so that the kingdom of Jesus may be expanded, He can still perform miracles with your contributions today. The important point is that you should be willing to dig your hand into your pocket. Are you willing to share your possessions with those people who really need them?

Lord, I pray that you will give me a caring heart, so that I may be willing to share all that I have with others. Thank You that I may know that, with my small contribution, You can do great things in Your kingdom. Amen.

Jesus and the Canaanite woman

A Canaanite woman came to him, crying out, "Lord, Son of David, have mercy on me! My daughter is suffering terribly from demon-possession" (Matt. 15:22).

We have seen how Jesus really cared about people and had compassion on them. Therefore, when the Canaanite woman, who was in such need, came to Jesus we would expect Him to help her immediately. Strangely enough, this does not happen. As a matter of fact, Jesus acts completely different to the way He usually does. First, He does not answer her at all. When He does answer her, His words seem rather heartless: *"I was sent only to the lost sheep of Israel"* (v. 24).

However, the distraught mother refuses to give up, although she must have thought that Jesus did not care about her. When she once again asks Him to help, Jesus tells her it is not right to take the children's bread and toss it to their dogs. Her answer totally disarms Jesus, *"Yes, Lord,"* she says, *"but even the dogs eat the crumbs that fall from the master's table."* (v. 27) Now Jesus knows that the woman truly believes in Him and He heals her daughter with these words, *"Woman, you have great faith! Your request is granted"* (v. 28).

Sometimes, God does not answer your prayers the first – or even the tenth – time that you pray. However, if you persevere in faith and prayer, He will eventually grant you the desires of your heart, if they are in accordance with His will.

Lord Jesus, I sometimes wonder whether You really care about me, because my prayers are not answered immediately. Please help me to persevere in praying and believing. Amen.

The little daughter of Jairus

> *Read Mark 5:21-23; 35-42*

Then one of the synagogue rulers, named Jairus, came there. Seeing Jesus, he fell at his feet and pleaded earnestly with him, "My little daughter is dying. Please come and put your hands on her so that she will be healed and live" (Mark 5:22-23).

A very important man named Jairus, knelt in front of Jesus and pleaded with Him to come and lay His hands on his terminally ill little daughter. Jesus accompanied him immediately, but on the way there was a delay. While Jesus was talking to a woman who suffered from bleeding, someone from Jairus's house arrived with the terrible news that the little girl had died.

Jairus probably thought that Jesus could not care much for either him or his little girl, because He had wasted so much time with a woman that He could just as well have healed later. But Jesus knew Jairus's thoughts, and He really cared about him and his little daughter. *"Don't be afraid; just believe,"* (v. 36) were His words to the distressed father. At the house of Jairus, Jesus told the mourners that the little girl was only sleeping. They laughed at Him, because they had seen for themselves that she was dead. When He took the little girl's hand, she came alive again.

Jesus cares enough about you to save you from sin and to offer you eternal life. Have you responded to His invitation yet?

Lord Jesus, thank You that I can rest assured in the knowledge that You love me and care about me, even though circumstances sometimes cause me to doubt Your love. I glorify You because I have everlasting life, because You sacrificed Your life for me. Amen.

The woman suffering from bleeding

Read Mark 5:24-34

And a woman was there who had been subject to bleeding for twelve years. When she heard about Jesus, she came up behind him in the crowd and touched his cloak. Immediately her bleeding stopped and she felt in her body that she was freed from her suffering (Mark 5:25, 27, 29).

On the way to Jairus's house, the people crowded around Jesus as usual. Among them was a woman who had been suffering from an illness that had been a source of great embarrassment to her for twelve years. She firmly believed that if she could just touch His clothes, she would be healed. And indeed, when she touched Jesus, a miracle happened. She could feel in her body that she had been freed from her suffering.

And Jesus? Even though there were dozens of people rubbing against Him and touching Him, He knew immediately when the woman touched His clothes. *"Who touched my clothes?"* (v. 30) He asked. Then the woman fell down at His feet and told Him the whole truth.

Although He was in a great hurry, Jesus found time for her. He listened to her and told her that her faith had healed her, and that she had been freed from her suffering.

You can take your personal problems to Jesus with the utmost confidence. He cares about you, He already knows about your crises and, should you reach out to Him in faith, He will grant you the wisdom to work through your problems.

Lord Jesus, thank You that I can come to You with all my problems, my anxieties and my doubts. I know for sure that You will listen to me and help me. Amen.

Four men bring their friend to Jesus

Read Mark 2:3-12

Some men came, bringing to him a paralytic, carried by four of them. Since they could not get him to Jesus because of the crowd, they made an opening in the roof above Jesus and, after digging through it, lowered the mat the paralyzed man was lying on (Mark 2:3-4).

These four men really cared about their paralyzed friend. They carried him to the house where Jesus was teaching, but when they could not reach Him because of the crowds of people, they made an opening in the flat roof and lowered their paralyzed friend in front of Jesus' feet.

When Jesus saw the faith of the four friends, He said to the paralyzed man, *"Son, your sins are forgiven"* (v. 9). When the teachers of the law who were sitting there rebuked Him because He seemed to be blaspheming, Jesus proved to them that He indeed had the authority to forgive sins. He said to the paralyzed man, *"I tell you, get up, take your mat and go home"* (v. 11).

Before the eyes of the astounded onlookers, the paralyzed man got up, took his mat and walked out. The people were amazed. They praised God, saying, *"We have never seen anything like this!"* (v. 12).

The caring attitude of the four friends toward their paralyzed friend resulted in his being cured. True faith does not mind sacrifice, especially not where others, who could be helped in this way, are concerned. Always be willing to help those who need your help.

Heavenly Father, help me to help others who are in need and to spare no pains to bring them to You. Amen.

Jesus and the little children

Read Mark 10:13-16

People were bringing little children to Jesus to have him touch them, but the disciples rebuked them. When Jesus saw this, he was indignant. He said to them, "Let the little children come to me, and do not hinder them, for the kingdom of God belongs to such as these. And he took the children in his arms, put his hands on them and blessed them (Mark 10:13, 14, 16).

When Jesus was on earth, society did not regard children as important. For this reason, the disciples tried to prevent the mothers from bringing their children to Jesus. They probably felt that the children would waste Jesus' time. However, Jesus was indignant about the actions of the disciples and passionately declared, *"Let the little children come to me, and do not hinder them, for the kingdom of God belongs to such as these"* (Mark 10:14).

Jesus went even further and told His disciples that anyone who will not receive the kingdom of God like a little child, will never enter it (see v. 15). Then He took the children in His arms, put His hands on them and blessed them.

Jesus demonstrated His caring love for children (and other people who were unimportant in the eyes of the world), by taking them in His arms and touching them. Remember that you should accept God's guidance and sovereignty like a child, and that you must believe in Him unconditionally if you want to be assured of a place in heaven.

Lord Jesus, thank You that You love children and that they are the most important people in Your kingdom. I pray that You will grant me the disposition of a child, so that I will accept Your guidance and sovereignty unconditionally in my own life. Amen.

Go and do likewise

"Which of these three do you think was a neighbor to the man who fell into the hands of robbers?" The expert in the law replied, "The one who had mercy on him." Jesus told him, "Go and do likewise" (Luke 10:36-37).

One of the most beautiful parables that Jesus told is that of the good Samaritan who was on a journey and found an injured man lying next to the road. Although a priest and a Levite had walked past the man, neither was willing to help him.

However, the Samaritan bandaged the man's wounds, put him onto his own donkey and took him to an inn. When he had to continue on his journey the next day, he left money with the innkeeper so that the man could receive further care.

We would have expected the priest and the Levite to help the injured man, but they walked past him. The Samaritan, who was actually an enemy of the Jew, was the one who cared about the injured Jew and helped him. In those days, it was totally unacceptable for a Jew to be touched by a Samaritan, because they looked down on the Samaritans. Therefore, Jesus' parable has a surprise ending. It is the person we least expect who demonstrates compassion for his neighbor.

With this parable, Jesus wants to teach you that you cannot choose your neighbor. Every person is your neighbor and is entitled to your caring love. Jesus expects you to follow the Samaritan's example and reach out to others – even though they may belong to a race or faith different from your own.

Lord Jesus, please teach me to truly care for other people. Not to hesitate in offering my help, but to reach out to those people who need help. Amen.

Mary anoints the feet of Jesus

Read John 12:1-8

Then Mary took about half a liter of pure nard, an expensive perfume; she poured it on Jesus' feet and wiped his feet with her hair. And the house was filled with the fragrance of the perfume (John 12:3).

Shortly before His crucifixion, Jesus had dinner with Simon the leper. While the guests were eating, Mary took out a jar of very expensive nard and poured it on Jesus' feet. With her unselfish, but rather extravagant deed, Mary gave her all to Jesus. She demonstrated her love for Him in a way that left no doubt.

When the lovely fragrance of the nard filled the room, the guests had no option but to become aware of Mary's deed of love.

Judas was the first to condemn her. He was of the opinion that the nard could have been sold for a lot of money and the money given to the poor. But Jesus disagreed. He knew that Mary's love for Him was sincere and that her offering came from her heart. "Leave her alone," He said to the disciples. *"[It was intended] that she should save this perfume for the day of my burial. You will always have the poor among you, but you will not always have me"* (John 12:7-8).

Mary demonstrated her care for Jesus in the form of a very expensive perfume which she poured on His feet. What do you do to assure Him of your love? Are you, like Mary, willing to be extravagant, or are you still calculating the cost?

Lord Jesus, thank You that You did not calculate the cost of Your love for me, but were willing to be crucified for me. Help me, like Mary, to offer You my all. Amen.

The criminal on the cross

Read Luke 23:32-33; 39-43

Then he said, "Jesus, remember me when you come into your king-dom." Jesus answered him, "I tell you the truth, today you will be with me in paradise" (Luke 23:42-43).

When Jesus was taken away to be crucified, there were two criminals with Him. The one was crucified on his right, the other on his left. One of the criminals ridiculed Jesus and asked Him, *"Aren't you the Christ? Save yourself and us!"* (v. 39) However, the other criminal rebuked him, saying: *"Don't you fear God? We are punished justly. But this man has done nothing wrong"* (v. 40-41). Then he turned to Jesus with a request, *"Jesus, remember me when you come into your kingdom."*

Although Jesus was suffering great physical and spiritual pain, He heard this request and granted it without delay. The criminal deserved the death penalty, but Jesus promised him heaven itself, *"I tell you the truth, today you will be with me in paradise,"* He said.

Grace is something that no one can earn, but it is freely given by God to people who believe in Him. The condemned criminal did not deserve Jesus' sympathy, but Jesus truly cared for him, irrespective of His own pain and suffering. On the cross, the criminal received God's gift of grace that opened the way to heaven.

You too, do not deserve God's grace. However, Jesus offers it to you because He loves you and cares for you. Do not hesitate to accept God's gift to you.

Lord Jesus, thank You for enabling me to be with You in paradise one day, although I deserve it as little as the criminal who was crucified with You. Amen.

Father, forgive them ...

> *Read Luke 23:33-38*

When they came to the place called the Skull, there they crucified him, along with the criminals. Jesus said, "Father, forgive them, for they do not know what they are doing" (Luke 23:33-34).

Jesus loved us so much that He not only sacrificed heaven to come and live on this earth as an ordinary man, but even died on the cross for us. Yet He was rejected by His own people, who even had Him crucified, although He was completely innocent. But Jesus did not stop caring for them. He prayed that His Father would forgive those who sentenced Him to death because they did not know what they were doing.

In contrast to Jesus' compassion and forgiving love for them, the behavior of those around Him was completely heartless. They divided up His clothes among them. The last sign of His human dignity was taken away from Him.

This is the kind of rejection that Jesus had to suffer in order to earn grace and salvation for those who believe in Him. This is how every believer can expect to be treated by a world that has rejected God's greatest gift.

Jesus demonstrated His love and compassion for you on the cross. Because He paid the price for your sins in full, God is now willing to forgive all of them. Don't you want to demonstrate your love for Him and your compassion toward others with your way of life?

Lord Jesus, thank You that You love me so much that You were willing to be crucified for me. Help me to demonstrate my love for You and my compassion toward others through my way of life. Amen.

A widow who opened her heart to others

> *Read Acts 9:36-43*

In Joppa there was a disciple named Tabitha (which, when translated, is Dorcas), who was always doing good and helping the poor (Acts 9:36).

Luke described Tabitha as a woman who demonstrated her compassion in everything she did for others. She was always doing good and helping those less privileged than herself. Her good deeds were proof of her loving heart. She did not only give of her possessions, but also of her time and energy. We read that she made clothes for the poor.

When she suddenly fell ill and died, the widows, to whom she had been so good were inconsolable. They called Peter to Joppa, took him to the room upstairs where her body was lying and told him how good she had been to them. They also showed him the clothing that she had made for them with her own hands. Caring people inspire other people to care for them in turn; if you give love, you always receive love in return.

Peter saw that the widows were truly sad about the death of their benefactor. He sent them out of the room and prayed fervently. Then he commanded, "Tabitha, get up," whereupon Tabitha opened her eyes and sat up. The widows were overcome with joy because God had given Tabitha back to them.

You can also serve God by doing good to others. Does your life bear testimony to the fact that you belong to God?

Heavenly Father, thank You that You take such good care of me. Grant me a heart that is open toward others, so that I, like Tabitha, may become aware of the needs of others and so that I will always do good. Amen.

One of the least

> *Read Matthew 25:34-40*

"The King will reply, 'I tell you the truth, whatever you did for one of the least of these brothers of mine, you did for me'" (Matt. 25:40).

Jesus concluded His last sermon before His crucifixion with a description of those things which will count the most with God during the last judgment. God sets a premium on the love and compassion that His children display toward others. When Jesus returns He is going to test the love and compassion that people demonstrated on earth. And this test will determine who will be allowed into His kingdom.

Jesus called the poor and the needy "brothers of mine" and He clearly stated that if you care about such people, it is proof of your relationship with Him. What you have done for them on this earth, you have done for Jesus. But the opposite is also true: That which you have neglected to do, you have not done for Jesus either.

Your conduct toward others is an indication of how much you care about Jesus. That which you do to others, you indirectly do to Jesus. Therefore we need to go and truly think about exactly what Jesus' words mean before we again refuse a request of someone who needs our help. When a beggar knocks on your door, remember that he is "one of the least".

Lord Jesus, You were always ready to help others. Please make me willing to do the same. Let me never forget that what I do to others, I also do to You. Amen.

Forgive one another

> *Read Colossians 3:12-17*

Bear with each other and forgive whatever grievances you may have against one another. Forgive as the Lord forgave you. And over all these virtues put on love (Col. 3:13-14).

Christians should bear with each other and be willing to forgive one another, Paul wrote to the Christians in Colosse. The Greek word that has been translated "bear with", implies giving someone a second chance. Jesus personally set us an example of forgiveness. He told Peter that we should be willing to forgive one another "seventy times seven" (Matt. 18:22). (In the Bible the number seven represents perfection. But Jesus multiplied this ten times.) Therefore, according to Jesus, forgiveness should have no limits.

If you truly care for other people you should be willing to forgive them when they have transgressed against you. You should not record their mistakes, but rather overlook them. If you do not carry God's love in your heart, you will try in vain to forgive. To forgive as Jesus requires of us, means that you will have to be willing to sacrifice many things. You should forgive everybody.

This kind of forgiveness is not part of human nature. However, this is the kind of forgiveness you will have to develop if you wish to be more like Jesus.

Lord Jesus, I pray that You will teach me to forgive like You, to be willing to offer my forgiveness freely – up to seventy times seven. I know that I will never be able to do this on my own – thank You that it is indeed possible through the working of Your Spirit. Amen.

Carry each other's burdens

Carry each other's burdens, and in this way you will fulfill the law of Christ (Gal. 6:2).

Many people today do not take notice of one another any more, because time has become a luxury. We simply no longer really care about each other, because of our hurried lifestyles. However, this is not how a Christian should live. You should really care about others and take notice when other believers suffer. Help them bear their problems. Do not let them wrestle with it all alone. This is what Jesus expects of us.

Therefore, to really care about others implies that you should be willing to place yourself in their shoes so that you will really know what they think and how they feel. In Romans 12, Paul gives a practical description of this kind of caring, *"Love must be sincere. Share with God's people who are in need. Practise hospitality. Rejoice with those who rejoice; mourn with those who mourn"* (vv. 9, 13, 15).

The way in which you treat other people reveals whether or not you belong to Christ. You should be a window of Jesus' caring love for others. When people observe the things that you do, they should notice Him. From now on, try to follow John's advice, *"Whoever claims to live in him must walk as Jesus did"* (1 John 2:6).

Lord Jesus, please enable me to care the way You cared, to live the way You lived, to notice other people's needs and help them. Amen.

Friends sharpen one another

Read Proverbs 27:9-17

Perfume and incense bring joy to the heart, and the pleasantness of one's friend springs from his earnest counsel. As iron sharpens iron, so one man sharpens another (Prov. 27:9, 17).

Two friends who really care about each other have a lasting influence on each other. Through their mutual interactions, they sharpen one another. If your friend is honest, your crooked transactions are going to result in your having such a guilty conscience that you would begin to do the right thing. If you know that your friend does not like you to use bad language, you will do your utmost to get rid of this bad habit.

But the opposite is also true. Undesirable friends can have a negative influence on your life. If your friends drink too much or use drugs, you might feel pressured to follow their example. Ensure that your influence on your friends is always positive. True friends should reprimand one another if necessary, even though it is not always easy or pleasant to do so.

Jesus set us the perfect example with regard to friends. *"Greater love has no one than this, that he lay down his life for his friends. You are my friends if you do what I command"* (John 15:13-14).

Do you care sufficiently about your friends to set a good example for them, and not to withhold your advice when you see that they are doing wrong? Then become Jesus' friend too by being obedient to Him.

Lord Jesus, thank You for friends who sharpen me. Make me a friend to them as You are a friend to me and help me to be totally obedient to You. Amen.

Submit to one another

Read Ephesians 5:1-30

Submit to one another out of reverence for Christ. Wives, submit to your husbands as to the Lord (Eph. 5:21-22).

Ephesians 5:22 is a verse that many women do not like, because not all of us like to submit to our husbands! However, if we read verse 21 first, we really should have no problem with this command. In the first place, husband and wife must submit to one another out of reverence for Christ. When He comes first in our lives, we become less important. Our relationship with Christ should be the cornerstone of our marriages and our relationships. The submission of which Paul speaks means that we will demonstrate our caring love for one other in marriage by being willing to yield and putting our marriage partner first.

A happy marriage requires two unselfish marriage partners who will demonstrate their caring love to each other in words and deeds every day. Tell your husband that you love him and admire him. Show him in a thousand and one little ways. Forget about your "rights" in marriage and do your utmost to make your husband happy. This kind of caring love is more infectious than measles and will cause him to assure you of his love. He will go out of his way to demonstrate that he really cares about you. And then it will be easy to submit to one another out of reverence for Christ.

Lord Jesus, thank You that You have given me a husband to love. Help me to demonstrate my caring love for him in our marriage by submitting to him. Amen.

September 29

Reach out to people in need

> *Read Isaiah 58:6-11*

If you spend yourselves in behalf of the hungry and satisfy the needs of the oppressed, then your light will rise in the darkness, and your night will become like the noonday (Isa. 58:10).

Thousands of people in the world die of hunger every day. Millions of people throughout the world live in extreme poverty. In the Indian city, Calcutta, there are millions of people who live on the streets and have to survive on charity. They do not have access to even the most basic facilities. In many other countries hundreds of thousands of homeless people live in desperate conditions. Because most of us live in comfortable houses, with enough food for every day, we can scarcely imagine how these people have to live.

God expects you to be willing to reach out to the poor. To share your food with the hungry, to provide the poor wanderer with shelter, to clothe the naked (v. 7). Get involved with relief schemes in your area. If you are willing to give to people in need and to extend a helping hand to them, you will be rewarded. Then the Lord promises to bless you, to guide you always, to satisfy your needs and to strengthen you (v. 11). You may gladly take Him at His Word – He always fulfills His promises!

Father, there are so many people around me who are in need that I sometimes feel it is not worth trying to help them. I pray that You will help me to meet their needs as You meet mine. Amen.

Comfort one another

Read 2 Corinthians 1:3-7

God, who comforts us in all our troubles, so that we can comfort those in any trouble with the comfort we ourselves have received from God (2 Cor. 1:3-4).

The people around you do not only have material needs, but also emotional needs. There are probably more people in your vicinity who need a hug or a sympathetic ear, than there are people who suffer from a lack of food. If your heart is truly open to others, you will quickly realize when there is someone close to you who needs comfort. Because you have been on the receiving end of God's comfort, you know full well how you, in turn, can comfort other people.

"Strengthen the feeble hands, steady the knees that give way; say to those with fearful hearts, 'Be strong, do not fear; your God will come'" (Isa. 35:3-4).

If there are some of your friends or acquaintances who need to be comforted, be there for them. Visit them, pray for them, but above all, tell them that God loves them and that He is there with them. Find time for others in your busy program. Be willing to listen to them, without offering too much advice. Sometimes people are only looking for someone who will really listen to them. Offer your sympathy to people who need to be comforted.

And, when you are in need, pocket your pride and go and talk to your friends.

Lord Jesus, thank You that You are always there for me. Teach me to notice the pain of others and to comfort them as You comfort me. Amen.

Prayer

I pray that You will give me a caring heart for others, that I may notice the distress of the people around me and satisfy their needs.

Help me to have compassion on others, to open my purse, home and heart to them, to be willing to offer my help, even though it may be at my own expense.

Grant that I will be willing to support my friends and family by word and deed, that I will not show the least of Yours the door – that I will help even strangers.

Make me obedient and willing to put myself at Your disposal, to forgive others unconditionally, as You forgive me.

Teach me to demonstrate my caring love to You through my way of life, to be unselfish in my marriage, and make me willing to comfort others as You comfort me every time I am despondent.

I know that I will never succeed by myself – please enable me to do so through Your Holy Spirit.

Amen.

October

Paul's letter of rejoicing

We all yearn for happiness. But worldly joy is a fleeting experience. When disasters come, worldly happiness quickly disappears.

Christian joy is different. It is built on the solid foundation of God's caring love for His children, and is not dependent on your physical circumstances. True joy is rooted in the unchanging and everlasting love of Jesus.

Therefore, God's children can be truly happy – even in times of suffering. *"Rejoice in the Lord always. I will say it again: Rejoice!"* Paul advises us in Philippians 4:4.

If you read this letter of rejoicing with the sincere desire to get to know Jesus better day by day, then He will shower you with eternal joy.

Joy is serious business!

Read Philippians 1:1-5

I thank my God every time I remember you. In all my prayers for all of you, I always pray with joy because of your partnership in the gospel from the first day until now (Phil. 1:3-5).

The word joy first appears in verse four of chapter one, setting the tone for the letter. Paul prays for the congregation in Philippi with joy, even though he was in jail when he wrote this letter.

There was a special bond between Paul and the church in Philippi, because when the Holy Spirit prevented him from going to Asia he founded the church in Philippi. Paul's joy comes from knowing that the Christians in Philippi were his partners in God's kingdom. They worked with him to spread the gospel of Jesus.

Selwyn Hughes declared, "Joy is the serious business of heaven."[1] And this should be the same on earth. God wants His children to be people of joy, to rejoice in Him and in His love for them. He wants us to pray for one another with joy. No one can take this joy away from you, because it comes from God.

Is the joy of God evident in your life? Develop the habit of praying with joy for your family and friends, as well as for those who preach the gospel.

Heavenly Father, teach me to live each day with joy, to intercede with joy for others and to preach Your gospel with joy. Amen.

God completes what He begins

Read Philippians 1:6-8

[I am] confident of this, that he who began a good work in you will carry it on to completion until the day of Christ Jesus (Phil. 1:6).

Another reason why Paul could pray with so much joy for the Christians in Philippi, was that he knew that they were on their way to heaven. God does not do anything by half-measures. Paul assured them that He would carry the good work that He had begun in them to completion.

Faith comes from God. *The Message* proclaims, *"There has never been the slightest doubt in my mind that the God who started this great work in you would keep at it and bring it to a flourishing finish on the very day Christ Jesus appears."*

When we tell others the joyous news of God's gospel, we do not always see the fruits of our labors. However, like Paul, we can be confident that God will carry the good work that He has begun to completion. It is in His hands.

All that we need to do is sow the first seeds. God is the One who will make them germinate and grow. In his book, *Joy, the Serious Business of Heaven*, Selwyn Hughes says that God does not write an unfinished symphony. He finishes that which He begins. And His work in the life of man can never be undone – regardless of how hard the devil may try.

Heavenly Father, thank You for the assurance that You will bring the good work, which You began in me, to completion. Thank You also that You will bless the work that I do for You. Amen.

A love that changes you

Read Philippians 1:8-11

And this is my prayer: that your love may abound more and more in knowledge and depth of insight, so that you may be able to discern what is best (Phil. 1:9-10).

After Paul declared his sincere love for the people of Philippi, he described what their love should be like. It should increase day by day. And as love increases Christians will be able to make the best choices.

Jesus brings His love into your life when He enters your heart. Love cannot be separated from Him because He is love. And this love turns you into a brand new person. We are not capable of loving others as God commands, but *"God has poured out his love into our hearts by the Holy Spirit, whom he has given us"* (Rom. 5:5).

When the love of Jesus enters your life, it changes everything – it turns you into a new person with new priorities. "Love is blind", the worldly saying goes. But the love of Jesus is never blind. It points your life in the right direction. Paul prays that our love may abound more and more in knowledge and depth of insight, so that we may be able to discern what is best.

The love that comes from Jesus is a love that longs to teach and guide you, a love that wants to show you what is really important. If you do not yet have that kind of love in your life, then pray for it!

Lord Jesus, I ask You to bring Your love, which changes everything, into my life and, through that love, to teach me the things that are truly important. Amen.

God reverses your situation

Read Philippians 1:12-17

Now I want you to know, brothers, that what has happened to me has really served to advance the gospel. As a result, it has become clear throughout the whole palace guard and to everyone else that I am in chains for Christ (Phil. 1:12-13).

Paul's unjust imprisonment seemed like a terrible setback. It looked as though his time in jail would hinder his ministry. But just the opposite was true: because of Paul's arrest, the gospel of Jesus was heard by more people. The members of the palace guard realized that Paul was being kept in captivity because of his faith. Paul had the opportunity to talk to them about Jesus, and people that had never heard about Jesus heard the Good News.

Instead of complaining about being treated unjustly, Paul saw God's plan in his situation and was a shining witness to the soldiers who kept him in captivity. Paul showed Christians that not only can we come to terms with suffering, but we can use it to advance the gospel.

You can learn to handle your negative situations in such a way that God's kingdom will benefit. You have probably already discovered that your personal suffering strengthens your willingness to testify, and that it draws you closer to God and increases your dependence on Him. With God's help, the crises in your life can be turned into victories.

Heavenly Father, thank You that, with Your help, I can use the crises in my own life to the benefit of Your kingdom. Help me always to recognize Your plan in my life when things go wrong. Amen.

To live is Christ!

Read Philippians 1:18-22

I hope that I will have sufficient courage so that now as always Christ will be exalted in my body, whether by life or by death. For to me, to live is Christ and to die is gain (Phil. 1:20-21).

In one of his sermons the well-known Welsh preacher, Christmas Evans, imagined that he went to Rome and asked Nero, "What does life mean to you?" "For me, life is power," Nero answered. When Evans asked the same question of the philosopher Seneca, he replied, "For me, life is thought." Evans then visited Paul in jail and asked him what life meant to him. *"For me, life is Christ,"* was Paul's reply. And then he added, *"And to die is gain."*

Paul was not afraid to die because He knew that Jesus had taken the sting out of death. If we know Jesus, then death is really a bridge to true life.

There are definitely not many among us who can, in all honesty, echo Paul's words. Life is very precious to us. We enjoy living so much that we are not ready to die now! But, Christians need not fear death. We know that God will accompany us through the valley of death into heaven where Jesus is preparing a place for His children.

Lord Jesus, thank You that I can know that life, for me, is Christ, and that I need not fear death. Thank You for preparing a place in heaven for me. Amen.

Life or death?

Read Philippians 1:22-28

Yet what shall I choose? I do not know! I am torn between the two: I desire to depart and be with Christ, which is better by far; but it is more necessary for you that I remain in the body (Phil. 1:22-24).

Paul could not decide which option was better: to carry on serving God and spreading the Good News, or to die and be united with Jesus in heaven. He decided that, if he continued to live, he would be a blessing to the Philippians and give the people reason to praise God. In the words of *The Message*, Paul says, *"So I plan to be around awhile, companion to you as your growth and joy in this life of trusting God continues. You can start looking forward to a great reunion when I come visit you again. We'll be praising Christ, enjoying each other. Meanwhile, live in such a way that you are a credit to the Message of Christ."*

None of us can choose when we want to die. When my grandmother was already quite old my father suddenly died from a heart attack. My grandmother could not accept his death. She kept saying that she longed to "go home" but the Lord had taken my father, who could still have achieved so many things on this earth. The Lord knows the right time for each of His children to depart for heaven. He has kingdom work for those who are still on earth.

Make sure that you do not neglect your work in His kingdom, but live in such a way that you will help others to find joy in Christ.

Lord Jesus, thank You for taking the sting out of death. I no longer need to fear death, and can live every remaining day with joy. Amen.

To suffer for Jesus

> *Read Philippians 1:27-30*

For it has been granted to you on behalf of Christ not only to believe on him, but also to suffer for him (Phil. 1:29).

The Bible teaches us that to suffer for Christ is to our benefit and that God can use our suffering to expand His kingdom. *"For just as the sufferings of Christ flow over into our lives, so also through Christ our comfort overflows. If we are distressed, it is for your comfort and salvation,"* writes Paul to the Corinthians (2 Cor. 1:5-6). In today's Scripture reading, he says that Christians should regard it as a privilege to suffer for their faith.

Christians in Paul's time were physically persecuted and even killed for being Christians. This is not the case in Western countries. But Christians in other parts of the world are often martyred for their faith.

Our "suffering" usually means having to endure ridicule when defending our beliefs in the workplace, on the sports field or among our friends. The greater the impact we have on society as Christians, the more we will be rejected by mockers. Perhaps you do not experience this kind of suffering because you do not share the gospel as much as you should – you keep quiet when you should speak up; you do not share your faith with a godless world.

Lord, I do not really understand what it means to suffer for You. Make me willing to defend my beliefs, even though it could mean that people will ridicule me. Amen.

One in Christ

Read Philippians 2:1-4

Then make my joy complete by being like-minded, having the same love, being one in spirit and purpose. Each of you should look not only to your own interests, but also to the interests of others (Phil. 2:2, 4).

Paul told the Philippians that they could make his joy complete by being like-minded. *The Message* makes it crystal clear, *"Agree with each other, love each other, be deep-spirited friends. Don't push your way to the front; don't sweet-talk your way to the top. Put yourself aside, and help others get ahead. Don't be obsessed with getting your own advantage. Forget yourselves long enough to lend a helping hand."*

This paragraph looks like a blueprint for the attitude shown by Jesus when He dwelt on earth. He never put Himself or His own interests first. He was willing to leave heaven and come to earth so that we could become God's children.

It is virtually impossible for selfish human beings to be like-minded. All of us are selfish from birth. We want to do things our way. Just look at how a two-year-old insists on having his own way. To be unselfish and like-minded is only possible if we are one in Christ. Only He can enable us to live unselfishly and put others first.

Lord Jesus, I pray for the unselfish disposition that You displayed. Teach me to put others first. Make me willing to be the least and help me to remain in You. Amen.

The same attitude as Jesus

Read Philippians 2:5-7

Your attitude should be the same as that of Christ Jesus: Who made himself nothing, taking the very nature of a servant, being made in human likeness (Phil. 2:5, 7).

In Philippians 2, Paul describes the attitude of Jesus. Although He was God, He did not hesitate to put aside His glory and come to this world as a human being. He was born in a dirty stable. He lived such a simple life that He did not even have a house to stay in. He died the most painful of deaths – on the cross – so that we could become God's children. Jesus lived the life of an ordinary human being. He humbled Himself, putting aside all the special privileges of Deity, and that is why many people disregarded Him.

He took on the *"very nature of a servant"*, says Paul. He, the King of heaven, was willing to wash the feet of His disciples – and He expects His children to be willing to serve others in the same way. Jesus' road of humiliation passed by the cross.

Jesus was humble, and God expects you to be too. Will you follow His example?

Lord Jesus, I glorify You for being willing to leave heaven and become a Man – for the sake of sinful mankind. Please help me to have the same attitude of humility and total obedience to God that You did. Amen.

Willing to serve

Read Matthew 20:20-28

"Whoever wants to become great among you must be your servant, and whoever wants to be first must be your slave – just as the Son of Man did not come to be served, but to serve, and to give his life as a ransom for many" (Matt. 20:26-28).

The great preacher, Charles Spurgeon, once said that it was a greater humiliation for Jesus to become a human being than it would have been for an angel to become a worm! Yet Jesus did not think so. His greatness does not lie in the fact that He wants to be served, but in that He is willing to serve.

Jesus' suffering was not limited to His crucifixion. It included serving others in the capacity of a slave. He was willing to serve others, even though it would cost Him His life. And if you want to walk in the footsteps of Jesus, you will also have to sacrifice your own self-importance and become a servant, reaching out to others to help them. *"You, my brothers, were called to be free. But do not use your freedom to indulge the sinful nature; rather, serve one another in love,"* Paul writes to the congregation in Galatia (Gal. 5:13).

Are you willing to follow Jesus' example and to be of service in His kingdom?

Lord Jesus, You, who are the King of heaven, were willing to serve others. Thank You for giving Your life as a ransom for me. I pray that You will help me to be of service, so that Your kingdom here on earth may grow. Amen.

Obedient unto death

Read Philippians 2:7-11

And being found in appearance as a man, he humbled himself and became obedient to death – even death on a cross! (Phil. 2:8).

When Jesus lived on earth, everyone humiliated Him. People insulted Him, told lies about Him, even twice accused him of being possessed by demons! (see John 7:20, 8:48). And what did Jesus do? He never answered back, but always remained obedient to His Father. He was obedient *"to death"*, as Paul explains.

Because Jesus was fully human, He feared this death on a cross, because of the terrible suffering it involved. That is why He asked His Father if the cup of bitterness could be taken away from Him. In this, too, Jesus was the perfect example of obedience. Although He felt that He could not drink the cup of bitterness awaiting Him, He was willing to make His own will subservient to the will of the Father. Crucifixion was the most degrading and painful death imaginable. Yet Jesus was willing to suffer it so that you and I could come to God.

Total obedience is never easy. Yet, God requires it of His children. *"Love for God is to obey His commands,"* writes John (1 John 5:3). Therefore, if you want to follow Jesus' example, you will have to be willing to follow the commands of God and to make your will subservient to the will of God.

Lord Jesus, I glorify You for being obedient unto death so that I could be saved. Make me, in turn, totally obedient to You. Amen.

Jesus is exalted

Read Philippians 2:9-11

Therefore God exalted him to the highest place and gave him the name that is above every name, that at the name of Jesus every knee should bow, in heaven and on earth (Phil. 2:9-10).

Because Jesus was obedient in all things, His Father glorified Him. God exalted Him to the highest place and gave Him a Name that is above every other name, so that, at the name of Jesus, every knee should bow, and every tongue confess Him as Lord – to the glory of God. At the end of time all people, even those who did not want to accept Jesus, will acknowledge Him as Christ the Lord.

Jesus is the radiance of God's glory and the exact representation of God's being. *"He became as much superior to the angels as the name he has inherited is superior to theirs,"* says the writer of Hebrews (Heb. 1:4).

If you belong to Jesus, you should also radiate this glory. *"And we, who with unveiled faces all reflect the Lord's glory, are being transformed into his likeness with ever-increasing glory, which comes from the Lord, who is the Spirit,"* Paul explains (2 Cor. 3:18).

If the glory of Jesus is not yet reflected in your own life, pray that the Holy Spirit will transform you into His likeness.

Lord Jesus, I worship You as the One to whom every knee will bow, in heaven and on earth. Please help me to radiate Your glory. Amen.

God at work

Read Philippians 2:12-13

Continue to work out your salvation with fear and trembling, for it is God who works in you to will and to act according to his good purpose (Phil. 2:12-13).

Once God has "begun a good work in us", we should do all we can to try and live as Jesus lived. We should do the things that Jesus did, and live in total obedience to the Father, as Jesus did. We cannot obey God in our own strength because we are sinners.

But God is involved in our growth as Christians. *The Message* says, *"When I was living among you, you lived in responsive obedience. Now that I'm separated from you, keep it up. Better yet, redouble your efforts. Be energetic in your life of salvation, reverent and sensitive before God. That energy is God's energy, an energy deep within you, God himself willing and working at what will give him the most pleasure."*

We do not obey God because we hope to be saved through obedience – we live according to God's will because we have been saved and want to bring our Father joy. To do this, we should co-operate with the Holy Spirit who lives in us, so that we can become a little more like Jesus every day. God is personally at work in the life of each of His children, helping us to make a little progress on the road to sanctification every day.

Heavenly Father, thank You for working in me, so that I can become more obedient to You day by day. Amen.

Make a difference!

Read Philippians 2:14-15

Do everything without complaining or arguing, so that you may become blameless and pure, children of God without fault in a crooked and depraved generation (Phil. 2:14-15).

God's children look different, act differently and are different from the rest of the world. *"Go out into this world uncorrupted, a breath of fresh air in this squalid and polluted society,"* The Message encourages us. Because God is holy and without sin, He expects His children to live a holy life. This is Paul's message to the congregation in Ephesus: *"Put on the new self, created to be like God in true righteousness and holiness"* (Eph. 4:24).

If you belong to God, you should make a positive difference in the community in which you live. You should not complain or argue, you must be pure and blameless. People watching how you live should recognize beyond any doubt that you belong to God.

We need to be careful how we live. Because we are all sinners from birth, it is very easy for us to let others down by the way we live. Even Christians often differ among themselves. We find it hard to live in peace and love one another.

Therefore, pray regularly with the psalmist, *"May those who hope in you not be disgraced because of me, O Lord, the Lord Almighty; may those who seek you not be put to shame because of me, O God of Israel"* (Ps. 69:6).

Lord Jesus, thank You for being an example worth following. Help me to live in a holy and righteous way, and to truly make a positive difference in my community. Amen.

Stars in a universe of darkness

Read Philippians 2:15-16

Shine like stars in the universe as you hold out the word of life – in order that I may boast on the day of Christ that I did not run or labor for nothing (Phil. 2:15-16).

Jesus Himself says that He is the light of the world and that whoever follows Him will never walk in darkness, but will have the light of life (see John 8:12). Paul takes this further: Christians shine like stars in the dark universe because they hold out the word of life.

When Robert Louis Stevenson was a small boy, he was watching the lamplighter in their street one evening at dusk. When his nurse wanted to know what he was doing, he replied, "I am looking at the man making holes in the darkness."

We should not hide the light of our faith, but we must live so that others can see that we believe in Jesus. In the Sermon on the Mount, Jesus says, *"You are the light of the world. A city on a hill cannot be hidden. Neither do people light a lamp and put it under a bowl. Instead they put it on its stand, and it gives light to everyone in the house. In the same way, let your light shine before men, that they may see your good deeds and praise your father in heaven"* (Matt. 5:14-16).

It is your duty to make holes in the darkness of a world filled with sin, to let the light of God shine brightly, wherever you may live.

Lord Jesus, I glorify You as the Light of the world. Help me to reflect Your light, so that, through Your gospel, I can help to light up a dark world. Amen.

Reason for joy

Read Philippians 2:16-18

But even if I am being poured out like a drink offering on the sacrifice and service coming from your faith, I am glad and rejoice with all of you. So you too should be glad and rejoice with me (Phil. 2:17-18).

Sacrifices and offerings formed a very important part of the Jewish religion. The priests had to bring offerings for the sins of the people, blood had to flow before their sins could be forgiven. Paul tells the Philippians that their faith is an offering in the service of God. An offering always goes hand in hand with sacrifice – it costs us something.

In living his faith to the full, Paul often suffered severely, but he made these sacrifices with joy. He was even willing to die joyously because his death could help the people of Philippi to serve God with greater devotion. He considers this a reason for rejoicing.

Through the ages all great believers have been willing to make great sacrifices for the sake of their faith. But we seem to have become lax. Our faith does not really require any sacrifices from us – it costs us relatively little. Yes, we do believe. But our faith does not make any real difference to the way we live our lives.

If you can say that your faith requires sacrifices from you, then you have reason for great joy in Christ!

Lord Jesus, help me to make any sacrifices that are necessary for my faith to become a real and living testimony to Your goodness – and grant that I will even succeed in rejoicing sincerely about it. Amen.

Rejoice in the Lord!

> *Read Philippians 3:1-2*

Finally, my brothers, rejoice in the Lord! (Phil. 3:1).

Christians are characterized by joy. "Joy is the banner flying above the castle as a sign that the King is home," Chas Cowman writes. It is only God's children who can hold onto their joy in times of sorrow. Because we know Jesus, He infuses His joy into our lives. We cannot hide it, it shines in our eyes and radiates from our smiles. We love life because we love God and we know that He loved us first.

The main reason for our joy is that we have God by our side. *"With joy you will draw water from the wells of salvation. Shout aloud and sing for joy, people of Zion, for great is the Holy One of Israel among you,"* the prophet Isaiah writes (Isa. 12:3, 6).

Because God is by our side, we know that nothing can happen to us unless He allows it to happen. We know that He is by our side even when we go through difficult times, when we face crises, when we are threatened by danger and sickness.

In spite of all these things we can still rejoice because we know that we are not alone. "No comfort is stronger than the assurance that, in the midst of your distress, you are embraced by the love of God," writes John Calvin.

For this reason, you can rejoice in your Lord every day!

> Lord Jesus, I praise You for the joy that forms part of my life because I serve and love You. Thank You that Your constant presence in my life enables me to rejoice forever. Amen.

The most important of all

Read Philippians 3:3-7

But whatever was to my profit I now consider loss, compared to the surpassing greatness of knowing Christ Jesus my Lord (Phil. 3:7-8).

Paul says that he has more reason to put confidence in the flesh than anyone else. He was circumcised on the eighth day, born of the people of Israel, of the tribe of Benjamin, a Hebrew of Hebrews and a Pharisee. He zealously persecuted the church and, as for legalistic righteousness, was faultless (see Phil. 3:4-6). However, his excellent CV could not guarantee Paul a future in heaven, and he was fully aware of this fact. For this reason, he regarded all other things of lesser importance so that he could live to the full for Christ.

When Paul became a disciple of Jesus, his priorities changed completely. Everything that he had previously relied upon, was now of no importance. What he valued most was knowing Jesus, following Him and obeying Him. Paul devoted his whole life to spreading the Gospel of Jesus so that people from pagan nations could hear the Good News of the Gospel of Jesus Christ.

There are many things that people today regard as indispensable. Very few of us are satisfied with Christ only – as Paul was. Perhaps it is time to do a spiritual survey: Which things enjoy the highest priority in your life? Is Jesus truly the most important Person in your life? Would you be willing to consider everything else a loss so that you could get to know Jesus even better?

Lord, there are still so many other things, apart from You, that are indispensable and very important to me. Please help me to get my priorities straight so that I will be willing to sacrifice all for Your sake. Amen.

What are your priorities?

> *Read Philippians 3:8-11*

I want to know Christ and the power of his resurrection and the fellowship of sharing in his sufferings, becoming like him in his death (Phil. 3:10).

Many of us "know" the president of the United States of America, the prime minister of Britain and the president of South Africa, but chances are slim that we have met them personally.

When Paul expressed his desire to "know" Christ, he was referring to a personal relationship with Jesus. He considered all other things in his life as of little importance compared to the surpassing greatness of knowing Jesus.

Paul sacrificed his personal status, suffered loss, torture and humiliation, and was willing to lay down his life to preach the gospel. When he got to know Jesus personally, his entire life changed. His greatest desire was to know Jesus more and more and to share in the power of His resurrection.

How well do you know Jesus? Does your knowledge of Him involve only factual knowledge, or do you have a profound relationship with Him? And what exactly are your priorities regarding Jesus? Is He more important to you than anybody or anything else – as was the case with Paul?

You might be required to suffer for Jesus. It might happen that you will be ridiculed as a result of your faith. Are you prepared to face such things for Jesus?

Lord Jesus, I want to get to know You better every day. Please speak to me through Your Word and make me willing to sacrifice all other things for Your sake, so that You will be my highest priority. Amen.

This heavenly prize could be yours!

Read Philippians 3:12-14

But one thing I do: Forgetting what is behind and straining toward what is ahead, I press on toward the goal to win the prize for which God has called me heavenwards in Christ Jesus (Phil. 3:13-14).

In this text Paul uses the metaphor of a race – and in this race he does two things: he forgets what is behind and he strains toward what is ahead. He does his utmost to reach the goal, so that he can be considered for the prize for which God has called him heavenwards.

Each Christian's life is a race. And in this race we must exert ourselves fully if we want to win the prize, namely eternal life. *The Message* interprets today's Scripture reading as follows, *"I've got my eye on the goal, where God is beckoning us onward – to Jesus. I'm off and running, and I'm not turning back. So let's keep focused on that goal, those of us who want everything God has for us."*

An athlete who continually glances behind him will never win the race. We too should be willing to leave behind the things of the past, to look ahead and to keep our eyes fixed on Jesus. The more things you do, the less likely that you will do each one well. Perhaps you should scale down, start doing less, so that you can function better in the kingdom of God.

Too many good things in your life could divert your attention from the best Thing. In the race of faith, you should choose the one Thing that can never be taken from you.

Lord Jesus, help me to run the race of faith without glancing behind me. Let my eyes be fixed on You, in order to ensure that I win the prize at the end. Amen.

Become spiritually mature

All of us who are mature should take such a view of things. And if on some point you think differently, that too God will make clear to you (Phil. 3:15).

The effort we put in to finish the race of faith and to gain the heavenly prize, is an indication of spiritual maturity. We must exert ourselves to claim God's promise for ourselves, to know Jesus and to experience the power of His resurrection. Paul encourages the Philippians to be spiritually mature by taking the same view of things as he holds.

There are six things that he emphasizes in his letter to the Philippians, which will enable you to grow spiritually.

Firstly, you should have a fervent desire to truly know Jesus personally. Secondly, you should carefully monitor your own spiritual progress. Thirdly, you should not be sentimental about your past, but be willing to regard the things of the past as of lesser importance, because the future with Jesus is more important. In the fourth place, it is necessary for you to regard everything else as unimportant, because Jesus is your highest priority now. You should furthermore focus on those things that really matter, so that you will have time for things of real importance. And lastly, you should not look back, but ahead, in order to complete the race of faith as the winner and, in so doing, gain the heavenly prize.

How many of these six things have you implemented in your life? Mark those that need attention and ask the Lord to help you to grow and become spiritually stronger every day.

Heavenly Father, please help me to grow and become spiritually stronger every day so that, eventually, I may be as perfect and mature as Jesus. Amen.

Hang in there!

Read Philippians 3:15-16

Only let us live up to what we have already attained (Phil. 3:16).

People participating in a race often get very tired and are left behind. In television broadcasts of ultra marathons, we see how dozens of people drop out along the road. The longer and the more difficult the race, the greater the number of people who cannot finish the race.

But, this should not happen in the race of faith that Christians are running. If you feel tired and despondent, you can prevent yourself from dropping out of this race of faith by keeping your eyes focused on Jesus. When we look at Him and realize how much He has sacrificed for our sake, then it is easy to continue running.

"Let us throw off everything that hinders and the sin that so easily entangles, and let us run with perseverance the race marked out for us. Let us fix our eyes on Jesus, the author and perfector of our faith. Consider him, so that you will not grow weary and lose heart," advises the author of Hebrews (Heb. 12:1–3). *"He who stands firm to the end will be saved,"* Jesus personally promises in Mark 13:13.

If the race of faith has left you tired and despondent, just hang in there for a short while. Look toward Jesus – then you will receive new strength to complete the race. You will not grow tired and fall by the wayside.

Lord Jesus, I am so tired at the moment. I pray to You for strength to keep going. Help me to persevere to the very end, so that I can claim the prize. Amen.

Imitate Jesus

Read Philippians 3:17-20

Join with others in following my example, brothers, and take note of those who live according to the pattern we gave you. For many live as enemies of the cross of Christ (Phil. 3:17-18).

Paul calls on Christians to follow his example in the race of faith. He can do so with confidence because he himself followed Jesus' example. And that takes some doing! Most of us are rather inclined to say, "Do as I say and not as I do." But Paul basically says, "Imitate me as I imitate Jesus. Follow the example which I set you."

In everything we do, we should imitate Jesus. We must try our utmost to become increasingly like Him every day, by following His example. By doing the things that He did, by speaking as He spoke, by helping as He helped, by serving as He served. Because we are selfish by nature, we cannot fully succeed in doing these things. Yet Jesus can give us the strength we need to follow His example. This, however, will require serious commitment from each of us.

Paul also directs a serious warning to his readers: we should not become enemies of the cross instead of cross-bearers (v. 18). Remember that heaven is your true homeland and that your time here on earth is transitory. Live in such a way every day that other believers can follow your example with confidence.

Lord Jesus, I try so hard to follow You, but I just cannot succeed. Please help me to live as You lived, so that those people who look at me will be able to see You. Amen.

Rejoice always!

Read Philippians 4:1-4

Rejoice in the Lord always. I will say it again: Rejoice! (Phil. 4:4).

Paul finds the congregation of Philippi a source of great joy. Every time he prays for them, he thanks the Lord for them. And it is his heartfelt desire that they should share in this joy. *"Rejoice! I will say it again: Rejoice in the Lord,"* Paul writes to the people of Philippi. And his life indeed bears witness to his testimony. Not only does he urge the Philippians to rejoice regardless of suffering – but he does so himself. When he and Silas were put in jail, they sang songs of praise to the glory of God. When Paul was tortured, when he suffered, he still kept his joy.

It is not difficult to rejoice when you experience the presence of God in your life every day. However, it does become more difficult when things take a wrong turn – if the way God answers your prayers is different from your expectations, if you pray incessantly and it feels as though He does not answer at all, or if you experience persecution in your own life.

Paul declares that we should rejoice even in those things that we would have changed. *"But we also rejoice in our sufferings, because we know that suffering produces perseverance; perseverance, character; and character, hope. And hope does not disappoint us"* Paul writes to the Romans (Rom. 5:3-5).

With God's help, you too can succeed in rejoicing always – even in times of suffering. Trust Him in this!

Lord Jesus, I glorify You for helping me to rejoice always, even in times of suffering, because I trust that You only want the best for me. Amen.

Let your gentleness be evident to all

Read Philippians 4:4-5

Rejoice in the Lord always. Let your gentleness be evident to all (Phil. 4:4-5).

Paul wrote this letter to the Philippians from prison. Yet his letter overflows with joy. Paul wants to teach us a valuable lesson with this letter: our heart's attitude should not depend on our external circumstances. Christians can succeed in rejoicing always, even when things turn out bad for them.

In verse 5 Paul gives us a tip on how to achieve this: *"Let your gentleness be evident to all."* This concerns your attitude toward others. *"Make it as clear as you can to all you meet that you're on their side, working with them and not against them,"* states *The Message's* version of our Scripture reading for today. Do not always insist on having your own way, be focused on the needs of others, accept them for what they are and give them some space to be who they are. Be flexible in your conduct and allow others the right to their own opinions.

All these characteristics were evident in Jesus' conduct. He even refused to criticize those people who persecuted Him and had Him crucified. Instead, He prayed for them till the very end. *"When they hurled their insults at him, he did not retaliate; when he suffered, he made no threats,"* Peter wrote (1 Pet. 2:23).

God's supernatural grace in your life should enable you to overcome your "natural" discontent with others and to be gentle toward all, so that you will become more and more like Jesus every day.

Lord Jesus, I pray that You will help me to be gentle toward all people, to refrain from always insisting on having my own way, and to allow others to have opinions that differ from mine. Amen.

The Lord is near

Read Philippians 4:5-7

Rejoice in the Lord always. I will say it again: Rejoice! Let your gentleness be evident to all. The Lord is near (Phil. 4:4-5).

The reason Paul succeeded in rejoicing always, in being so gentle toward all people, was that he lived in the presence of the Lord. There are few things that give a Christian such a feeling of safety and security than the knowledge that God is near, that He will never forsake us, but that He is always there to support and help us.

Neither difficult people nor unpleasant circumstances can deprive us of this security. We know that if we have God by our side, nothing can really harm us. He is there to support and help us through our difficult times.

Another heartening fact is that when we draw closer to God, He, in turn, will also draw closer to us. *"Come near to God and he will come near to you,"* writes James (James 4:8). If, at times, you feel as though God is far away from you, it could be because you have not taken sufficient time and sufficient trouble to live close to Him. Find the time to study His Word, to speak to Him in prayer, and to meditate on Him.

When you are busy with the things of God, a miracle happens and, like James, you will discover that He will draw near to you. *"The LORD is near to all who call on him, to all who call on him in truth,"* the psalmist promises (Ps. 145:18). Spend time today in His presence.

Heavenly Father, thank You for Your promise that when I want to come near to You, You, in turn, will come near to me. Teach me to live in Your presence every day so that I may be aware of Your guidance. Amen.

Do not be anxious

> *Read Philippians 4:6-7*

Do not be anxious about anything, but in everything, by prayer and petition, with thanksgiving, present your requests to God (Phil. 4:6).

A survey confirmed that most people worry unnecessarily. Forty percent of people worried about things that never happened; thirty percent worried about things in the past over which they had no control; twelve percent worried unnecessarily about their health; ten percent were also (unnecessarily) worried about their families. Only in eight percent of all cases were their worries justifiable.

There are dozens of reasons why people walk around with burdens of worry on their shoulders. There have been few periods in history in which there were as many reasons for anxiety as there are right now. Therefore, when Paul urges us not to be anxious, it is a command that is rather difficult to obey. But worry indicates that we are attempting to change our circumstances ourselves; that we are relying on ourselves. And this never works.

Trust, on the other hand, implies that we will gather all the necessary information regarding an issue and then consult God about it. That we will allow Him to bring about solutions for our problems. Take careful note of how this should be done: *"By prayer and petition, and with thanksgiving."* While requesting God to take care of your troubles, you can be so sure that He will help you, that you can thank Him at the same time!

Lord, there are still so many things that I worry about. I want to tell You about each and every one of them. Thank You that I can trust in You to take care of all my troubles. Amen.

The peace of God

Read Philippians 4:6-7

And the peace of God, which transcends all understanding, will guard your hearts and your minds in Christ Jesus (Phil. 4:7).

The result of prayer, accompanied by thanksgiving, is that *"the peace of God, which transcends all understanding, will guard our hearts and minds in Christ Jesus,"* writes Paul to the church in Philippi. But there is a world of difference between what the world regards as peace and the nature and content of the peace that God brings about in the human heart.

The peace that comes from God is never only a cease-fire – it is an attitude toward life. We can experience this peace even when we are in the midst of a storm. People who have the peace of God in their hearts, know that God is in control, that no matter what happens, that He only wants the best for them, and He is completely capable of caring for them, even though they may be surrounded by darkness.

When Jesus promised His disciples His peace, He said, *"Peace I leave with you; my peace I give you. I do not give to you as the world gives. Do not let your hearts be troubled and do not be afraid"* (John 14:27).

The peace of Jesus in your life drives away every fear. And this peace can be part of your life every day. All you need to do is look at your situation from God's perspective. Jesus wants to give you His peace – are you willing to make it your own?

Lord Jesus, I pray that You will grant me the peace which transcends all understanding, in my heart and in my life. Help me to be at peace because I know that nothing can happen to me without first having to get past You. Amen.

Think about what is right!

> *Read Philippians 4:8-9*

Finally, brothers, whatever is true, whatever is noble, whatever is right, whatever is pure, whatever is lovely, whatever is admirable – if anything is excellent or praiseworthy – think about such things (Phil. 4:8).

Those things that we think about determine our thoughts as well as our actions. Therefore, our thoughts play a very important role in our lives. Before we do anything, good or evil, we first have to think about it. Paul admonishes the Philippians to focus their thoughts on those things that are good and right. *"Summing it all up, friends, I'd say you'll do best by filling your minds and meditating on things true, noble, reputable, authentic, compelling, gracious – the best, not the worst; the beautiful, not the ugly; things to praise, not things to curse,"* says *The Message*.

I have caught myself on more than one occasion being thankful that people could not read my thoughts! We get to know ourselves through the things that we think about. And usually, you are what you think! Positive people attract positive things to them, while negative people frequently discover that nothing goes right for them.

What does your thought-life look like? Should we not begin to think about what is right? *"We take captive every thought to make it obedient to Christ,"* writes Paul in 2 Corinthians 10:5. If you can attain that in your life, you will find that the result of your positive thoughts will be that the *"God of peace will be with you"* (Phil. 4:9).

Lord Jesus, I pray that You will take every thought of mine captive, making it obedient to You, so that the peace of God can be present in my life every day. Amen.

Empowered by His strength

Read Philippians 4:10-13

I have learned to be content whatever the circumstances. I can do everything through him who gives me strength (Phil. 4:11, 13).

The fact that God's children can do everything through God who gives them strength, is a message that they learned very well over the years. Their victories over their enemies were the work of God. It was He who fought on their side, who preserved them from danger, who gave them strength to solve every problem.

God works like that today. All power and strength "in heaven and on earth" belong to Him. And the magnitude of that power is immense. Paul describes it in the first chapter of Ephesians: *"I pray also that the eyes of your heart may be enlightened in order that you may know his incomparably great power for us who believe. That power is like the working of his mighty strength, which he exerted in Christ when he raised him from the dead and seated him at his right hand in the heavenly realms"* (Eph. 1:18-20).

It is comforting to know that you can succeed in everything you do because God will assist you. You no longer need to rely on your own strength because you have God's miraculous power at your disposal. And once you have realized the magnitude of God's power, you will want to lay claim to that power in order to succeed with everything in future!

Lord Jesus, thank You for Your power that resides in me. Thank You that I may know that I can succeed in everything, that I can move mountains, that I can be successful in all that I do, because I have Your power at my disposal. Amen.

God meets your needs

> *Read Philippians 4:14-20*

And my God will meet all your needs according to his glorious riches in Christ Jesus. To our God and Father be glory for ever and ever. Amen (Phil. 4:19-20).

Paul concludes his letter of rejoicing by putting into words his joy and gratitude about the tangible evidence of the Philippians' concern for him. He expresses his thanks for the contributions that they have sent him on a number of occasions. But the money that they have sent him is not his primary focus. He rejoices because God will bless them because they have been so good to him. Their gifts are a fragrant offering, an acceptable sacrifice, and pleasing to God, Paul testifies. And God will meet all their needs according to His glorious riches in Jesus.

The secret of abundance is to have God in your life. He is capable of taking care of you every day, of meeting all your needs. And God does not just give what you need, but He provides abundantly for your physical, as well as your spiritual needs. Because He is your Shepherd, you will never be in want of anything. *"You have given me the heritage of those who fear your name"*, writes the psalmist (Ps. 61:5).

If you know and glorify God, you can rejoice in living, because He will meet all your needs, and because He will fulfill all your desires – provided they are in line with His will for your life.

Heavenly Father, I praise You for providing so abundantly for all of my physical and spiritual needs that there is nothing I am in want of. Thank You for the magnitude of Your grace in my life. Amen.

Prayer

Lord Jesus,

I praise You for the joy that I have because I love You.

Thank You that the joy that comes from You does not depend on my circumstances, because it is rooted in You.

Thank You for the assurance that no one can ever take away this joy, even though crises and disasters may come against me; that, in the midst of suffering and sorrow, I can still look to You, filled with joy, because I know that You love me and that You will take care of me, that You will abundantly meet all my needs.

Help me to rejoice always – even about those things that I would have preferred to be different.

I pray that You will help me to focus my thoughts on those things that are of importance to You, that I will cease my constant worrying, and instead discuss my concerns with You.

Thank You for the peace that transcends all understanding and for providing in my need.

I know that I can do everything through You who gives me strength.

Amen.

November

Get to know yourself in the psalms

There are psalms for every season of life, for every emotion we experience.

Most of the psalms are songs of praise and gratitude, but there are also a considerable number of psalms that relate to negative emotions such as fear, sorrow, anger, jealousy and doubt.

It is in these psalms that we come face to face with ourselves.

It is these psalms that help us to come to terms with our negative emotions, to express our doubts about our experiences of God's love, to tell Him that we do not always understand Him, to cry in times of sorrow, and to honestly show our anger and anxiety.

Above all, these psalms help to confirm our confidence that God will never forsake us no matter what we might feel.

This month we will explore a few of the "darker" psalms and, so, get to know ourselves better.

Share your thoughts with God

Search me, O God, and know my heart; test me and know my anxious thoughts. See if there is any offensive way in me, and lead me in the way everlasting (Ps. 139:23-24).

Sometimes our minds are filled with things we would like to hide from God, as well as from other people. But there is nothing you can say to God that could shock Him. He already knows all your thoughts, before you have even formed them. Therefore, you can confidently share your negative feelings with God. You can tell Him when you think that life is unfair; when things go wrong for you personally, when the unbelievers experience prosperity; when disasters strike you and your family.

In such times, like the psalmist, examine your own heart. Are you living close to God? Are you willing to obey His voice? The writer of Psalm 139 wants to assure you that God is by your side even when you are feeling all alone, that He knows your heart and your anxious thoughts. Therefore, He will keep you from following any offensive ways. And, because He is so involved with you, you can confidently believe that He will ensure that everything works out for your good in the end, that you will live closer to Him each day, and that you will stay on the right path.

Heavenly Father, You know me so well that I can hide nothing from You. You know that I am feeling bitter and aggrieved today. Thank You for noticing my anxious thoughts and for helping me in all I go through. Amen.

Trust in God when you are afraid

Read Psalm 56

When I am afraid, I will trust in you. In God, whose word I praise, in God I trust. By this I will know that God is for me (Ps. 56:3-4, 9).

When we look at the psalms of lamentation, we see a reflection of ourselves time and again. We recognize ourselves in the psalms in which the psalmists lay their negative emotions before God. We can identify with their feelings, precisely because we experience similar emotions every day.

Some Christians find their negative emotions a source of embarrassment, because they think that these indicate a lack of trust in God. But this is not true. You are allowed to be afraid, you are allowed to doubt, you are allowed to be angry and filled with sorrow, as long as you take your fears to God and trust in Him. When you do this, you discover that God is there for you and He is on your side.

Toward the end of this psalm, the poet discovers that God has been aware of his fear and sorrow all the time: *"Record my lament; list my tears on your scroll – are they not in your record?"* (v. 8). You can claim this promise for yourself today: In times of trouble, when it feels as though God is not taking any notice of you, He is still by your side. He is aware of your distress, He keeps a record of your tears and He will help you – as He has always done in the past.

Heavenly Father, thank You that I can come to You with my fears. How good it is to know that You are aware of my pain and suffering, that You keep a record of each one of my tears. Amen.

God comes to the rescue

Read Psalm 40:1-5

I waited patiently for the Lord; he turned to me and heard my cry. He lifted me out the slimy pit, he set my feet on a rock (Ps. 40:1-2).

In Psalm 130, the psalmist declares, *"Out of the depths I cry to you, O Lord; O Lord, hear my voice. Let your ears be attentive to my cry for mercy"* (vv. 1-2). When he finds himself in the deepest distress, he calls out to God, and God listens to him and helps him.

In Psalm 40 God turns to him, lifts him out of the slimy pit and sets his feet on a rock. This distress call to God is based on the psalmist's previous experience – he knows that God has always helped him in the past, and therefore he believes that God will do so again. And God does not disappoint him – He gives him a firm place to stand and puts a new song in his mouth.

If you find yourself in distress, your only way out is to ask God for help. He will lift you out of the "slimy pit" and set your feet on a rock. Moreover, He is a rock that you can hold onto, His constant love will keep you standing firm in any circumstance. *"When I said, 'My foot is slipping,' your love, O Lord, supported me,"* writes the psalmist in Psalm 94:18.

And in Psalm 40:4, he once again confesses, *"Blessed is the man who makes the Lord his trust."*

Heavenly Father, how good is it to know that I can call on You in situations of distress, that You will set my feet on a rock again. Please do this for me today. Amen.

Support in times of distress

When I was in distress, I sought the Lord; at night I stretched out untiring hands and my soul refused to be comforted (Ps. 77:2).

The psalmist prays through the night, but his soul refuses to be comforted. When he thinks about God, his thoughts are filled with despair. He groans as sleep escapes him. He is too troubled to speak. His greatest sorrow lies in the fact that God does not seem to act as He did in the past. But then, when the psalmist remembers the miracles that God has performed he finds new courage and rediscovers God's greatness and holiness.

Often we pray fervently in distressing circumstances, and it seems that the Lord does not answer our prayers. The Lord seems far away, and we find it hard to see the loving God, who has always come to our rescue. We are almost too scared to admit it to ourselves, but we are disappointed in God. It seems to us as though He has changed, as though He no longer cares about us and has forsaken us. If it seems that the Lord has turned His back on you.

Should you feel this way, turn away from your negative situation and focus on God's miracles in nature, as well as in your own life. God loves you, He wants to be a shepherd to you and guide you (v. 20).

Heavenly Father, forgive me for feeling as though You no longer love me. Help me to see Your miracles anew and to believe that You are still my Shepherd. Amen.

Confess your sins

Read Psalm 32

When I kept silent, my bones wasted away through my groaning all day long. For day and night your hand was heavy upon me; my strength was sapped as in the heat of summer (Ps. 32:3-4).

The psalmist fails to confess his sins to God and finds that life goes badly for him. His tension manifests itself as a disease; his bones waste away and his strength is sapped. Only then does he acknowledge his sins and confess his transgressions to the Lord.

Sin always leads to estrangement between us and God. *"But your iniquities have separated you from your God; your sins have hidden his face from you,"* writes Isaiah (Isa. 59:2).

Strains and stresses have a major influence on our lives, as well as on our health. When we bottle them up, our physical condition deteriorates. If your relationship with the Lord is not in order, everything else also goes wrong. But if you are willing to be open with the Lord, and to confess your sins, He not only forgives your sins, but your health improves significantly.

If you are battling some or other form of disease at present, make sure that it is not the result of hidden sins. Confess your sins before God, one by one. He is always willing to forgive your sins and to restore your health.

Heavenly Father, forgive me for not confessing my sins. I now want to confess them to You, one by one, and ask You to forgive me and restore my health. Amen.

When God hides His face

Read Psalm 44:10-27

Awake, O Lord! Why do you sleep? Rouse yourself! Do not reject us for ever. Why do you hide your face and forget our misery and oppression? (Ps. 44:23-24).

In this psalm, the psalmist expresses his anger toward God. He feels as though God has rejected him, as though God is asleep, although he has remained true to God. *"Yet for your sake we face death all day long. We are considered as sheep to be slaughtered,"* he complains (v. 22). And then he asks God a whole lot of questions. Why does God sleep? Why does He hide His face from him? Why does He forget his misery?

Many believers find it incomprehensible that bad things can happen to them, even though they love God and serve Him. In times of adversity they try in vain to find sense in their crises.

We can freely express our anger to God, as long as disaster and adversity bring us closer to Him. Psalm 44 concludes with the thought that, regardless of the poet's circumstances, God's unfailing love remains constant. You can hold onto this promise, regardless of how hopeless your situation may seem at the moment, because God does love you. Even though it may feel to you as though He is asleep and hiding His face from you, He is aware of all your suffering and, eventually, He will bring an end to it.

Lord, today is such a bad day that I want to ask where You are, why You continually reject me and hide Your face from me. Please help me, so that I can be assured again of Your unfailing love for me. Amen.

When God seems far away

Read Psalm 22:2-11, 22-23

My God, my God, why have you forsaken me? Why are you so far from saving me, so far from the words of my groaning? O my God, I cry out by day, but you do not answer, by night, and am not silent (Ps. 22:1-2).

In this psalm David expresses how hurt he feels because the Lord seems to be so far away, and because He does not answer David's call. The fact that God has helped his forefathers makes the fact that he is not being helped even worse. Eventually, his feelings of hurt turn into a full-scale depression: *"But I am a worm and not a man, scorned by men and despised by the people"* (v. 6). And yet, toward the end of the psalm, he finds that God has heard his prayers.

The most intense pain that a believer could experience is the feeling that God has forsaken him. Perhaps you can identify with David, because you have, at times, felt forsaken by God. Because you have also experienced feelings of hurt when looking at how other people are being helped and blessed by God, while your life takes a turn for the worse. It hurts deeply that the God who is supposed to love you, seems so far away when you need His help the most.

On the cross Jesus asked the same question as David: *"My God, my God, why have you forsaken me?"* God forsook His Son in the hour of His deepest distress so that you may always have Him by your side in times of distress. God will answer your prayer in His perfect way.

Father, forgive me for thinking that You have forsaken me. Thank You that I now know that this is not the case, that You have answered all of my prayers. Amen.

Refrain from anger

Read Psalm 37:1-8

Be still before the LORD and wait patiently for him; do not fret when men succeed in their ways, when they carry out their wicked schemes. Refrain from anger and turn from wrath; do not fret – it leads only to evil (Ps. 37:7-8).

Sometimes, things happen that enrage you. You feel angry toward people who offended you, and angry toward God who allowed these things to happen to you. If He is omnipotent, He could have prevented it, right?

How do you handle your rage when you are angry and disappointed? In Psalm 37 the psalmist teaches you what to do.

In the first place, you must be willing to continue trusting in the Lord, even though things don't turn out well for you. Trust comes easily when life treats you well, but in a crisis it is rather difficult to hold on to God's promises if they do not come true for you.

In the second place, you must refrain from getting angry. God wants to use all the negative things in your life so that you can move closer to Him. You probably pray more often in a crisis than when all goes well. Try to identify the lesson that God wants to teach you through the crisis that you are facing.

In the third place, it is unnecessary to fret. All of us experience crises at one time or another. If you love God, you can rest assured that He is by your side in a crisis, and that He will carry you through it.

Lord, crises are never pleasant. They leave me angry, as well as disappointed in You. Teach me to trust You, to refrain from anger and not to fret. Thank You for the assurance that You are by my side in this crisis. Amen.

In times of danger

Read Psalm 55:1-9, 23

Listen to my prayer, O God, do not ignore my plea. My heart is in anguish within me; the terrors of death assail me. Fear and trembling have beset me; horror has overwhelmed me (Ps. 55:1, 4-5).

The psalmist was deeply troubled when writing this psalm. He was threatened by his enemies and found himself in grave danger. Therefore, he called on God to help him. Have you ever been so scared that you choked with fear, your mouth was bone-dry and you thought that your final moment had arrived?

When we face danger, our first reaction is normally to flee. *"I said, 'Oh, that I had the wings of a dove! I would fly away and be at rest – I would flee far away and stay in the desert,'"* writes the psalmist (vv. 6-7).

David often found himself in life-threatening situations. Saul intently followed him, his own son wanted to kill him, and he had dozens of enemies who pursued him. Therefore, he knew very well what it felt like to be assailed by the terrors of death. And every time that he found himself in a dangerous situation, he turned to God in-stead of fleeing into the desert! He therefore testifies in verse 22: *"Cast your cares on the Lord and he will sustain you; he will never let the righteous fall."*

If you find yourself in a life-threatening situation, you too can call on the Lord for help. Remember that God will never allow you to fall. He will sustain you and protect you.

Heavenly Father, thank You for being a refuge to me in dangerous situations, that You always promise to protect, to rescue and to help me as You did David. Amen.

God is your Strength

Read Psalm 59:10-18

O my Strength, I watch for you; you, O God, are my fortress, my loving God. But I will sing of your strength, in the morning I will sing of your love; for you are my fortress, my refuge in times of trouble (Ps. 59:9, 16).

For the psalmist, God is a hiding place, a fortress where he can take refuge when his life is threatened by his enemies. For this reason, he places his hope in God, even in hopeless situations. Because he has his God by his side, he can live fearlessly in a dangerous world. God is his Strength: *"You, O God, are my fortress, my refuge in times of trouble,"* he testifies.

We often fear things because we lose control over our situations. And all of us want to be in control at all times! In the world in which we live, there are many reasons to be afraid. Every day we hear of muggings, burglaries and incidents of violence in our communities. Not one of us is really safe from possible danger. The fact that our lives may be in danger, scares us. We install burglar guards and alarm systems in our homes, and yet we still live with fear in our hearts.

God wants to be a refuge for you in times of danger. He wants to be your Strength. And God is in complete control – regardless of what may happen. There is nothing that falls outside His jurisdiction. Tell Him about your fears and lean on Him in times of danger. He can and will rescue you.

Heavenly Father, I glorify You for being a fortress to me, a refuge in times of trouble. Thank You for preserving me when I find myself in danger. Amen.

In times of sickness

Read Psalm 30

O Lᴏʀᴅ, my God, I called to you for help and you healed me. You turned my wailing into dancing; you removed my sackcloth and clothed me with joy (Ps. 30:2, 11).

In this psalm, the psalmist tells how God has delivered him by turning his negative situation around, by healing him and by removing his sorrow and clothing him with joy.

There are few things as frightening as an illness you can do nothing about. After my husband had suffered a serious heart attack, he wrote that illness leaves its mark on a man. It affects his body and spirit. His entire life is affected by it. Sometimes, you bombard God with 'why questions' and He does not answer. However, you can be entirely sure of one thing: the best and most satisfactory answer to all your questions is a new, personal encounter with God.[1]

Psalm 30 offers an answer to prayer in times of distress. When you fall ill or suffer affliction, the Lord will hear your supplication and, eventually, remove your sackcloth and clothe you with joy. If negative things in your life bring you closer to God, then they are actually profitable. And although God does not always heal His children who are ill, we can know that, eventually (even though it may only be in heaven one day), He will put an end to all sickness and suffering.

Heavenly Father, I praise You for healing me. Thank You for all the positive lessons of life that I can learn from my illness, as well as for the fact that it has brought me into a deeper relationship with You. Amen.

Refrain from envy

> Read Psalm 73:2-5, 13-26

I had nearly lost my foothold. For I envied the arrogant when I saw the prosperity of the wicked. They have no struggles; they are not plagued by human ills (Ps. 73:2-5).

Envy usually manifests itself when we compare ourselves to others who are better off than us. And if these people are unbelievers, then it is even harder not to be jealous of their prosperity! The psalmist even began to doubt the goodness of God when he saw the prosperity of unbelievers. He could not understand why life treated them so well, while he struggled. He complained to God that he was being plagued all day long and punished every morning. But then he realized what the final destiny of these prosperous people is, and he discovered that there is nothing better in this world for him than God.

Perhaps you are experiencing the same problems as the psalmist. You seem to be the only one suffering, while those who do not serve God experience only prosperity. It is better not to compare yourself to others. Your faith in God offers you an inner security that unbelievers will never have, regardless of how well life may treat them.

Rather testify with the psalmist that, although your flesh and your heart may fail, God is the strength of your heart and being in the presence of God is the only thing you truly need.

Father, please forgive me when I so easily become envious of unbelievers. Assure me once again that I will belong to You for ever. Amen.

How good is God?

Read Psalm 73:13-24

Surely in vain have I kept my heart pure; in vain have I washed my hands in innocence. All day long I have been plagued; I have been punished every morning (Ps. 73:13-14).

How can God be good if life is so unfair, the psalmist wonders. We are so often confronted by corruption that it is sometimes difficult to believe that God is really good to His children.

Yet we cannot measure God's goodness toward us by what happens to us. When we live an exemplary life and yet we do not prosper, we need to become quiet in God's presence once again and ask what He wants to teach us through the injustice we suffer.

The psalmist finds his answer within the sanctuary of God: The wicked have no future prospects. A terrible destiny awaits unbelievers for whom things are going so well now. When the Lord arises, He will pass over them. Therefore, it is foolish to be bitter. Life is not fair. Christians do not always get what they deserve. But we can rest assured in the knowledge that God loves us and cares for us.

Is life treating you badly at present? God wants to guide you by His counsel and give you the assurance that when you die, you have a future with Him because heaven is awaiting you.

Heavenly Father, I apologize that, when things really turn out for the worse, I question Your love and goodness toward me. Thank You that I can know that You are preparing eternal glory for me in heaven. Amen.

Do not sin!

Read Psalm 4

In your anger do not sin; when you are on your beds, search your hearts and be silent (Ps. 4:4).

While praying, the psalmist confesses his anger to the Lord. He asks the Lord to give him relief from his distress, as He has done in the past. Unbelievers are telling lies about him, but he believes that God's ability to help him is greater than their accusations, as well as his own anger. Toward the end of the psalm, the psalmist decides to trust in the Lord. Because he knows that God will hear his cause, it is possible for him to calm down, free of trouble, and to sleep peacefully (v. 8).

All of us get angry when people accuse and malign us. One of the hardest lessons to learn is to keep your peace and to refrain from saying things in anger that you will later regret. If people treat you unjustly, guard against falling prey to the sin of slandering out of helpless rage.

Take note of the psalmist's warning: Do not sin! It is difficult, but try to leave the matter in God's hands. He is completely able to solve your problems. You no longer need to spend sleepless nights, but you can sleep peacefully because you can rest assured in the knowledge that God will let you live in safety.

Heavenly Father, You know how aggrieved I feel at the moment because people have offended me. Please help me to refrain from wanting to retaliate. Help me to calm down. Amen.

Be merciful to me, Lord

> *Read Psalm 6*

Be merciful to me, LORD, for I am faint; O LORD, heal me, for my bones are in agony. My soul is in anguish. How long, O LORD, how long? (Ps. 6:2-3).

The psalmist is suffering from sickness and sorrow. *"I am faint, my bones are in agony, I am worn out with groaning; all night long I flood my bed with weeping and drench my couch with tears,"* he complains in verses 2 and 6. The real reason why life is treating the psalmist so badly is that his relationship with God is troubled. His enemies are causing problems for him and he asks God to come to his rescue. And God listens, *"The LORD has heard my cry for mercy; the LORD accepts my prayer"* (v. 9).

Sickness and sorrow could have far-reaching consequences in your life. They could even cause you to doubt God's love for you. People who offend you could leave you embittered. When you are sick and filled with sorrow, if life treats you unfairly, it is easy to become distressed and throw in the towel. It is also quite normal to start doubting God's love for you in hard times.

But it is better to follow the psalmist's advice. Present your complaint to the Lord. He can heal and comfort you. He will not allow His children to be treated unjustly for ever. Recognize that your situation is in God's hands and that He has promised to defend the fatherless and the oppressed (Ps. 10:18). He will answer your prayers.

> Lord, it is difficult to continue trusting in You when I am sick and filled with sorrow. Be merciful to me and please assure me once again that you will deliver me and answer my prayers. Amen.

Put your hope in the Lord!

Read Psalm 88:1-10

For my soul is full of trouble and my life draws near the grave. I am counted among those who go down to the pit; I am like a man without strength. You have put me in the lowest pit, in the darkest depths (Ps. 88:3-4, 6).

This psalm is regarded by some theologians as the most melancholy in the entire Bible. The psalmist's soul is deeply troubled, he is nearing the end of his strength and it feels to him as though God has forsaken him. He wants to know why God has rejected him, why he has had to suffer from such a young age.

The psalmist is being driven to despair by his suffering, his *"life draws near the grave"*. The psalm does not tell us that the Lord has heard his prayers. And yet a tiny flicker of hope remains. He addresses his melancholy prayer to the Lord *"who saves me"* (v. 1).

Usually, it takes a long time before we lose hope altogether. And people who put their hope in the Lord have never been completely disappointed. The prophet, Jeremiah, could declare from experience: *"So I say, 'My splendor is gone and all that I had hoped from the Lord.'"* Yet, only six verses further, he testifies: *"I say to myself, 'The Lord is my portion; therefore I will wait for him'"* (Lam. 3:18, 24).

If you find yourself in the depths of despondency, you can hold on to God *"who saves you"* and continue putting your hope in Him!

Heavenly Father, You know me so well and, therefore, You also know how faint my hope is at present. Thank You that I can hold on to You; that I still believe that You will come to my rescue. Help me to keep on putting my hope in You. Amen.

I put my hope in God

Read Psalm 39:1-13

But now, LORD, what do I look for? My hope is in you (Ps. 39:7).

A man's life is as transient as a breath. And if God were to justly punish people for their sins, then very little hope would remain for us. The psalmist declares that his hope is in God. He asks God to deliver him from his sins and to withhold his deserved punishment. He is solely dependent on God, because He takes care of him.

The painter, G. F. Watts, created a painting which he called Hope. This painting is of a blindfolded woman sitting with a bowed head on a globe of the world. In her hand she holds a lyre. Only *one* string of the lyre is not broken and, in the sky above her, there shines a single star. The woman in the painting is near to reaching the end of all hope, but as long as there is one string remaining on the lyre, as long as *one* star continues to shine, she does not lose hope.

When you feel despondent, ask God to forgive your sins and give you hope. God's children know that, no matter how badly things turn out for them, they can still have hope, because God is there. He is our only hope. And, because you believe in Him, you can hold onto hope – even in the most perilous of circumstances. Hope is always focussed on the future. You need never lose hope. You can rest assured in the knowledge that heaven is awaiting you one day!

Heavenly Father, thank You for being my only hope. That I can hope, regardless of how dark things may seem, because I know that You have prepared a place in heaven for me. Amen.

Hold onto God's love!

Read Psalm 116

The cords of death entangled me, the anguish of the grave came upon me; I was overcome by trouble and sorrow. I believed; therefore I said, "I am greatly afflicted." And in my dismay I said, "All men are liars." (Ps. 116:3, 10-11).

The psalmist was anxious, anguished and troubled when he wrote this psalm. He was disillusioned when he discovered that all men are liars. In his hopeless condition, he calls on the Lord and the Lord rescues him from his distressing situation. *"Be at rest once more, O my soul, for the Lord has been good to you. For you, O Lord, have delivered my soul from death, my eyes from tears,"* he prays in verses 7-8. He then undertakes to prove through his way of life that God has been good to him.

When things go wrong for you, if people defraud and disappoint you, you can call on the Lord with confidence and continue believing in Him. You can gladly hold onto His love for you. The Bible assures us that there is nothing on earth that could separate us from this love. *"For I am convinced that neither death nor life, neither angels nor demons, neither the present nor the future, nor any powers, neither height nor depth, nor anything else in all creation, will be able to separate us from the love of God,"* testifies Paul (Rom. 8:38-39).

God is the same merciful God that He has always been. He will support you in hard times and carry you through crises. Trust Him in this – and remember to emphasize your gratitude by your deeds.

Heavenly Father, how good You are! Thank You that, like the psalmist, I can hold onto Your love always. You have saved me, supported me and carried me through my crises. Amen.

Loneliness

Read Psalm 25:1-22

Turn to me and be gracious to me, for I am lonely and afflicted. The troubles of my heart have multiplied; free me from my anguish (Ps. 25:16-17).

There are few things that cause one to feel so totally destitute as loneliness. The poet, Rupert Brooke, tells how lonely he was when he had to leave Liverpool for New York. At the quay-side there was not a single person to bid him goodbye. Rupert spotted a young boy in rags among the crowd, and offered him a sixpence if he would wave to him as the ship was leaving the harbor. The little boy waved fiercely when the ship departed, and Rupert no longer felt lonely. He had someone to wave him goodbye.

In Psalm 25 the psalmist expresses his own feelings of loneliness. He asks God to turn to him and be gracious, because he is lonely and afflicted. He continues to trust in the Lord because he knows that God is by his side.

Many of us feel lonely at times, especially as we become older and many of our friends have passed away. But God's children need never be lonely. You can use the times when you are alone to come closer to God. If you belong to God, then you have His promise that He is always by your side, and that He will never leave you nor forsake you (Josh. 1:5, 9). He lives in you through His Holy Spirit. He promises to support and help you every day. Remember this whenever you feel lonely again!

Heavenly Father, I thank You that Your children need never feel lonely. Thank You that You will never forsake me, but that You are by my side every moment of every day, to support and help me. Amen.

In grave danger

Read Psalm 109:22-31

*For I am poor and needy, and my heart is wounded within me.
Help me, O LORD my God; save me in accordance with your love*
(Ps. 109:22, 26).

David often found himself in life-threatening situations. When
people were after his life, time and again he sought refuge with God,
and the Lord rescued him from his enemies every time. When he
wrote this psalm, he was in a wretched state. *"My knees give way
from fasting; my body is thin and gaunt. I am an object of scorn to
my accusers"* (Ps. 109:24-25). Then, like so many times before, he
turned to the Lord. In spite of the grave danger in which he found
himself, he trusted that the Lord would help him and he promised
to greatly extol God once he has been rescued.

Like David, we are often dismayed about the things that people
do to us. Some time ago all our savings were embezzled by a
financial advisor whom we had trusted. It was quite a while before
the reality of his betrayal really sunk in. It was too ghastly to
contemplate! And yet when we eventually realized that we would
have to make do without this security, we were confident that
the Lord would help us, that He would take care of us as He had
promised.

You can gladly turn to God with your personal burden of pain
and suffering. He *will* listen to you and help you.

Heavenly Father, thank You for being absolutely faithful. Thank
You that You will never leave me in the lurch, but that I can always
turn to You for help and advice. Amen.

Out of the depths

Read Psalm 130

Out of the depths I cry to you, O LORD; O Lord, hear my voice. Let your ears be attentive to my cry for mercy. I wait for the LORD, my soul waits, and in his word I put my hope (Ps. 130:1, 2, 5).

Things such as sickness, suffering and sin, sometimes cause us to feel as though we are sitting in a dark pit. This is how the psalmist feels in this psalm. His burden of sin weighs heavily on him, but he knows that the Lord will forgive his sins. Therefore, he confesses his sins and cries out of the depths to the Lord for mercy. He puts his trust in God and he is willing to wait for help from the Lord.

The psalmist does three things when he faces a crisis: He confesses his sins, he trusts in the Lord to end his crisis, and he is willing to wait on the Lord to redeem him.

When you find yourself in a pit, you can gladly take these three steps: *Confess your sins to God*. Perhaps it is your sins that prevent God from intervening in your situation and listening to your prayers. *Trust in the Lord to help you*. He is omnipotent and capable of helping, even though things may seem impossible to you. Lastly, *be willing to wait* until the Lord rectifies things for you in His chosen time.

Long ago, guards were posted on the walls of cities to watch for the dawning of a new day. Similarly, you should wait patiently until the Lord changes your dark circumstances for the better.

Heavenly Father, today I cry out of the depths to You. Please help me, forgive my sins, enable me to steadfastly trust in You and to wait patiently on You. Amen.

When God feels far away

Read Psalm 10:1, 12-18

Why, O LORD, do you stand far off? Why do you hide yourself in times of trouble? (Ps. 10:1).

In the first part of this psalm, the psalmist complains that God stands too far off from him, that He hides Himself, especially in times when he needs Him most. He tells God about the arrogance of the wicked and calls on Him to break their grip of power.

In the second part of the psalm, the psalmist discovers that God has been aware of his suffering and sorrow all along, that He was never far away but close by, and that He is ready to bring an end to his suffering. *"You hear, O LORD, the desire of the afflicted; you encourage them, and you listen to their cry,"* he testifies in verse 17.

When inexplicable disasters strike you, you too, probably feel as though God has turned His back on you, as though He does not listen to your prayers, and as though He is standing far off. But God's children never need to rely on their feelings. You can rest assured that, although it may not seem so to you at the moment, God is still there for you. He not only takes note of your suffering and sorrow, but promises to put an end to it. And even if your opponents think that God is unaware of their schemes, He actually sees everything they do.

Does God feel far away from you at this moment? Remember that He is close to you, He wants to renew your courage today, hear your prayers and cause justice to triumph.

Oh Lord, You feel very far away today, and I need You so much. Please help me, take note of my sorrow and suffering, and answer my prayer. Amen.

Can God forget about you?

> *Read Psalm 13*

How long, O LORD? Will you forget me forever? How long will you hide your face from me? (Ps. 13:1).

The psalmist is totally despondent because he thinks that the Lord has forgotten about him; that He is no longer aware of him. His heart is filled with sorrow because he is left to his own devices. Then he turns to the Lord for help. He tells Him that he trusts in His unfailing love, that his heart rejoices in God's salvation – even though his situation has not changed.

God *cannot* forget His children. *"Can a mother forget the baby at her breast? Though she may forget, I will not forget you! See, I have engraved you on the palms of my hands; your walls are ever before me,"* God promises in Isaiah 49:15-16.

If you are in distress, stop focusing on your circumstances. Look beyond them, as the psalmist does here. Think about all the times when the Lord has helped you. He will do so again. And even if your distress does not dissolve immediately, you will gain a new perspective. No situation is so disastrous that it cuts you off from God's grace.

If you can remember this, nothing will seem dark to you any longer. Then, like the psalmist, you will succeed in singing a song to the glory of the Lord because He has been good to you.

Lord, at the moment it feels as though You have forgotten about me. I am surrounded by darkness. Please help me to look away from the darkness and become aware of You. To sing a song of praise to You, regardless of my problems. Amen.

How long, O Lord?

Read Psalm 79

How long, O LORD? Will you be angry forever? How long will your jealousy burn like fire? (Ps. 79:5).

In this psalm, the psalmist laments the destruction of Jerusalem by God's enemies. God's people had become objects of reproach to their neighbors. But God's anger toward His disobedient people still did not subside. The psalmist wants to know how long God's wrath toward His people will last. He pleads for God to have mercy on Israel for the sake of His name. He concludes his prayer with a promise, that if the Lord preserves them, they will show their gratitude through their deeds.

If our suffering continues for a long time, we might become completely despondent. But, if we know that the suffering will not continue forever, then it is easier to bear. Like the psalmist, we also need to run to God when confronted by a crisis. We plead for His mercy and we make promises of what we will do if He answers our pleas.

We know that Jesus has deflected God's wrath about our sins on the cross, and our sins are forgiven. We also know that our suffering in this world will not last forever, but will come to an end. *"For our light and momentary troubles are achieving for us an eternal glory that far outweighs them all,"* writes Paul to the congregation in Corinth (2 Cor. 4:17).

Father, thank You for the assurance that my troubles will not last forever, but will result in eternal glory. Amen.

Joy after suffering

Read Psalm 51:1-11

Against you, you only, have I sinned and done what is evil in your sight. Let me hear joy and gladness; let the bones you have crushed rejoice (Ps. 51:4, 8).

Psalm 51 is one of the best-known prayers of repentance in the Bible. After his adultery with Bathsheba, David confessed his guilt to God with a sincerity that touches our hearts. He confessed that he had sinned against God only and asks for forgiveness so that he may once again experience God's joy and gladness in his life. He prays that the God who has crushed him, will let him rejoice again. He also promises that he will serve the Lord with new fervor.

Sin always separates God from people. When you sin, you experience the same negative emotions that David describes here: a lack of joy and intense feelings of guilt. Yet if you confess your sins as David did, God is willing to forgive you your sins time and again and to restore your joy. However, confession of sins also requires a changed way of life from you. Only then will you be able to rejoice in God again.

God promises His children joy after sorrow. *"Weeping may remain for a night, but rejoicing comes in the morning,"* writes the psalmist in Psalm 30:5. Although God does not safeguard His children against suffering, for a Christian, suffering always ends in joy. Even though your fate may not change here on earth, you can still put your hope in heaven where all suffering will be something of the past forever.

Heavenly Father, I wish to confess my debt of sin to You. Please forgive me and restore Your joy in my life. Thank You for promising Your children that joy will replace sorrow. Amen.

Joy in the presence of God

> Read Psalm 42:6-12

My tears have been my food day and night, while men say to me all day long, "Where is your God?" Why are you downcast, O my soul? Why so disturbed within me? Put your hope in God, for I will yet praise him (Ps. 42:3, 5).

Psalm 42 starts with a longing for God. *"As the deer pants for streams of water, so my soul pants for you, O God."* The psalmist longs for God's presence in his times of suffering. His need for God's presence is as pressing and as much a matter of life and death as a deer's need for water. He finds it difficult when unbelievers ridicule him and ask him where his God is. For this reason, his soul is downcast and he cries out to God.

However, even though his circumstances are so negative, a spark of hope remains, *"By day the LORD directs his love, at night his song is with me – a prayer to the God of my life"* (v.8). In spite of everything, the psalmist trusts that the Lord will once again deliver him.

Our joy in the Lord is founded on God's presence. Even in the deepest distress, Christians find comfort in God's presence. Do you still long for God? The early church called the Sunday between Ascension Day and Pentecost the "Sunday of longing". They reserved this Sunday to express their longing for God.

Your sincere longing for God is the key to true joy. It will change your vision of life and cause you to think anew about your Christianity.

Heavenly Father, I long for Your presence. Thank You for the joy which Your presence awakes in me. Help me to sing to You even in the darkest night. Amen.

Joy passes by a sacrificial altar

> *Read Psalm 43*

Vindicate me, O God, and plead my cause against an ungodly nation. You are God my stronghold. Why have you rejected me? (Ps. 43:1-2).

Psalm 43 expresses the fluctuation between hope and doubt that is so characteristic of people facing a crisis. The psalmist prays that God will rescue him from his enemies. He feels cut off from God, and therefore he asks the Lord to send forth His light and His truth to guide him to the temple, and he asks that God will enable him to praise Him yet again. He believes that God is his Savior and that he will soon be able to experience the goodness of God in his life again.

When life treats you very badly it is possible that you could start to doubt God and to lose His joy. God promises His children joy, but the joy that God gives is very precious. It sometimes enters our lives by the road of suffering. As we trust in God, eventually we learn to look beyond our circumstances. Often it is when circumstances are at their darkest, that God sends His light to lead us from despair.

True joy comes from the cross. Our joy rises from Jesus' sacrificial altar. Because He died for us, we have every reason to be joyous. Jesus sacrificed His life so that you and I can live joyously. Is your joy founded in Him?

> Lord Jesus, thank You for dying for me so that I can live a joyous life. Help me to see beyond my difficult situation and to become aware of You. Amen.

In times of darkness

Read Psalm 119:105-112

Though I constantly take my life in my hands, I will not forget your law. Your word is a lamp to my feet and a light for my path (Ps. 119:109, 105).

When the psalmist wrote this beautiful song extolling God's law, things were not going well for him. *"I have suffered much; preserve my life, O Lord, according to your word. Though I constantly take my life in my hands, I will not forget your law,"* he testifies in verses 107 and 109. He is surrounded by darkness, but in this darkness he relies on the Word of God, which is a lamp to his feet and a light for his path. He contrasts the circumstances threatening his life to his obedience to the law and the Word of God, in which he still rejoices.

It could be dangerous to try to find your way in the dark without a light. You can only travel safely in the dark if you have a light that can banish the darkness and enable you to see the dangers surrounding you.

We are often confronted with dangerous situations in our lives. Yet, for us too, God's Word can still be a lamp to our feet and a light for our path in times of darkness. If, like the psalmist, you undertake to obey God's law, He will preserve you in dangerous situations. With the Lord's Word as a light, you can travel through the dark times and places of life with joy.

Heavenly Father, thank You that Your Word remains a light for my path through life in times and places of darkness. I know that I will always get the right counsel from You. Amen.

What has your suffering taught you?

Read Psalm 119:71-77

It was good for me to be afflicted so that I might learn your decrees. I know, O LORD that your laws are righteous, and in faithfulness you have afflicted me (Ps. 119:71, 75).

The psalmist complains because the Lord allows him to go through intense suffering. He asks for comfort and the Lord hears his prayer and comforts him. The psalmist gains a whole new perspective on his affliction. He is struck by the fact that this affliction, which he fought with all his might, was good for him in the end. It helped him to learn God's decrees and it was a sign of God's faithfulness.

None of us can escape affliction or suffering, and most of us fight it as the psalmist did! Yet we eventually discover that the suffering taught us to be more dependent on God, that our troubles brought us a new awareness of His love and faithfulness, and that it taught us to live close to God and not simply to accept His grace as a matter of course.

What has the suffering in your life taught you? If it contributed to a greater spiritual maturity, as well as to spiritual growth, then, in the end, it was more than worth the trouble. Therefore, should you have to go through a time of suffering again, remember that God is omnipotent and holds your life in His hands. Ask yourself what the Lord wants to teach you through it, instead of complaining and groaning about your suffering.

Heavenly Father, thank You that I can know that, in the end, it was good for me to be afflicted, because it taught me to hold on to You alone, and not to trust in myself any longer. Amen.

November 30

Praise God for His love and faithfulness

Read Psalm 108

I will praise you, O LORD, among the nations; I will sing of you among the peoples. For great is your love, higher than the heavens; your faithfulness reaches to the skies (Ps. 108:3-4).

This month we focused on the "dark" psalms that reflect the psalmists' negative emotions. We should not dwell on them for too long, but should progress to the psalms of praise, in which we thank God for His undeserved love and mercy.

Time and again, when facing a crisis, the psalmists realized that God is on their side, that He supports them and hears their prayers. If, like the psalmists, you have acknowledged your own pain, sorrow, anger and fear to God, the time has now come for you to praise God because He has been with you through all your suffering, and He assures you of His love and faithfulness every day.

In Psalm 108, the psalmist sings a song about his God. As he looks at the past, he is compelled to testify to God's caring love and His faithfulness that reaches to the skies. He feels secure in the presence of God even though he is still facing danger.

And today you can join the psalmist in singing this song. God is by your side, He preserves you in situations of danger, He comforts you in times of sorrow, He causes your anger to subside and banishes your fear. Therefore, you can end this month by testifying in unison with the psalmist, *"With God we shall gain the victory, and he will trample down our enemies"* (Ps. 108:13).

Lord, I praise You for Your support and faithful love, as well as for the fact that I can be more than victorious, because You are on my side. Amen.

Prayer

*H*eavenly Father,

Thank You that, during the past month, I was able to recognize myself in the negative emotions portrayed by the psalmists.

It is a great relief to me that I may, with confidence, share my doubts and concerns, my fear and anger, my anxiety and sorrow with You.

Sometimes, it feels as though You are far away from me, as though You do not hear my prayers, as though You hide Your face and are unaware of my sorrow.

I cannot understand why life sometimes treats unbelievers so much better than it treats me.

I pray that You will deliver me, that You will hear my prayers and support me.

Thank You for always being by my side in times of suffering and when I feel all alone, that You promise me joy after suffering, that You rescue me from situations of distress and never forsake me, that You heal my sickness and that I can hold onto Your love at all times.

I want to keep on putting my hope in You, Lord, because I know that You guarantee me a place in heaven.

Together with the psalmist, I want to praise You for Your love and faithfulness.

Amen.

December

Christmas is a festival of joy!

Christmas is the one festival of the year that replaces our many fears with joy.

We would all benefit greatly if we could exchange our feelings of oppression and fear for lasting joy in God.

This is what Christmas is all about!

Share the message of joy with everyone around you this year: "Jesus was born, the Son of God became a Man, so that you and I may be God's children!"

Because He came to dwell on this earth, you need not fear anything.

He guarantees you joy and security in a world that has forgotten the meaning of joy and safety.

"Surely you have granted him eternal blessings and made him glad with the joy of your presence," proclaims the psalmist (Ps. 21:6).

At Christmas, God comes near to you.

Therefore, this Christmas season, you can confidently exchange your fears for the joy of God that no one can ever take away from you.

Never be lacking in zeal!

Read Romans 12:9-17

Never be lacking in zeal, but keep your spiritual fervor, serving the Lord (Rom. 12:11).

For a profound relationship with God, fervor, faithfulness and zeal are required. *"Don't burn out; keep yourselves fueled and aflame. Be alert servants of the Master, cheerfully expectant,"* says *The Message*.

The people of Israel often lost their enthusiasm for the God of the Covenant. Therefore, speaking through the prophet Jeremiah, the Lord says to them, *"I remember the devotion of your youth, how as a bride you loved me"* (Jer. 2:2). Unfortunately, Israel's "honeymoon love" for God steadily decreased. And because they had lost their fervor for God, things became increasingly worse for them.

Be careful not to lose your first love for the Lord. It is easy to start your relationship with God with great enthusiasm but then gradually this enthusiasm wanes – almost without your realizing it. When this happens, your quiet time becomes nothing more than a good habit and you pray out of habit because it is part of your routine. But the excitement of a living relationship with God, and looking forward to time spent with Him, has been lost.

The word "enthusiasm" is derived from *"en theos"*, which quite literally means: *"God inside me"*. Always remember that the wondrous God, in whose presence you find yourself when you pray and study His Word, lives within you. And never be lacking in zeal for Him!

Lord Jesus, I have to admit that I am no longer as enthusiastic about my relationship with You as I was at first. Please forgive me and rekindle my first love for You. Amen.

Do you truly love the Lord?

Read John 21:15-19

When they had finished eating, Jesus said to Simon Peter, "Simon son of John, do you truly love me more than these?" "Yes, Lord," he said, "you know that I love you." (John 21:15).

Jesus asked Peter three times whether he truly loved Him. (Perhaps that was because a short while before, Peter had disowned Him three times). Peter answered, "Yes Lord," three times, and each time received a command – to take care of God's sheep.

God's children know that God loves them. In this Christmas season, we are focusing on the miracle of God's love that compelled Him to send His only Son to this world so that you and I could find Him. But do you truly love Him? The proof that you love Him is the fact that you obey His commandments. *"This is love for God: to obey his commands,"* writes John (1 John 5:3).

If you truly love God, like Peter you will be willing to get personally involved in the expansion of His kingdom, to take care of His sheep, feed His lambs and to fulfill the commands in His Word. During this Christmas season, reflect anew on your love for God. Decide how you can demonstrate this love in the future, and especially in the month that lies ahead.

Heavenly Father, I glorify You for Your infinite love for me. But Lord, my own love is sadly lacking. Make me obedient to Your commands, so that others may recognize my love for You. Amen.

Prove your love through your way of life

Read 1 Thessalonians 1:2-8

We always thank God for all of you, mentioning you in our prayers. We continually remember before our God and Father your work produced by faith, your labor prompted by love, and your endurance inspired by hope in our Lord Jesus Christ (1 Thess. 1:2-3).

In this letter Paul gives a beautiful testimonial of the people of Thessalonica – they have lived in such a way that others could see that they belonged to Christ. *"You became imitators of us and of the Lord. And so you became a model to all the believers in Macedonia and Achaia,"* he writes in verses 6 and 7.

The Christians of Thessalonica truly loved other people, they held onto Jesus' promise that He would return, and they served the loving God with their whole heart. They were "slaves" of God, willing to perform His commands and to be used by Him.

And that is precisely what faith is all about. The lives of Christians should be exemplary. You should not only let others know that you love Jesus by talking about it, but also – and especially – by the way in which you live. It is a difficult command, but your life should testify so clearly to your faith that words should not really be necessary.

Do you still pay only lip service to the Lord, or do you live in such a way that other people can see from the example that you set that you truly love Him?

Lord Jesus, forgive me that my life is not yet a clear testimony to my faith, for all to see. Help me to actively live my faith to the full in all that I say and do. Amen.

The discipline of love

> *Read 1 Corinthians 13:4-13*

Love is patient, love is kind. It does not envy, it does not boast, it is not proud. It is not rude, it is not self-seeking, it is not easily angered, it keeps no record of wrongs (1 Cor. 13:4-5).

The love that Paul writes about here is definitely a supernatural kind of love. There is not one person who is patient, modest and forgiving by nature – we regard ourselves as far too important for that. Paul offers practical examples of what our love for one another should be like, as well as how we can demonstrate God's love to others. Christmas should be a time of love. Therefore, it is the right time of year to learn how God's love can be shown to others in practical ways.

The Christmas season is the time of year that you receive many opportunities to pass the love that God has for you on to others. This month you should try to act like Jesus toward every person who crosses your path. Work on your own patience, kindness, forgiving disposition and modesty. If you are God's child, then you are related to Jesus. "Christianity means the manifestation of a strong family likeness to Jesus," writes Oswald Chambers.[1] In a nutshell, this means that you show the same kind of love to others that Jesus gives to you.

Go out and live like Jesus. Show love – even to those people who have willfully caused you harm, so that others can recognize that Jesus is in your life. Live in such a way that you become a window through which other people can see Jesus' love for them.

Lord Jesus, I want to be a window of Your love for other people this Christmas. Please help me to apply the discipline of love. Amen.

Witnesses amidst suffering

Read 1 Thessalonians 1:2-10

You became imitators of us and of the Lord; in spite of severe suffering, you welcomed the message with the joy given by the Holy Spirit (1 Thess. 1:6).

The congregation in Thessalonica was very dear to Paul. He continually expressed gratitude toward God for *"your work produced by faith, your labor prompted by love, and your endurance inspired by hope"* (1 Thess. 1:3). They followed his example and, in their way of life, he could see how people who had been made new in Christ lived. Moreover, these people from Thessalonica welcomed the message of Christ with the joy given by the Holy Spirit – in spite of severe suffering.

Christians are the only people who can continue to rejoice in God amidst difficult circumstances.

God often uses difficult circumstances to deepen the faith of His children and to spread the gospel. When Paul was put in jail, the whole palace guard heard about Jesus (Phil. 1:13). Moreover, Paul's imprisonment made the Christians' trust in God stronger and they were encouraged to speak the word of God more courageously and fearlessly (Phil. 1:14).

You can also be a witness when you suffer. When bad things happen in your life, ensure that you retain your inner joy and faith. Hold onto the promise that it is precisely these things that you find difficult to handle that God uses to strengthen you spiritually and to expand His kingdom.

Lord Jesus, help me to live in such a way that I will utilize my problems to expand Your kingdom, and help me to continue rejoicing in You. Amen.

Imitators of Jesus

You became imitators of us and of the Lord; in spite of severe suffering, you welcomed the message with the joy given by the Holy Spirit (1 Thess. 1:6).

Yesterday, we saw that the Thessalonians had become an example of godly living through their lifestyle. The gospel bore fruit because people who heard about Jesus saw their example, and came to believe in God. So powerful was their living testimony, that there was no need for Paul and his associates to say anything more about it (v. 8). Other people testified how the example of the Thessalonians had converted them away from idols and how they were now serving the living God.

These Christians of Thessalonica became imitators of Paul and therefore, also of Jesus. They served Him fervently and willingly. They discovered the secret that He had to be the most important Person in their lives.

"Whoever claims to live in him must walk as Jesus did," writes John (1 John 2:6). How effective is your example to others? Are you an imitator of Jesus? Can people see Him in you?

Try to live and act in such a way during this Christmas season that you will truly become more like Jesus every day.

Lord Jesus, I wish to become more like You. Please help me to imitate You in everything I do so that my example will inspire others to love and follow You. Amen.

The First and the Last

Read Revelation 22:12-17

"Behold, I am coming soon! I am the Alpha and the Omega, the First and the Last, the Beginning and the End" (Rev. 22:12-13).

In Revelation 22, Jesus declares that He will be coming soon, that He is the First and the Last, and that nothing exists or happens outside the sphere of His presence. He acts with the authority of God, because He is God.

When the congregation in Colosse began to accept the heresy that Jesus was not really all that important, Paul repeated what Jesus said about Himself: *"He is the image of the invisible God, the firstborn over all creation. For by him all things were created: things in heaven and on earth. He is before all things, and in him all things hold together"* (Col. 1:15-17).

Wherever Jesus is, God is there as well. Jesus is the visible image of the invisible God. He came to show us how God wants us to live.

Is Jesus truly the First and the Last in your life? How important is He to you? What do you think about most often; on what do you spend most of your time? *"Seek first his kingdom and his righteousness, and all these things will be given to you as well,"* Jesus promises in the Sermon on the Mount (Matt. 6:33). If you are willing to give Jesus the first and the last place in your life, you can take hold of His promise that you will have all you need.

Lord Jesus, You know that I love You, but You also know that there are still so many other things, besides You, that are important to me. From now on, please be the First and the Last in my life. Amen.

Jesus is the Highest

> Read Philippians 2:5-11

Therefore God exalted him to the highest place and gave him the name that is above every name, that at the name of Jesus every knee should bow, in heaven and on earth and under the earth ... (Phil. 2:9-10).

Precisely because Jesus was willing to make Himself nothing by taking on the very nature of a servant, and being made in human likeness (Phil 2:7), God exalted Him and gave Him a Name that is above every name, so that at His name every knee should bow, in heaven and on earth. *"God exalted him to his own right hand as Prince and Savior that he might give repentance and forgiveness of sins to Israel,"* proclaims Peter in Acts 5:31.

Oswald Chambers wrote the classic devotional, *My Utmost for His Highest*. He then wrote another devotional, *Still Higher for the Highest*. Jesus Christ is the Highest, he explains. Your life can never be really safe and secure if you do not worship Him as the Highest.

If complications arise in your life, you must not do anything before first consulting the Highest.

Are your thoughts beginning to reflect the heart of Jesus? Can Jesus be seen in the things that you do? In your circumstances? asks Chambers. If not, pray until He personally gives you clarity on what course of action to take. "Our Lord can trust anything to the man or woman who sees Him," writes Chambers.[2]

Lord Jesus, teach me to wait on You, to make You the most important Person in my life, so that I may be able to see You in my circumstances. Amen.

What Jesus came to do for you

Read 1 Corinthians 1:18-31

It is because of him that you are in Christ Jesus, who has become for us wisdom from God – that is, our righteousness, holiness and redemption (1 Cor. 1:30).

Quite a few of the Corinthians were sidetracked. Paul gave them practical advice on how they should really live as Christians. In the first chapter of Paul's letter to the Corinthians, he writes in detail about the message of the cross. Jesus' crucifixion makes sinners right with a holy God, enables ordinary people to live a holy life and enables us to have everlasting life. We have the definite promise that Jesus will return to this world one day to come and fetch His children.

"Everything that we have – right thinking and right living, a clean slate and a fresh start – comes from God by way of Jesus Christ," says *The Message*.

Only by believing in Jesus, could the people of Corinth succeed in living the way God wanted them to live. He is the Key to God's wisdom, He delivers us from sin, makes us holy and enables God to forgive us. Do you believe in the only Person who can make you right with God? Only by believing in Him, will you succeed in living fully for God.

Lord Jesus, I glorify You for being wisdom from God to me, that You have redeemed me from my sins and enabled me to be God's child. Amen.

Live in Jesus

Read Colossians 2:6-15

So then, just as you received Christ Jesus as Lord, continue to live in him, rooted and built up in him, strengthened in the faith as you were taught, and overflowing with thankfulness (Col. 2:6-7).

Paul presents two comparisons here. The first is drawn from agriculture: the believer must be rooted in Jesus, like a plant in the soil. The second image comes from the building industry: Jesus is the foundation on which we are built. Without Him, we would have no real security.

We all experience things that try our faith in Jesus at times. In such times of difficulty, it helps if you live close to Jesus, if you are rooted and built up in Him. Should you find it difficult to have faith, look past those things that cause your faith to falter and look toward Jesus. Work on your relationship with Him.

If you do this, then you will receive fullness in Christ and you will be circumcised with the circumcision done by Jesus. In other words, you will gradually succeed in ridding yourself of your sinful human nature and living in holiness like Jesus. Furthermore, you have the promise that you will live with Him.

Lord Jesus, teach me to live in You, rooted and built up in You, so that I can receive Your fullness and be raised from the dead to be with You one day. Amen.

Lack of faith is an impediment

Read Matthew 13:53-58

And they took offence at him. But Jesus said to them, "Only in his hometown and in his own house is a prophet without honor." And he did not do many miracles there because of their lack of faith (Matt. 13:57-58).

The people of Nazareth, Jesus' hometown, were skeptical about Him. Was He not simply the son of the carpenter who grew up in their midst? Was his mother not Mary and his brothers James, Joseph, Simon and Judas, they asked. Where would He have learned the things that He wanted to teach them? Matthew reports that they took offence at Him (v. 57). Their lack of faith was an impediment to Jesus. *"And he did not do many miracles there because of their lack of faith,"* today's Scripture verse explains. Because they refused to recognize Jesus as the Messiah, they could not experience the blessing that He wanted to give them.

Your lack of faith could also be an impediment that prevents God from performing miracles in your life. Jesus wants His children to persevere in faith, regardless of their physical circumstances. This is not always easy, especially when we do not receive those things we believed we would.

"Everything is possible for him who believes," Jesus assured the father who brought his ill son to Him. Perhaps it is necessary for you to join the father in his prayer today, *"I do believe; help me overcome my unbelief!"* (Mark 9:23-24).

Heavenly Father, You know that I find it difficult to continue believing when those things that I believe in do not come to pass. Help me to persevere in believing, so that You can perform miracles in my life. Amen.

Prayer for forgiveness

But Moses sought the favor of the LORD his God. "O LORD," he said, "why should your anger burn against your people, whom you brought out of Egypt with great power and a mighty hand? Turn from your fierce anger; relent and do not bring disaster on your people" (Exod. 32:11-12).

The Lord instructed Moses to return to the people because they had sinned against God by worshiping a golden calf as an idol. He also declared that He wanted to destroy the people and make Moses into a great nation. However, Moses sought the mercy of God and asked Him to forgive His stubborn people.

Today, God is still judged by the conduct of His children. If people looking at us can see that we have absolute trust in God, they know that the God whom we worship is truly faithful.

Sinning has become so commonplace that it does not really upset us. Like Moses, it is still necessary for you to ask God's forgiveness for your own sins, as well as for the sins of your people. Will you do so?

Heavenly Father, I pray that You will forgive my sins and that You will also make me an intercessor for others. Thank You for Your mercy which You bestow on us so abundantly. Amen.

Do not be afraid

And there were shepherds living out in the fields nearby. An angel of the Lord appeared to them, and they were terrified. But the angel said to them, "Do not be afraid. I bring you good news of great joy that will be for all the people" (Luke 2:8-10).

The group of shepherds outside Bethlehem were terrified when an angel suddenly appeared before them. However, the angel put them at ease, *"Don't be afraid. I'm here to announce a great and joyful event that is meant for everybody, worldwide: A Savior has just been born in David's town, a Savior who is Messiah and Master,"* says *The Message*.

We have more reason than ever before to live in fear. Life has become unsafe for all of us. When our house was broken into some time ago, we were terribly shocked because we had always assumed that the complex in which we live was totally secure. During the month following the burglary, our sleep was disturbed and we were awoken by the slightest sound at night.

The angel's joyful Christmas message is still valid for fearful human beings today: Do not be afraid – the Son of God is here! He is always the guarantee for your safety. Even though your house may be burgled, even though you may find yourself in a life-threatening situation, even though you may lose your life, you are safe forever because Jesus has given you everlasting life.

"I am the resurrection and the life, He who believes in me will live, even though he dies; and whoever lives and believes in me will never die," is Jesus' promise to Martha (John 11:25-26). Make this promise your own during the Christmas season.

Lord Jesus, thank You that I no longer need to fear anything, because You guarantee my safety for all eternity. Amen.

Reconciliation, hope and peace

> *Read Colossians 1:19-23*

But now he has reconciled you by Christ's physical body through death to present you holy in his sight, without blemish and free from accusation – if you continue in your faith, established and firm, not moved from the hope held out in the gospel (Col. 1:22-23).

There is no real future for us or for the world if we are not re-conciled, through Christ, with God and with one another. People continuously search for fulfillment in a world sadly lacking in peace and hope – two words that should play a very important role in the lives of Christians. In one of his Christmas sermons, my husband said that hope expects a better tomorrow. Hope lights a shining star on the dark, closed door of the future.

"Christ (is) in you, the hope of glory," writes Paul to the Colossians (Col. 1:27). Because you love Him and believe in Him, you can confidently hope that His promises will be fulfilled. *"For God was pleased to have all his fullness dwell in him, and through him to reconcile to himself all things, whether things on earth or things in heaven, by making peace through his blood, shed on the cross,"* Paul promises (Col. 1:19-20).

Godly peace always involves being made whole. When Jesus came to earth, He made us whole, and our broken relationships with God and other people were restored. Reconciliation is only possible if we look past the current conflicts toward the future with hope in our hearts, so that we can find true peace.

Heavenly Father, I pray that You would make me a minister of Your reconciliation here on earth. Thank You for sending Jesus so that I could inherit peace and put my hope in You. Amen.

Lasting reconciliation

Read Ephesians 2:13-18

For he himself is our peace, who has made the two one and has destroyed the barrier, the dividing wall of hostility. For through him we both have access to the Father by one Spirit (Eph. 2:14, 18).

Jesus died to reconcile us with God. When He died, the curtain of the temple, which separated the Most Holy from the Holy of Holies, tore from top to bottom. Jesus' death gave us free access to God forever. The process of reconciliation, initiated by the death of Jesus, includes us all.

With the Fall, our relationship with God and with one another was broken. Reconciliation is the act of mending broken relationships. Therefore, reconciliation includes all relationships: your relationship with God, with your partner in marriage, with your neighbors and with your friends. Reconciliation is an ongoing process, because we keep on sinning.

God allowed His Son to die so that we could be reconciled with Him and with one another. *"His purpose was to create in himself one new man out of the two, thus making peace, and in this one body to reconcile both of them to God through the cross, by which he put to death their hostility"* (Eph. 2:15-16).

Have you accepted God's reconciliation in your life? And do you live at peace with your neighbor?

Lord Jesus, I praise You because Your crucifixion put to death the hostility between God and me, as well as between other people and me. Help me to pass Your reconciliation on to others. Amen.

Reconciliation requires sacrificial love

> *Read 2 Corinthians 5:16-21*

All this is from God, who reconciled us to himself through Christ and gave us the ministry of reconciliation: that God was reconciling the world to himself in Christ, not counting men's sins against them (2 Cor. 5:18-19).

When God reconciled the world to Himself through Christ, the price was high – the life of His Son. Our reconciliation with God cost Jesus His life. Reconciliation always comes at a price, it always requires a sacrifice from us. And we have been entrusted with this message of reconciliation, writes Paul.

Reconciliation is demonstrated through our actions. Reconciliation may be the gateway to peace and hope for you, but it is going to require sacrificial love from you. It turns you into a new person and makes you want to be more like Jesus every day.

True reconciliation is only achieved when people turn toward one another and live in harmony. Jesus was willing to put others first and, if you really are in earnest with your task of reconciliation, you will have to be willing to wash the feet of other people and to be willing to serve them.

Resolve to live in reconciliation with others, so that people looking at you will see that you have become a new person through Christ. This is a near impossible challenge, but it is possible if the Holy Spirit takes control of your life.

Heavenly Father, I am so much in need of reconciliation with You, as well as with other people. Help me to go out and live Your reconciliation to the full, so that people will see You in my life. Amen.

God's miracle

Read Luke 1:26-38

He will be great and will be called the Son of the Most High. The Lord God will give him the throne of his father David, and he will reign over the house of Jacob forever; his kingdom will never end (Luke 1:32-33).

Mary knew that the message the angel brought to her was not humanly possible. "How will this be?" she asked the angel. And indeed, the events surrounding the birth of Jesus are impossible with man. It was a miracle – God's miracle. Mary's pregnancy, the virgin birth and the angel's announcement are all miracles, supernatural events, that only God can do.

And these miraculous events summarize the meaning of Christmas. The events of Christmas remain a miracle – a miracle that we should never take for granted. God Himself left heaven and came to dwell on earth, so that sinners could become children of God.

Christmas is always a special time. Families get together to share the wonder and joy of the season. Usually, Christmas also comes in a special package: Christmas music, ribbons, gifts, candles, bells and lights. But, it is far more than just a merry festival that loved ones share with one another. The true meaning of Christmas is lost if Jesus does not form the center of our Christmas festivities.

Lord Jesus, thank You for the miracle of Your birth. Make this Christmas time a celebration of You. A festival that will bring us closer to You. Amen.

Spread the news of the miracle

Read Luke 2:15-20

When the angels had left them and gone into heaven, the shepherds said to one another, "Let's go to Bethlehem and see this thing that has happened, which the Lord has told us about" (Luke 2:15).

When the shepherds heard the angel's message they immediately forgot their fear of the extraordinary events. They were eager to spread the miraculous message they had seen and heard. They hurried straight to Bethlehem, where they found Joseph, Mary and Jesus in the stable, just as the angel had said. When they had seen them, Luke writes, they told others what they had heard about this Child: that He was the long-awaited Savior, Christ the Lord!

Jesus' parents must have been overjoyed that the angel's message to Mary has been confirmed in such a special way. The shepherds returned to their flocks of sheep, glorifying and praising God for all the things they had heard and seen (v. 20).

Jesus expects His children to spread the Good News of His birth in the world around us, to tell others that He is the only Savior, the only way for us to get to heaven. The Christmas miracle is not a miracle that we should keep to ourselves. Tell it to all you come into contact with during this Christmas season. The miraculous message must be told to all people who have not yet heard it.

Make it your Christmas mission to tell at least one other person about the miracle: God became Man, so that human beings can become children of the King.

Heavenly Father, like the shepherds, I want to tell others about Your miracle. I praise You for becoming a Man, so that I can be a child of the King. Amen.

Amazed about the miracle

Read Luke 2:15-20

All who heard it were amazed at what the shepherds said to them. But Mary treasured up all these things and pondered them in her heart (Luke 2:18-19).

Every person who heard the miraculous message of the Messiah's birth was amazed by it. And this message changed their lives. The shepherds would never be the same again. They had a new relationship with God and they glorified and praised Him for all the things they had seen and heard.

Mary and Joseph must have spent much time thinking about the events of the past few months. Mary treasured the words of the shepherds in her heart and often thought about them. Joseph probably thought about the dream in which the angel had told him that the Son Mary was expecting came from the Holy Spirit and that He would redeem His people from their sins.

Two thousand years later, the miracle of Jesus' birth still leaves us filled with amazement. The fact that God, the great Creator, loved human sinners so much, that He sent His only Son to dwell on this earth as an ordinary human being and be crucified, so that you and I may become children of God, still leaves us speechless. The fact that Jesus chose to leave heaven and to be born in a dirty stable, the fact that He did not shun the most cruel of all executions, but was willing to be crucified for you and me, is even more incomprehensible. But the Bible assures us that it is all true. What a miracle!

Heavenly Father, I glorify You for the miracle of Christmas. Help me never to take this miracle for granted, but to reflect on it and to speak to others about it. Amen.

This miracle is for ordinary people

Read Luke 2:10-20

But the angel said to them, "Do not be afraid. I bring you good news of great joy that will be for all the people. Today in the town of David a Savior has been born to you; he is Christ the Lord" (Luke 2:10-11).

Bethlehem was an ordinary town and the shepherds were ordinary people. They were neither rich nor important, and they were terrified when they heard the angel's announcement on the first Christmas night. When they responded to the angel's message and went to Bethlehem, following the announcement of the birth of the Messiah, they found neither rich nor important people there. Instead of a stately home, a beautiful baby's room or dainty baby's clothing, they found a simple couple who had to spend the night in a dirty stable, and a Baby wrapped in cloths and lying in a manger.

The first Christmas message was addressed to ordinary people. God did not look for kings or rulers or governors to tell them that the Savior had been born. The gospel of Jesus is still meant for everybody – ordinary people, such as you and me. Years later, after His crucifixion and resurrection, Jesus told His disciples to spread His message. *"Therefore go and make disciples of all nations, teaching them to obey everything I have commanded you,"* (Matt. 28:19-20).

What are you doing with that message? Are you willing to spread it during this Christmas season?

Lord Jesus, thank You for coming to this world for ordinary people; for enabling ordinary people to become God's children. Help me to spread Your Good News to ordinary people this Christmas. Amen.

Glory to God!

Read Luke 2:13-14

Suddenly a great company of the heavenly host appeared with the angel, praising God and saying, "Glory to God in the highest, and on earth peace to men on whom his favor rests" (Luke 2:13-14).

Listen carefully to the message of the angel on the very first Christmas: he did not mention the Christmas decorations, Christmas trees, expensive gifts and extravagant festivities that we have become accustomed to when celebrating Christmas. He spoke about God's glory and veneration. The choir of angels rejoiced in the joyous message that is too overwhelming to express in ordinary words. Their song of joy puts the spotlight fully on God: *"Glory to God in the highest, and on earth peace to men on whom his favor rests."*

If we desire true peace in our hearts today, then the recipe is easy – and the same as during that first Christmas. We should glorify and praise God. The very heart of our festivities should still be aimed at praising God because He sent His Son to become a Man, so that we could find Him. We must kneel in wonder before such an awesome God this Christmas, we must bow before His glory and majesty, we must acknowledge Him as King of our lives and glorify and praise Him.

If you are willing to glorify Him through your life and in your Christmas festivities, then God will grant you His everlasting peace in your heart and life.

Is *Glory to God* the signature tune in your heart?

Heavenly Father, I pray that You will help me to pay less attention to outward trappings this Christmas and to concentrate on Your glorification and veneration. Please grant me Your peace in my life. Amen.

Christmas is a time for missionary work

> *Read Isaiah 11:1-3*

A shoot will come up from the stump of Jesse; from his roots a Branch will bear fruit. And he will delight in the fear of the LORD (Isa. 11:1, 3).

The prophet Isaiah had a message for God's people: Although they found themselves under God's judgment, He would bring about a miracle – from the dead stump of Jesse a shoot would come up that would bear fruit. God sent His Son to establish a new Kingdom here on earth, a Kingdom in which the harmony between God and man will be restored and every citizen will have access to God.

This thought inspired me to experience Christmas in a brand new way. I began to link Christmas with the spreading of God's message of redemption. On that very first Christmas, God put into action His plan to allow sinners to become His children.

Because Jesus came to dwell on this earth as the Son of Man, we can be part of God's family too. Every person now has access to God.

Christmas teaches us to follow the example of the shepherds and spread the good news that Jesus brought.

During this Christmas season share God's message of redemption with at least one other person. Remember, Christmas is a perfect time for missionary work.

Lord Jesus, I glorify You for becoming a man, so that I could become a child of God. Help me to spread Your message of redemption to others. Amen.

Acknowledging God

Read Hosea 6:1-3

"Let us acknowledge the LORD; let us press on to acknowledge him. As surely as the sun rises, he will appear; he will come to us like the spring rains that water the earth" (Hos. 6:3).

God's children often become more aware of their Christianity during the Christmas season. We attend Christmas services, we reflect upon the advent of Jesus to this world and we once again read the prophesies of the birth of Jesus in the Old Testament, as well as the narratives of His birth in the New Testament. Moreover, we experience the love and caring of other Christians in the giving of presents and times of togetherness during Christmas. We live in the evidence of God's love and of our love for one another.

Christmas is therefore pre-eminently that time of the year when we should renew our relationship with God. When we realize once more what it cost God to enable us to celebrate Christmas. Christmas is also the right time to acknowledge God anew and, in unison with the choir of angels of long ago, decide to glorify God through our way of life from now on.

My Christmas prayer for you is Paul's beautiful prayer in 1 Thessalonians 5:23 and 24, *"May God himself, the God of peace, sanctify you through and through. May your whole spirit, soul and body be kept blameless at the coming of our Lord Jesus Christ. The one who calls you is faithful and he will do it."*

Lord, from now on, I want to glorify You through my way of life every day. Please help me to acknowledge You to the full, so that all that I say and do will be in line with Your will for my life. Amen.

Peace on earth

Read Luke 2:8-15

Suddenly a great company of the heavenly host appeared with the angel, praising God and saying, "Glory to God in the highest, and on earth peace to men on whom his favor rests" (Luke 2:13-14).

People have turned the concept of peace into a political idea that requires the conflict between nations to come to an end. The world is yearning for peace, for someone who will ensure us peace in a world that is inundated with strife.

The angel's announcement of peace on that first Christmas has a condition attached to it – it is not an unqualified promise: God's peace is meant for those people on whom His favor rests. *The Message* states, *"Peace to all men and women on earth who please him. Therefore, the peace of which the angel speaks, is a biblical peace. And biblical peace means to be whole, to be healed from the brokenness that sin has brought into this world. This peace only comes by the Way of the Cross."*

It does not seem as though the angel's announcement of peace on that first Christmas has became a reality in our lives. We cannot see it yet. We still live behind high fences and security gates because we want to protect ourselves, we want to bring about peace for ourselves. But this is never going to work. Before you can experience God's peace in your life, you must first make peace with Him and your neighbor.

Lord Jesus, thank You that You brought about peace between God and man. Make me a peacemaker in this world, so that Your peace can reside in my life. Amen.

From crib to cross

Read Isaiah 53:1-6

But he was pierced for our transgressions, he was crushed for our iniquities; the punishment that brought us peace was upon him, and by his wounds we are healed (Isa. 53:5).

Jesus' journey through this world started in Bethlehem, but ended at Golgotha, where Christ died, so that the world could have peace. God always punishes sin with death, and Jesus' blood had to flow on the cross so that our burden of sin could be removed.

Jesus took our suffering upon Himself, He carried our burden, and the punishment that guaranteed us peace was upon Him. His wounds brought us healing. Jesus was crucified so that peace could exist once again between a holy God and sinners. He carried the punishment for our sins so that we could be redeemed forever. *"For he himself is our peace,"* writes Paul to the Ephesians (Eph. 2:14).

If you want to experience God's peace during this Christmastime, there are a number of questions that you will have to ask yourself: Do you believe in the Child of Bethlehem? Have you made peace with God and the people around you? Do you know the crucified Jesus? If you can answer yes to all these questions, then the angel's promise of peace is for you. Not because of Christmas, but because of Good Friday.

Lord Jesus, how can I thank You for dying so that I can have everlasting life? Thank You that I can experience Your peace this Christmas, because on the cross You redeemed me from my sin. Amen.

Cultivate a Christmas disposition

Read 1 John 4:7-16

This is how God showed his love among us: He sent his one and only Son into the world that we might live through him. And so we know and rely on the love God has for us (1 John 4:9, 16).

Christmas – the season to celebrate God's love for us – is over. We should never let Christmas pass us by without it changing us. If we want to know how much God loves us, all we need to do is look at Jesus. At no time of the year are we more aware of this love than at Christmas, when we celebrate Jesus' advent to this world. We can summarize this love in one sentence: The Son of God became Man, so that sinners can find God.

"Christmas is not merely another day, an occasion that has to be observed, soon to be forgotten again," writes William Parks. "It is an attitude of the heart that should characterize every day of our lives. To believe that the message of Christmas can indeed change lives, and to work toward achieving it in the lives of all people, is the essence of our faith."

Therefore, ensure that this year's Christmas events will bring about a change in your heart – and that you will carry the spirit of Christmas the whole year through, so that it will affect all that you do and all whom you come into contact with. May the peace and joy of Christmas remain with you every day of the year!

Heavenly Father, thank You for Your love for me. Help me to keep the spirit of love, peace and joy that Christmas injects into my life, for the rest of the year. Amen.

A Shepherd for the year ahead

Read Revelation 7:13-17

"For the Lamb at the center of the throne will be their shepherd; he will lead them to springs of living water. And God will wipe away every tear from their eyes" (Rev. 7:17).

The Bible often describes God as a Shepherd. This portrays the special relationship between God and believers. If we have this Shepherd by our side, we also have the assurance that we will not be in want of anything, that He will walk the road of life ahead of us, protecting us from dangers, and that He will lead us beside quiet waters and take care of us.

The year is almost at an end. Because we live in times of uncertainty, none of us can know for sure what is awaiting us during the year ahead. However, we can know Who will accompany us on the road through the new year.

Jesus wants to be your Shepherd in the year ahead. He has already demonstrated His love for you by laying down His life for you. He wants to provide in all of your needs, He wants to offer you the Living Water free of charge and, moreover, He wants to put an end to all your sorrow and pain. He guarantees you everlasting life. He promises that no one will ever be able to snatch you from His hand.

If you know Jesus as your Shepherd, you can face the year ahead with complete peace of mind. With this Shepherd by your side, you will be victorious.

Lord Jesus, thank You for being my Shepherd. Thank you that You laid down Your life for me, that I am not in want of anything because You take care of me, and that I can rest assured in the knowledge that You guarantee me everlasting life. Amen.

Looking back, looking ahead

Read Psalm 90

Teach us to number our days aright, that we may gain a heart of wisdom. Satisfy us in the morning with your unfailing love, that we may sing for joy and be glad all our days (Ps. 90:12, 14).

At the end of every year we survey the year that is past, but we also look ahead and dream about the future awaiting us. We will need wisdom to make the right decisions in the year ahead – God's wisdom. In the Old Testament, wisdom was considered the key to a happy life. The gift granted by God to people to enable them to make the right choices, and the discernment to know what is right and what is wrong. Proverbs 1:7 teaches us that wisdom is living righteously before God and doing His will.

If you truly want to be successful, you will need God's wisdom in the new year. Ask Him for it. Remember that all that you have achieved during the past year is through the grace of God. You did not achieve success on your own and your hopes and dreams for the future are dependent on His grace.

What do you want from the year ahead? Success, health, wealth? In Psalm 90 Moses asks God to teach him to number his days aright, so that he may gain a heart of wisdom. Make this prayer your own for the new year.

Heavenly Father, I pray for Your wisdom in the year ahead. Teach me how to live, how to do Your will, how to make the right choices – and always help me to give You the glory for all my successes. Amen.

Focus on God

Read Psalm 90:1-4

Before the mountains were born or you brought forth the earth and the world, from everlasting to everlasting you are God. For a thousand years in your sight are like a day that has just gone by, or like a watch in the night (Ps. 90:2, 4).

Everything is always changing. We cannot really depend on anything, but God is still the same as when this psalm was written. God is totally trustworthy. He is eternal. He is constant. Through the ages, He has remained the same. You do not have to get used to a "new" God every year, as is the case with new computer programs or new websites. The God whom you worship is still exactly the same as before. His promises are still true.

If you look back on the past year, it is quite possible that you did not always get what you asked of God. Always remember that He has a different perspective from you. God looks at us from His perspective of eternity. He sees the total picture, while we only see a section of the present. If God has not brought all your dreams to pass, He most likely wants to surpass your dreams! Your tears of disappointment during the past year are also part of God's plan for your life. In time, you will find that He has comforted, strengthened and encouraged you during those times that you needed Him most.

Heavenly Father, I glorify You because You are great and constant and omnipotent. Thank You for holding my life in Your hands and that I can entrust my future unreservedly to You. Amen.

The human perspective

You sweep men away in the sleep of death; they are like the new grass of the morning – though in the morning it springs up new, by evening it is dry and withered (Ps. 90:5-6).

Psalm 90 gives a rather somber portrayal of people. All people are transient and dying. We don't like to think of ourselves like that. From our day of birth, all of us suffer from a deadly illness – sin. We are born with it. It wears us down day after day. In contrast to God who is eternal and constant, we are like grass that springs up new in the morning, but by evening it has withered.

God hates all sin. For this reason, man's time spent here on earth is never free of misery. God can never make peace with sin, nor can He ignore the brokenness of the world since the Fall. Sin destroys the relationship between God and man, as well as between man and man. It makes our lives incomplete.

However, God wants to heal you. He is extending His arms of love to you today. He invites you to come to Him as His child again. On the cross Jesus canceled your sin and He enabled you to become God's child. He made it possible for a holy God and sinners to walk through life together.

If you accept God's offer of grace, you are no longer as transient as the grass, but a child of God with an eternal future.

Heavenly Father, thank You for Your gift of grace. I dearly want to accept it. Thank You for the assurance that I can look forward to an eternal future with You. Amen.

A prosperous New Year!

Read Psalm 90:12-17

Satisfy us in the morning with your unfailing love, that we may sing for joy and be glad all our days. Make us glad for as many days as you have afflicted us, for as many years as we have seen trouble (Ps. 90:14-15).

Today is the very last day of the year. It is our heart's desire that the year ahead will be prosperous. Tomorrow we will all wish one another a "prosperous New Year". This new year's greeting has a bright glow. God wants His children to be happy, He wants to offer us His caring love.

It is my wish for you that, in the year ahead, you will be embraced by love every day, and that you will be able to see God's hand in your life every day. Because God loves you, you can hope that the year ahead will be a year of jubilation, even though the one that is almost past may have been filled with pain and suffering. Even though pain and disappointment might be your portion, you can rest assured in the knowledge that God will remain the same in the year ahead – that He will be with you in times of sorrow, and that He will be aware of every one of your tears.

Today He wants to tell you that, should you get tired and worn out: "Come to Me, with Me there is tranquility." God wants to take care of you in the year ahead, He wants to make you happy, He wants to carry you day after day, He wants to satisfy you in the morning with His unfailing love.

Heavenly Father, I praise You because You were by my side every day during the past year, and You carried me through times of suffering and times of joy. Please do the same for me in the year ahead. Amen.

Prayer

Lord Jesus, it is December – the month in which we celebrate Your birth.

Thank You for the joy, freedom from fear and security that Your presence guarantees me.

I praise You because You were willing to leave heaven for me, and to be born as an ordinary human being, so that sinners can become children of the King.

Help me never to lose my love and zeal for You, to love You unreservedly, and to demonstrate this love through my way of life.

Make me an imitator of You, so that I can become more like You every day.

I glorify You as the First and the Last, as the Highest One before whom every knee should bow.

I want to live in Your presence, rooted and built up in You.

Forgive me for my sins that still create a divide between You and me, and banish my numerous fears, because You guarantee me eternal safety.

Thank You for reconciling me with God and other people, for the miracle of Your birth that has changed my life.

I now wish to devote myself totally to You and glorify You.

I pray for peace in my heart and life.

Be a Shepherd to me in the year ahead, guide me, teach me and take care of me, and satisfy me in the morning with Your unfailing love.

Amen.

Endnotes

JANUARY
1. Henri Nouwen quoted in Raymond Croucher (ed.). 1991. *Rivers in the Desert*. p. 56.
2. C. S. Lewis. *Discipleship Journey*.
3. Jörg Zink. 1984. *Pad na die gebed*. Cape Town: Tafelberg. p. 74.
4. Don Postema quoted in Raymond Croucher (ed.). 1991. *Rivers in the Desert*. p. 58.
5. Brenda Waggoner. 1999. *The Velveteen Woman*. Colorado Springs: Cook Communication. p. 144.
6. Lewis B. Smedes. 1982. *How Can It Be All Right When Everything Is All Wrong?* Colorado Springs: Harold Shaw Publishers.
7. Don Postema quoted in Raymond Croucher (ed.). 1991. *Rivers in the Desert*. p. 55.
8. Brother Lawrence adapted from Raymond Croucher (ed.). 1991. *Rivers in the Desert*. p. 57.
9. Taken from *Toward Jerusalem*. p. 83.
10. Brenda Waggoner. 1999. *The Velveteen Woman*. Colorado Springs: Cook Communication. p. 137.

FEBRUARY
1. Erwin Lutzer. 2000. *Getting Closer to God*. Michigan: Servant Publishing. p. 177.

MARCH
1. Piet Naudé. 2000. *Stories vir die lewe*. Cape Town: Lux Verbi.

APRIL
1. Max Lucado. 2001. *Six Hours One Friday*. Cape Town: Struik. p. 298.
2. Karl Barth quoted in Johan Cilliers. 1991. *Glo en leef*. Cape Town: Lux Verbi. p. 104.
3. Johan Cilliers. 1991. *Glo en leef*. Cape Town: Lux Verbi. p. 104.
4. Henri Nouwen. 1996. *Bread for the Journey*. San Francisco: HarperCollins Publishers.

MAY
1. Henri Nouwen. 1996. *Bread for the Journey*. San Francisco: HarperCollins Publishers.

JUNE

1. Charles Swindoll. 1994. *Active Spirituality.* Dallas, Texas: Nelson Word. p. 11.
2. Charles Swindoll. 1994. *Active Spirituality.* Dallas, Texas: Nelson Word. p. 110.
3. Johan Smit. 2000. *Beloftes van vriendskap en omgee.* Vanderbijlpark: Carpe Diem. p. 155.

JULY

1. Hennie Symington quoted in Burger, Smit, et al. 2000. *'n Nuwe jy.* Vanderbijlpark: Carpe Diem: p. 320.
2. Helmut Thielicke. 1992. *Die gebed wat die wêreld omspan.* Cape Town: Tafelberg. p. 79.
3. Lewis B. Smedes. 1982. *How Can It Be All Right When Everything Is All Wrong?* Colorado Springs: Harold Shaw Publishers.
4. Ibid. p. 28.
5. Phil Bosmans quoted in Nina Smit. 1996. *'n Keur van wysheid.* Vereeniging: Christian Art Publishers. p. 75.
6. Johan Smit. 1994. *Liefde verander alles.* Vereeniging: Christian Art Publishers. p. 31.
7. I. L. de Villiers quoted in Nina Smit. 1996. *'n Keur van wysheid.* Vereeniging: Christian Art Publishers. p. 75.
8. Johan Smit. 1994. *Liefde verander alles.* Vereeniging: Christian Art Publishers. p. 39.
9. Ibid. p. 32.
10. Henri Nouwen. 1996. *Bread for the Journey.* San Francisco: HarperCollins Publishers.
11. Henri Nouwen. 1996. *Bread for the Journey.* San Francisco: HarperCollins Publishers.
12. Johan Smit. 1994. *Liefde verander alles.* Vereeniging: Christian Art Publishers. p. 93.
13. Phil Bosmans quoted in Nina Smit. 1996. *'n Keur van wysheid.* Vereeniging: Christian Art Publishers. p. 73.

AUGUST

1. Willem Nicol. 2000. *Godsdiens wat werk.* Cape Town: Lux Verbi. p. 20.
2. Heinrich Jung-Schilling quoted in Nina Smit. 1987. *Skuiling teen vrees.* Cape Town: Lux Verbi.
3. 1995. *A Basket of Hope.* Christian Art Gifts: Vereeniging.

SEPTEMBER
1. Henri Nouwen. 1996. *Bread for the Journey*. San Francisco: HarperCollins Publishers.

OCTOBER
1. Selwyn Hughes. 2001. *Joy, the Serious Business of Heaven.* Surrey, England: CWR. 4 March.

NOVEMBER
1. Johan Smit. 1988. *Siekte, 'n uitdaging om te lewe.* Cape Town: Lux Verbi. p. 36.

DECEMBER
1. Oswald Chambers. 1970. *Still Higher for the Highest.* London: Marshall, Morgan and Scott. p. 18.
2. Ibid. p. 7.